Alternative Communities in Nineteenth Century England

Alternative Communities in Nineteenth Century England

Dennis Hardy

Longman
London and New York

Longman Group Limited London

*Associated companies, branches and representatives
throughout the world*

*Published in the United States of America
by Longman Inc., New York*

© Longman Group Limited 1979

First published 1979

Library of Congress Cataloging in Publication Data

Hardy, Dennis.
  Alternative communities in nineteenth-century England.
  Bibliography: p. 254.
  Includes index.
  1. Collective settlements—England—History.
2. Utopias—History. I. Title.
HX695.A3H37   335′.9′42   77-26279
ISBN 0-582-50212-6
    0-582-50216-0 ppr

Printed in Great Britain by Richard Clay (The Chaucer Press) Ltd, Bungay, Suffolk.

Contents

6 Appraisal   211

Preface

'So how do you get to a place where people live in harmony, and manage without money' – asked a visitor to one of the communities – 'by *railway* or by *rainbow*?' The question was asked in the nineteenth century, but the doubts which lay behind it strike a familiar note today. Can alternative communities be regarded as a realistic means of achieving change, or are they mere dreams? It is for its topical as well as for its historical interest that the question is pursued – how far and in what ways were alternative communities effective as a force for changing the prevailing social and economic form of organisation?

What follows is an account of small groups of people (sometimes part of a wider movement) who were united in their rejection of established patterns of nineteenth-century society. In most cases this amounted to an explicit rejection of capitalism and, even where the critique was not framed in these terms, it was still primarily from those who suffered most from the inequities of the system that the communities drew their greatest support. As a political strategy the communities went beyond mere criticism of what already existed and were, in themselves, experiments in alternative forms of organisation – living examples of a new reality that the rest of society might see and follow.

Many of their ideals proved to be illusory, but their own existence was real enough. An attempt is made to show where the communities were located, and to record their own histories. Moreover, where there is field evidence of their former existence – in the form of cottages and plots, tombstones and towers, plaques and place-names – this, too, is recorded. In looking for local evidence, there is a parallel with both classical and industrial archaeology, where artefacts are used as contributions to particular fields of enquiry and, more recently, as items of growing interest for a wider public. The scattered remains of the alternative communities can provide an accessible and unusual view into a world that may be found to hold a surprising relevance for the contemporary observer.

My own interest in the subject has stemmed from a variety of sources – from the experience of teaching various aspects of nineteenth-century urban history, in an environment that is conducive to interdisciplinary work; from a number of earlier visits to community sites in Essex, which had always seemed so full of interest yet neglected by comparison with more conventional historical sites; and, not least of all, from a political attachment to the essential ideas of 'decentralised socialism' which so many of the communities embrace.

In coming to the subject and in writing this book I owe a debt to many friends (though this is not to imply that they will all agree with all that has been written). Above all I wish to thank Madeleine Wahlberg, who has been involved in the project from the outset. Others who have given me invaluable help at various stages are Greg Andrusz, Dot Davies, Ted Lewis, Alison Shepherd, George Tasker and Ian Welsh. Librarians and archivists have been generous, without exception, in providing me with information; so, too, have the many people I contacted on the sites of former communities. Linda Baker, Cathy Boon and Mary Hayden typed the manuscript and to them I am very grateful.

At home, Bronwen carried more than her fair share of work while the book was written and, on top of all that, has found the time and interest to prepare the index. Rowan, Gemma and Alexis have kept it all in perspective!

Acknowledgements

We are grateful to the following for permission to reproduce copyright material:

The British Library for Fig. 1.2, for Fig. 2.14 from 'The Comick Almanack', 1843, for Fig. 3.1, for Fig. 5.1 from 'The New Order', 1897, for Fig. 5.8 from 'The New Order'; The C. W. Daniel Company Ltd. for Figs. 5.14 and 5.17 from *Whiteway* by Nellie Shaw; David and Charles (Holdings) Ltd. for Figs. 3.9, 3.18 and 3.22 from *The Chartist Land Company* by A. M. Hatfield; Clifford Harper for Figs. 6.2 and 6.3; The Illustrated London News for Figs. 3.14, 3.19, 3.20 and 4.2; The London School of Economics and Political Science for Fig. 3.33 from 'The Clarion', 1892; Manchester Central Library for Fig. 5.11 from 'The Free Commune' reproduced with the permission of the Cultural Services Committee from an original copy in Manchester Central Library; New Lanark Conservation and Civic Trust for Fig. 2.2; Norfolk County Library for Fig. 3.30 from 'The Cable', March 1895; The Ordnance Survey (Crown Copyright Reserved) for Figs. 3.5, 3.10, 3.15, 3.23 and 3.35; The Robert Owen Museum for Fig. 2.1; Sheffield Newspapers Ltd. for Fig. 5.4 photograph by courtesy of Sheffield Newspapers Ltd.; University of London Library for Fig. 2.4 from *Practical Directions for the Speedy and Economical Establishment of Communities* by W. Thompson, Fig. 2.10 from 'The Working Bee', 1840 and Fig. 2.17 from 'The New Age', 1843, by courtesy of the University of London Library; Mr Ronald Webber for the photographs reproduced in Fig. 3.34 and Fig. 3.35; Oscar Zarate for Fig. 3.2.

We regret we have been unable to trace the copyright holder of Fig. 4.15 from P. G. Rogers *The Sixth Trumpeter* and any information which would enable us to do so would be appreciated.

Cover illustrations: View of Snigs End – Illustrated London News
                        Aerial View of Burnley – Aerofilms Ltd.

Chapter 1

Context

The intention of this chapter is to outline a context for looking at the various forms of alternative community in nineteenth-century England. Firstly, the idea of alternative communities is explained in relation to a tradition of practical schemes that have sought to transpose the imaginary world of utopia into reality. Secondly, a rationale is offered for treating alternative communities in nineteenth-century England as a distinctive form of settlement. Thirdly, a typology is presented that, in turn, provides the framework for subsequent chapters; and, finally, before looking at individual communities, note is made of some of their recurring characteristics.

1.1 Alternative communities as 'practical utopias'

The argument is developed that nineteenth-century communities can themselves be located in the context of a continuing relationship between 'alternative communities', 'utopian thought' and 'historical circumstances'.

In the first place, alternative communities can be seen as attempts to implement utopian visions. Whereas communities are immediate and practical attempts to change reality, utopias remain as dreams of the imaginary society – the one is rooted in possibility, the other in fantasy. The term 'practical utopia' to describe the communities is, in this sense (as a fusion between possibility and fantasy) contradictory. But both concepts are about changing society, and communities derive from utopian thought the essential 'orientation which transcends reality and which at the same time breaks the bonds of the existing order'[1]. Communities can, therefore, be seen in a relationship with utopias, where the latter provides the ideological framework for local action [2]. This is not to imply that all utopias necessarily envisage an alternative society formed of communities, nor that all attempts to establish communities went beyond the discussion stage. But where groups of people did succeed in coming together, even for a short time, and laying what was in their terms the foundations for a new society, reference will be made to their utopian origins as well as to the characteristics of the communities themselves.

The communities derive their mandate, not so much from a

spontaneous reponse to local grievances, as from a total vision of an alternative reality. They represent the efforts of groups of people who are agreed on the nature of an alternative society, and on the efficacy of the community as a method of achieving it. Communities can, therefore, be seen both as a method of social change and as an end in themselves – contrasting with other methods such as individual dissent, State reformism or mass revolutionary movements.

There is also an important relationship with the precise historical circumstances in which utopias and community schemes are framed. While utopias envisage an alternative society they are, at the same time, conceived in relation to the material conditions of existing society. There is a 'parallel history' of utopia and reality, with the former representing a response to the particular conditions of established society. Community experiments differ in type and intensity at different points in time, and it is not sufficient to explain this simply in terms of corresponding variations in utopian thought. Instead, it is necessary to look beyond the specific details of community schemes and utopian ideas, and to consider them both in the wider context of a recurring search for secular and religious freedom.

From the end of the mediaeval period this history of communities is one that is rooted in part on the potential of human achievement in a new age of scientific, spiritual and terrestrial discovery; in part on a changing class structure and the potential of new forces released in the political revolution of the seventeenth century; and in part on a direct response to religious persecution. In the nineteenth century the source of utopian thought and practice is to be found more squarely within the contradictions of industrial capitalism, but it will be argued that the links with an earlier tradition are never wholly severed. An explanation of the communities will, therefore, be framed in relation to past experience as well as in relation to conditions surrounding the communities in their own time.

Paradoxically, the late-mediaeval period marks the start of a new phase of utopian thought and, at the same time, in its own social characteristics a cherished ideal to which later communitarians frequently turned [3]. It was a transitional period between a static world where people could hope for little more than their own salvation after death, and one where a more humanist view prevailed with scope to initiate material change in their own lifetime. This new role for human activity as a positive force opened the way for revolutionary dreams of earthly change.

As long as the clerically and feudally organised mediaeval order was able to locate its paradise outside of society, in some other worldly sphere which transcended history and dulled its revolutionary edge, the idea of paradise was still an integral part of mediaeval society. Not until certain social groups embodied these wish-images into their actual conduct, and tried to realise them, did these ideologies become utopian [4].

And yet, at the same time as utopian thinking enters a new humanist phase, it is often to a romantic vision of the fourteenth-century commune that later writers return for their model of community. As the real history is forgotten – that of a hierarchical society, of the constraints of the established Church on the scope for human growth, and of the prevalence of material poverty, disease and war – its memory is replaced by one of perfect integration between town and country, of the freedom of the commune when the rigid structure of feudal society disintegrated, of an intimate relationship between worker and product, and of a general sense of 'communitas'. It is this latter notion which persists, especially in the nineteenth century, when the scale and nature of capitalist industrialisation served to sharpen the profile of what had been 'lost'. The mediaeval commune is an important but by no means the only model used by the later utopians. Others returned to the primitive Christian Church – before it became weighted by an established hierarchy of clerics and their organisation, administering lands and extracting dues from the populace. They looked to the ideal of community that was associated with Jesus Christ and his disciples, leading simple lives and sharing all between them. Another favoured model was that of tribal society, where an image was formed of small groups of people living communally in close association with nature, and sharing the products of their labour within their own group.

The monastery, too, is sometimes recalled as an ideal to be emulated in future society. It is presented as a small, cooperative community, where patterns of work and social contact are governed by spiritual doctrine. Its physical separation from the rest of society reinforces its spiritual purity, the manifestation of a doctrinal attempt to separate soul from matter as a precondition for salvation. Whether communities need to be physically detached from 'corrupt' society is, in itself, a recurring question in utopian thought. The importance of the monastery is, perhaps, increased as a result of their dissolution in the sixteenth century, in that they could more easily be portrayed in memory as paradise lost. For instance, 'as for community, with the monasteries expired the only type that we ever had in England of such an intercourse. There is no community in England; there is aggregation, but aggregation under circumstances which make it, rather, a dissociating than a uniting principle' [5].

The notion of community in utopian thought is also nourished by a vague but persisting recollection of a past Golden Age, a Garden of Eden of material abundance and natural beauty, separated in time and space from the realities of common life. In English social history this is often intermingled with a nostalgic reminiscence of rustic harmony, and of village life in particular, with successive generations idealising their faded memories of a rural background. The eighteenth-century poet, Oliver Goldsmith, is illustrative of this tradition, lamenting the loss of 'rural virtues' and cherishing the image of happier days in the village of his childhood:

... loveliest village of the plain,
Where health and plenty cheer'd the labouring swain,
Where smiling spring its earliest visit paid,
And parting summers lingering blooms delayed;
Dear lovely bowers of innocence and ease,
Seats of my youth, when every sport could please [6]

Contributing to an explanation of what amounts to a retrospective vision of a simpler and better England, Christopher Hill (1958) (C) draws attention to the persisting idea of the 'Norman Yoke'. It rested on the original portrayal of an Anglo-Saxon society where people lived as free and equal citizens, governing themselves through representative institutions. This ideal form of society was brought to an end in 1066, when the Normans replaced egalitarianism with the tyranny of an alien king and landlords. But the memory of what was lost persisted, erupting in various forms for centuries after the Norman Conquest [7].

Finally, there is also in the idea of community a sense of salvation and regeneration. Since the biblical legend of Noah it has been presented at various times in utopian form as a small place, where the purification of the world can start afresh. There is consistently a spirit of new growth, immune from the corrupt influence of the old society – the 'ark in the flood' that symbolises both escape and rebuilding.

For a variety of these reasons, the ideal of the community has appeared as a consistent element in utopian thought and practice. A classic precursor of later models is that of Thomas More's *Utopia* (first published in 1516). It contains what is to become a familiar blend of criticism of existing society, coupled with the presentation of an alternative form of organisation. Significantly, the alternative society, 'Utopia', is represented in the form of an island, contained in itself and separated from the rest of civilisation. Within its forbidding boundaries (where 'without a Utopian pilot it's practically impossible for a foreign ship to enter the harbour'), social cooperation and physical order prevailed. Work is shared on an equitable basis, town and country are in balance, and there is a strict code of conduct designed to serve the common interest. It is a pattern of order and containment which may well bear the marks of More's own experience of monastic life.

The use of an island in utopian imagery is of interest, not only as a representation of community, but also as an illustration of the qualitative separation of alternative society from that which was known and realisable. It is a technique which was not new to this period (a classical example being Plato's 'Atlantis'), but in an age of discovery the popularity increased. The process of exploration and discovery was itself rich ground for imagination and, so long as large parts of the world remained uncharted, there was still the real possibility of coming across the perfect society. Utopian literature in the seventeenth century, especially, produced various examples of fictional lands in this mould – for instance, Francis Bacon's island of 'Bensalem', Samuel Hartlib's 'Macaria', Samuel Gott's 'Nova Solyma' and John Sadler's 'Olbia' [8].

In the sixteenth century the utopian island is still as much a product of

Fig. 1.1 Utopia and community: A classical model is that of Thomas More's *Utopia*, where a distant island is used to emphasise the separation of a utopian existence from the realities of mainstream society.

mediaevalism as it is of the new humanism. The humanist element is to be found in the endeavour of discovery, but something of the mediaeval presumption that things are ordained rather than achieved persisted in the notion that paradise could be 'found' rather than 'created' by human achievement. In the seventeenth century, while this schism still exists, the specific context of the English Revolution and the new opportunities

Fig. 1.2 Utopia and community: Another variation is exemplified by Edward Calvert's *The Primitive City*, where innocence and unity in Nature are lodged in the image of a past Golden Age.

offered for further political change, shift the balance of utopian thinking more squarely towards the humanist camp. The political opportunities for immediate achievement lead to a fusion between utopia and community that does not recur with anything like the same intensity until the early years of the nineteenth century. Increasingly, it is not the chance discovery of a tropical paradise that will transform the world, but the full exercise of human reason.

The preconditions for political and social change already existed before the revolutionary decades of the mid seventeenth century, but it was the events of the Civil War which opened the way for their outward development. With the execution of Charles I there followed a period of, arguably, unparalleled dissent and popular revolt; the old order was discredited, and attention now turned to the new form of society that might replace it. In the words of Gerrard Winstanley, 'the great searching of heart in these days is to find out where true freedom lies, that the commonwealth of England might be established in peace' [9].

Religious and secular dissent were closely intertwined, and the popular utopias that emerged bore the marks of both sources. Winstanley's rhetorical question asking 'why may we not have our Heaven here (that is, a comfortable livelihood in the Earth) and Heaven hereafter too?' [10], went straight to the heart of both established religious doctrine and accepted patterns of property relationships. In challenging the orthodox belief in the separation of body and soul, it reflected the views of a number of sects in this period, which preached that God existed on earth and that men and women might recapture the state of innocence which existed before the Fall. For Winstanley, God could be equated with Reason. At the same time, the very idea of 'a comfortable livelihood in the Earth' was incompatible with the reality of existing material inequalities. In place of these differences within society what emerged from a variety of sources were proposals for new communist forms of organisation. 'Meum et tuum divide the world into factions, into atoms; and till the world return to its first simplicity . . . covetousness will be the root of all evil' [11].

But although it was an atmosphere in which utopian thought flourished, it was also one of political immediacy – a vacuum existed which could yet be filled by the schemes of idealists. The fall of the monarchy was variously interpreted by sectarian organisations as a sign that the Kingdom of God on earth was imminent, and even Winstanley's practical programme for the communal appropriation of the land was not divorced from millennial inspiration. He claimed that his own venture on to St George's Hill at Weybridge in Surrey in 1649 was the product of divine inspiration as well as a moral and legal claim on the land:

in that we begin to dig upon George Hill to eat our bread together by righteous labour and sweat of our brows, it was shewed us by vision in dreams and out of dreams that that should be the place we should begin upon. And though that earth in view of flesh be very barren, yet we should trust the spirit for a blessing. And that not only this common or heath should be taken in and manured by the people, but all the commons and waste ground in England and in the whole world shall be taken in by the people in righteousness, not owning any property; but taking the earth to be a common treasury, as it was first made for all [12].

The community of Winstanley's 'Diggers' (or 'True Levellers', in contrast to the reformist 'Levellers' in the New Model Army) was a modest venture in itself, but it was clearly intended that the example should be followed by the poor elsewhere. While the pattern did not spread to the extent envisaged, there is certainly evidence of comparable schemes at this time. Largely, it seems, as a result of appeals by Winstanley, other Digger colonists were established at Wellingborough in Northamptonshire, Cox Hall in Kent, Iver in Buckinghamshire, Barnet in Hertfordshire, Enfield in Middlesex, Dunstable in Bedfordshire, Bosworth in Leicestershire, and at other sites in Gloucestershire and Nottinghamshire [13].

On removing the monarchy, the very heart of the old order, waves of dissent spread outwards, extending the call for change far beyond that of mere constitutional reform. But, although it may well be true to say that the 'seventeenth century volcano was at white heat' [14], in the event, for the English peasantry it failed to explode. Instead, the gains of revolution belonged to the bourgeoisie, and in a new alliance of merchants, financiers and landowners, the eighteenth century saw a steady accumulation of capital. This was not a period to nourish the hopes of utopian achievement, and writings were more about abstract issues exploring the idea of a 'state of nature' and issues of political right than about imminent revolution. It was by no means, though, a century of tranquillity and not only were the foundations laid for the new capitalist system of production which, in itself, was to engender a new phase of social and political turbulence, but constitutional revolutions in both North America and France were to have their own repercussions in England.

An early illustration of a new phase of utopian thought and practice, with the hallmarks of the eighteenth century but also with elements that were to reappear in nineteenth-century schemes, is that of 'Pantisocracy', brainchild of Samuel Taylor Coleridge and Robert Southey [15]. It was, in itself, a scheme to put a utopian notion of society directly into practice, using land already purchased at Loyaloak on the Susquehanna River in Pennsylvania. On the basis of three hours labour each day it was envisaged that enough would be produced to support the community. The produce would be stored and shared communally, and property would be 'generalised'. Leisure would be spent in liberal discussions and educating their children. There would be complete freedom of political and religious views, though marriage was retained as a basic relationship in the new society.

Twenty-seven men and women pledged themselves to 'Pantisocracy' (described by Coleridge as the equal government of all), but within a year of its conception in 1794 the group disbanded without having even left England. As an illustration of a new wave of utopian schemes, though, there are some interesting lessons.

Its conception at the time of the French Revolution is in itself significant. The events in France aroused new hopes for political justice and freedom and (as will be shown in the following chapter) was to have a profound effect on early nineteenth-century utopianism. Southey had claimed that he would be much happier 'on the frontiers of France every hour exposed to death in a cause I must feel to be just' [16]. A second point of interest is the growing attraction of North America for those who wanted to free themselves from the traditions of the Old World, and to recreate society in the virgin soils of the new land:

Where dawns, with hope serene, a brighter day
Than e'er saw Albion in her happiest times
... Free from the ills which here our peace destroy
Content and bliss on Transatlantic Shore [17]

Thirdly, 'Pantisocracy' reflects an interest in the ideas of two writers who are to have an influence on later schemes as well, namely, Rousseau and Godwin. Amongst some of Rousseau's more romantic followers his hypothesis that virtue and true freedom flourished in more natural conditions, erroneously came to assume the status of historical fact and normative ideal. North America – its new lands as near to a state of nature as the European romanticist could imagine – was an obvious location for the fulfilment of these ideals, a world where Coleridge could happily dream of 'criticising poetry when hunting a buffalo and writing sonnets whilst following the plough' [18]. Coleridge and Southey also turned for inspiration to William Godwin, with his ideas for a society without centralised government – an alternative system of a society composed of voluntary communities [19].

Finally, there is also a millennial side to their aspirations. As the likelihood of the practical realisation of their scheme receded, so the prospect of a miraculous transformation at some unspecified point in the future came to the fore. The change of society would not be gradual but sudden and cataclysmic – 'Pantisocracy is no longer the question – its realisation is distant – perhaps a miraculous millennium' [20].

Although there are elements in this romantic expression of an alternative which are to recur in nineteenth-century schemes, 'Pantisocracy' is still essentially an eighteenth-century vision. What Coleridge and others failed to foresee was the immense material transformation of society that was already under way, and which was to provide a new context for political ideas in the nineteenth century. With the presence of a well-established bourgeoisie and an accumulation of capital over a long period of overseas trade, the foundations for the new urban industrial enterprise had already been laid. What began to take form towards the end of the eighteenth century was the shadow of a new society, built upon an economic system of owners of capital and wage labour concentrated into new factories and towns devoted to mass production. Whereas towns had previously served the countryside, in various ways they now assumed a more dominant role, absorbing labour as well as capital from the land. The sharpening class division between capitalists and workers was expressed in the factories and mines in terms of the economic separation of the workers from the full product of their labour, in the new areas of housing in terms of their physical separation from employers and supervisors, and in Parliament in terms of political control for the dominant economic class.

In this context, alternative communities emerge not simply as a rejection of, say, 'town life' or 'bad working conditions', but as a rejection of the whole capitalist system, and as an attempt to replace it with something new. As 'alternatives' they were necessarily conceived within and in relation to the contradictions of 'established' society. In a dialectical relationship with emergent capitalism the history of alternative England becomes, in one sense, a history of established society itself.

But the attraction of 'community', in particular, as a central feature of utopianism was greatly increased in the nineteenth century. For the realisation was not simply that society was changing in itself, but that this change was at the expense of something that had already largely disappeared. And in the lost order could be seen the fading image of community. In place of a society composed of small, integrated groups where people were assumed to have experienced a sense of belonging, the character of the new society was one of an increasing scale of organisation and growing detachment for the individual. The focus of the old order – family life, the village and the small town – gave way to large cities and State bureaucracies. This was conceptualised towards the end of the nineteenth century by Tönnies in terms of a shift from *Gemeinschaft* to *Gesellschaft* – from a world of organic fellowship, where individuals related to each other in a common system of traditions and mutual ties, to one of commercial bourgeois society, where individuals themselves became units in the new chain of production. It is 'in the organisation and order of *Gemeinschaft* that folk life and folk culture persist. The state, which represents and embodies *Gesellschaft*, is opposed to these in veiled hatred and contempt, the more so the further the state has moved away from and become estranged from these forms of community life' [21].

As the gap between locality and state widened, so the ideal of community gained a new hold in the popular imagination. It was an ideal with both conservative and progressive tendencies – the one dwelling on a distorted image of what had already passed, the other rejecting its feudal associations while seeking to retain the essence of close contact. In the practice of nineteenth-century communitarianism, this tension – between something lost, and something yet to be created – is never wholly dispelled.

1.2 New communities in nineteenth-century England

The essence of the approach in the following chapters is to concentrate on the English alternative communities, but within a comparative setting where account is taken of other forms of settlement, related developments in other countries, and roots which often extend back well before the nineteenth century.

Firstly, alternative communities can be distinguished from other forms of small settlement in nineteenth-century England. The most obvious difference lies in the relative insignificance of their numbers and physical impact, but there are more important qualitative considerations. These can be illustrated by locating alternative communities at one end of a spectrum, extending through three 'ideal types' – from the many 'mainstream' communities built in the main thrust of capitalist industrialisation, through the 'model' communities which sought in their improved standards to idealise and sustain capitalist enterprise, to the very few examples of communities which were manifestations of alternative ideologies.

Mainstream communities: most of the small settlements built in this period were little more than unplanned collections of houses with factories, mines or railways. They were constituent elements in the overall process of urbanisation, a process which, although governed by the general forces of capitalist production, was in practice composed of numerous local decisions and actions by the owners of productive units and by speculative builders. Such developments represented a simple application of the principles of a market economy, in which the low standard of dwellings, the absence of communal services, and proximity to workplace met the new standards of 'minimum cost of production' and 'maximum yield of labour'. They were communities only to the extent that wage-earners and their families were inextricably bound to their workplace in closely-knit local networks of dependency. These small settlements were sometimes isolated, but often coalesced into larger urban complexes. In some instances they were little more than districts or appendages to larger towns, with barely their own identity – like the 'ragged hills ... bespangled with groups of houses inhabited by the working cutler' that William Cobbett observed around Sheffield in 1830 [22]. Or they were the mixture of small towns and villages that Engels visited in Lancashire in the 1840s:

Bolton, Preston, Wigan, Bury, Rochdale, Middleton, Heywood, Oldham, Ashton, Stalybridge, Stockbridge, etc. ... almost wholly working people's districts, interspersed only with factories, a few thoroughfares lined with shops, and a few lanes along which the gardens and houses of the manufacturers are scattered like villas. The towns themselves are badly and irregularly built ... [23].

And, later in the century, they appear in D. H. Lawrence's mixed Nottinghamshire landscape of colliery winding-gear and blackened chapels, of rows of little cottages and a disappearing country life – 'a curious cross between industrialism and the old agricultural England' [24].

Model communities: in contrast with the unplanned character of most of the new settlements there was a limited distribution of 'model communities'. They were established, mainly in the second half of the century, by industrialists with capital amassed, quite simply to reflect their sponsors' notions of what industrial society should be like. They usually represented a substantial improvement in environmental standards, but there was no question of challenging the existing system of society. On the contrary, they set out to reinforce those very qualities upon which the future of capitalism would be assured – such qualities as loyalty to employer, retention of a class system, hard and honest labour, disaffection with talk of revolution, respectability, thrift and religious belief. They were paragons of capitalist industrial society – conscious attempts to re-establish the assumed harmony of village life in an industrial setting, this time with the factory and mine-owner usurping the role of the feudal landlord.

Some of the best-preserved examples that exist are those of the West Riding, particularly in the area of Bradford and Halifax. The industrialists associated with these – Sir Titus Salt (at Saltaire), Colonel Edward Akroyd (at Copley and Akroydon), and the Crossleys (in the West Hill Park area of Halifax) – had family and business links with each other, had been Lord Mayors of Bradford and Halifax, were staunch Congregationalists, had all amassed industrial fortunes, and had not been above calling in troops to resist threats to their property in times of unemployment. There are also the influential model settlements built on fortunes in soap and chocolate, at Port Sunlight, Bournville and New Earswick.

These and a variety of other model settlements associated with mine and factory are documented in Gillian Darley's *Villages of Vision* (1975) (A). She also points to the growing number of 'estate' villages in the countryside built by landowners with improved standards of housing in mind; and, in the late nineteenth century, to the use of model communities for charitable institutions such as orphanages, almshouses and centres for the physically and mentally handicapped. The countryside was also the location for a number of 'land colonies' at this time. They took the form of cottages with smallholdings or a communal estate sponsored by philanthropists and religious groups. The religious colonies generally reflected a more critical approach towards the exploitation of labour, though they were still essentially reformist – endeavouring to regenerate body and soul through a return to the land [25].

Alternative communities: in contrast to both the mainstream and model communities, were those planned communities inspired by ideologies opposed to the established order of society. Attention will be concentrated on groups that gathered in one place, as opposed to 'communities' of scattered individuals (such as political or religious movements whose members continued to live in their own home). In defining the use of the term more closely, Raymond Williams (1976) (A) shows that although 'community' is a word which has been used in this country since the fourteenth century, its sense of 'immediacy' or 'locality' became much stronger in the nineteenth century, distinguishing the world of direct contact from more distant relationships with the State. In this later period, 'community' was the word normally chosen for experiments in an alternative kind of group-living [26]. Moreover, 'community' continues to have this meaning in contemporary use, though it has been joined in a more limited sense by 'commune'.

In the following text, the spirit of this development of terms is acknowledged – with 'communities' used to refer to the schemes, and 'communitarians' to describe the participants. Where it is necessary to stress this particular application (in contrast to the more general meaning of 'community', denoting simply a sense of identity and shared characteristics), then the term 'alternative community' is preferred. Additionally, regard is paid to the variations in how communities were described at the time – as 'colonies', 'estates' or simply by the name of their location or beliefs – with the original term given precedence.

As a distinctive form of development, their physical impact on the changing nineteenth-century landscape was extremely modest. They were small in number, and their individual membership was normally measured in tens. In some cases there were grandiose ideas for much larger settlements and for new forms of architecture and physical layout, but seldom did these dreams come anywhere near to fruition [27]. Apart from a few extravagant exceptions, it was commonly a story of the communities collapsing well before they had constructed either their physical or their social utopia.

In a number of instances the communitarians made use of existing groups of buildings – sometimes for reasons of economy, and sometimes because the physical layout was, in any case, of relatively little importance to their aspirations (something that was especially true of the anarchist communities towards the end of the century). Where they lived and what they did manage to build will be recorded, but it is primarily as political and social experiments rather than as design achievements that their place in nineteenth-century urbanisation will be assessed.

In addition to distinguishing alternative communities from other forms of small settlement, reasons can be given for concentrating on the English communities – at a time when there were, undoubtedly, comparable experiments elsewhere in Europe and North America. The first reason is, quite simply, that the additional material that would need to be gathered for a wider study would merit a book of its own. But there does, in any case, seem good reason for treating the communities in any one country as an individual case. This is in no way to deny or ignore the fact that alternative communities in the nineteenth century can, in one sense, be regarded as a universal form of response to the same general forces of capitalism, and that it may seem artificial to isolate examples on the basis of national boundaries. At the same time, within what can be seen as a general process, there were also important cultural variations – the form and impact of capitalism differing between countries, and between different parts of the same country. To the extent that alternative communities will tend towards the inverted values of mainstream society, it is reasonable to expect that they will vary in themselves according to the particular cultural milieu in which they are formed.

In the case of the English communities, although they occur in a variety of locations, their ties were seldom restricted to their local setting. It has been found that they were often associated with national political and religious movements, and to this extent the particular context of English history provides a relevant focus in its own right. It is no less important, however, to retain a comparative perspective, and reference will be made to related examples elsewhere. There were some instances where communities, clearly of the same origins as those in England, took root in other parts of Britain – like the Ruskinite community at Barmouth in Wales, or the Owenite communities at Orbiston in Scotland and Ralahine in Ireland. In cases like these, reference will be restricted to an explanation of their part in the broader movement, with their English counterparts receiving the more detailed treatment [28].

There is also an important relationship between the English communities and many of those that were established in the United States. The intensity of community formation in the new lands – where, according to Ralph Waldo Emerson, there was a time when 'not a reading man but has a draft of a new community in his waistcoat pocket' – far exceeded that in any of the European countries. Numbers involved have been put at as high as 100,000 participants, with as many as 300 communities [29]. European influence in these developments was not insignificant, and the view is generally taken that although 'the communitarian idea came to fullest flower in the New World ... its seeds were brought from the Old' [30]. What is more, the seeds had been carried across the Atlantic for many years before the nineteenth century – initially by religious groups from Central and Western Europe, in search of a more tolerant environment. Successive groups were attracted, not simply by this greater degree of tolerance, but also by the tangible advantage of cheap and plentiful land. In one of the main waves of American communitarianism – between 1820 and 1850 – sectarians (many of whom continued to come from Germany) were joined by political groups, notably, the utopian socialists originating in England and France. Later in the century, there is evidence of a reverse flow, with ideas gleaned from experience of American communities stimulating fresh experiments in the Old World. This theme will be developed in relation to the anarchist communities of the 1890s and, more recently, to the upsurge of communitarianism in the 1970s.

The final point in this section, as to why attention is directed to the nineteenth century, can be answered briefly. In English history the nineteenth century saw both the rise of industrial capitalism and, at the same time, the emergence of new patterns of dissent. It was a formative period both for mainstream society and for its very antithesis, and it is as part of this critical dialectic that alternative communities will be located. To place this relationship, in turn, within a broader historical perspective, reference will also be made to the origins of alternative communities which often extend well back into earlier periods, and to the continuing evidence of communitarianism in the twentieth century.

1.3 Typology

Within the limits outlined in the previous section, a total of twenty-eight alternative communities has been identified [31]. These communities are listed in the order of their date of inception in the Appendix (p. 238), and their distribution is illustrated in Fig. 1.3. Although there are apparently clusters both in terms of chronology (the 1840s and the 1890s being periods of especially intense activity) and in terms of place (Essex and the West Riding attracting a disproportionate number of the

�֍ ALTERNATIVE COMMUNITIES IN NINETEENTH-CENTURY ENGLAND

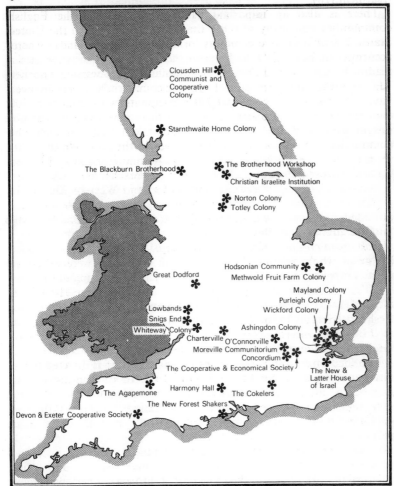

Fig. 1.3 Alternative communities in nineteenth-century England.

communities), given the small numbers involved, generalisations are better based upon qualitative considerations.

In particular, in view of their role as a challenge to the established order of society, the question might be asked as to whether they were purely idiosyncratic, or whether they reflected any broader ideological coherence. Were the communities floating individually outside the main currents of radical thought and action, or were they simply tactical variations in a wider struggle?

There is much that is eccentric in the history of the communities; but, equally, there is much that is not. In either case, an explanation cannot rest solely on the extent of their 'eccentricity'. That alone would fail to explain why communities have been more numerous at some periods rather than at others – why, for instance, the 1840s was an active period not only in England but also in France and the United States. Instead, we must look beyond 'eccentricity' to examine the specific relationship between community formation and the conditions in society at that time. A general relationship between utopian thought, historical circumstances and alternative communities has already been outlined, and this will now be pursued in relation to the communities in nineteenth-century England. It is this relationship which is the basis of the following typology:

1. *The communities of utopian socialism*, which were advocated in the early years of working-class action as both a means and an end for achieving social change. The communities considered in this category are: the Cooperative and Economical Society (1821); the Devon and Exeter Cooperative Society (1826); the Hodsonian Community (1838); Harmony Hall (1839); Concordium (1842); and Moreville Communitorium (1843).

2. *The communities of agrarian socialism*, which reflected a belief in 'getting back to the land' as the source of both moral regeneration and a more egalitarian society. The communities considered are: O'Connorville (1846); Lowbands (1846); Charterville (1847); Snigs End (1847); Great Dodford (1848); Totley Colony (1876); Methwold Fruit Farm Colony (1889); Starnthwaite Home Colony (1892); and Mayland Colony (1896).

3. *The communities of sectarianism*, referring to religious groups that withdrew from society in order to prepare either for the Kingdom of God on earth, or to ensure their own privileged salvation after death. The five communities in this category are: the Agapemone (1846); the Cokelers (1850); the Christian Israelite Institution (1857); the New Forest Shakers (1872); and the New and Latter House of Israel (1875).

4. *The communities of anarchism*, where there is a specific rejection of the State and other forms of centralised control, and where communities represent the basic unit of the new cooperative society. Those included in this category are: the Clousden Hill Communist and Cooperative Colony (1895); Norton Colony (1896); Purleigh Colony (1896); the Brotherhood Workshop (1897); Ashingdon Colony (1897); Wickford Colony (1898); Whiteway Colony (1898); and the Blackburn Brotherhood (1899).

The intention of the typology is not to obscure the many variations between individual communities but to clarify what various groups have in common. Nor is it intended to suggest that these are watertight compartments; inevitably, some categories will be more satisfactory than others. The 'utopian socialist' communities, for instance, over a twenty-five year period, are clearly identifiable both in terms of their incidence at a time when comparable schemes were occurring elsewhere, and because they subscribed explicitly to the same general doctrine. The 'sectarian' communities, though more scattered in time, are also unmistakable in their commitment to extreme religious doctrines. In contrast, the 'agrarian socialists', while having much in common with each other, did not recognise themselves as necessarily part of the same tradition. Finally, the 'anarchist' communities were all in the last decade of the century, had considerable contact with each other, and generally admitted to the same philosophical basis. In the following four chapters these various groups of communities will be considered, both in themselves and in relation to their historical situation.

In addition to these ideological variations, however, there are also certain characteristics which recur from one to another. Before going any further to explain their differences, a profile will be drawn of a hypothetical nineteenth-century community, 'Allopia' (meaning 'other place'). While reflecting all the details of no single community, Allopia may serve to highlight something of what many of them had in common.

1.4 Allopia

In its seven years Allopia attracted a total of 100 participants. After four years, when the community was at its height, there were as many as sixty people living in the little cluster of brick-built cottages.

In spite of its limited duration and size the community was remarkably active and observers were consistently impressed by the high level of commitment, especially during the first few years of its existence. A great deal of the credit for this observed cohesion, and for the associated achievements, must be attributed to the charismatic leadership of Henry Allos, founder of the community and driving force during its formative years.

Allos, before his years in the community, had been a trader in Sheffield. He was by no means wealthy but had amassed a modest capital which served in time to acquire the land and to get the buildings under way. He was widely read – being greatly impressed by Robert Owen, less so by Karl Marx – but probably his greatest asset was his powers of oratory. He attended meetings in and around the West Riding, using his immense charm and energies to persuade others that the ability to create a better society lay in their hands, not in Parliament or the hereafter. 'We shall acquire some land, and with our own hands, show others that the smoke and greed to which we have all been subjected need persist no more.' His belief in reason and persuasion was absolute. It was this unshakable belief which held the community together and persuaded others to join them in the early years when the first cottages were being built.

Yet even the charisma and ideas of Henry Allos proved inadequate in the face of both internal and external difficulties. A constant shortage of capital was the main problem. Believing that, if the community was to convince others it would have to be of at least 500 people, Allos invested heavily in an ambitious infra-structure of brick-fields and associated railway, roads to link with the Sheffield routes, and extensive water and drainage channels. As his own capital dried up, and in advance of any revenue from the newly-planted crops and fruit trees, he appealed to local farmers and industrialists. While he never hid his distaste for the capitalist system, he sought to win their support by arguing that there would always be a place for men of their initiative in the type of society which Allos envisaged. And better, he would argue, that they should involve themselves in a peaceful transition of society, than allow free rein to the mob. Occasional donations are recorded, but far from enough to stave off the growing financial crisis within Allopia. With few exceptions, the attitude of local farmers and villagers was, in any case, generally hostile.

Apart from a shortage of capital the tensions within Allopia are depressingly familiar. Most of the communitarians themselves had come from the factories and workshops of Sheffield, and were ill-suited to the rigours and requirements of farm life. During the first winters it was the excitement of new housing of their own and the momentum of collective enthusiasm which kept them together, in the face of extreme physical hardships. The early unity gave way in time to factional splits, more on the basis of personal than of ideological differences. But, paradoxically, the greatest threat to the survival of the community came from Allos himself. His power within the community, which all had seemingly been happy to accept at the outset and which he had in any case been willing to share, over the years became authoritarian. He was increasingly away from the community, lecturing in other parts of the country, and he protected his position by tightening procedures to ensure that no decisions could be made in his absence. And as the collapse of the community became more imminent, the extravagance of his schemes grew – to the point where it was finally the result of bad debts which led to its formal dissolution. It is sad to reflect that Allos spent the last years of his life in an asylum.

But in its heyday there were few who had not heard of Allopia. Apart from his own lecturing tours, for a period the community even printed its own weekly newspaper (*Harmonia*) which was circulated widely within the West Riding and in the industrial towns across the Pennines. It carried features on rationalist ideas, on community schemes elsewhere, and on the progress of Allopia itself. There were articles, too, in national publications such as *The Illustrated London News* which monitored its progress under headings of 'A strange colony of working men' and 'The vision of Henry Allos'. In the summer months organised visits would be arranged for Sheffield workers to view the achievements of the community, and, hopefully, to persuade some to follow the example. At one time there were even plans to buy land elsewhere for future communities of this nature, but apparently these came to nothing.

Apart from garden plots with the few pigs, cows and chickens that were individually owned, the main income was derived from a potato crop that was the result of cooperative effort. It was envisaged that the community would steadily extend its activities from crops, notably potatoes, which could yield a quick return, to fruit trees, which were planted in the first winter but which would not mature for several years. In time the early rural preoccupation would be balanced by a growth in craft activities, as workers who had been used to the factories learnt new skills for work that could be done in small groups. Allos believed that there was no product essential to society that could not be produced in groups of ten or twenty at the most.

Many of the communitarians had received little or no previous education, and one of the more noteworthy achievements in Allopia's brief history was the effort directed to redressing this. In spite of all the other difficulties and shortage of capital, a small school-house was built in the first winter, and Allos arranged for a visiting school teacher to provide instruction for all age groups. The well-heated building acquired a modest collection of books, and was a popular point for discussion and meetings as well as quiet study.

The community never reached a size which enabled the achievement of an equal division of labour between men and women as intended. That part of the scheme had depended on the communal care of babies and young children to release mothers, but the numbers involved were too small to merit the special rooms and nurses that were needed. Some economy was achieved through communal cooking and eating arrangements, but the more serious problem of self-esteem for the women in the community was never effectively tackled.

On the question of diet, Allos himself was a great proponent of vegetarianism, though his enthusiasm was, according to observers, clearly not shared by all. In the end it appears that a compromise was reached (Allos yielding on economic grounds) in which animals that were individually owned – pigs being the mainstay – could be killed to supplement the winter diet. The issue of dress reform was also one of compromise. Allos had been responsible for a number of articles in *Harmonia*, condemning conventional forms of clothing as being unhygienic and impractical. For a short period, visitors to the community reported that both men and women wore a kind of loose-fitting, green tunic – but the practice was clearly not popular within the community and, with the advent of winter, most of them had resorted to their old ways.

Though it is now more than a century since the community dispersed, the little brick cottages remain, the former garden plots now proving attractive to retired people especially. There is little evidence of ancillary buildings, though the school-house, used for a time as a chapel, has since fallen into poor repair and is now used by a local farmer to store winter hay.

Chapter 2

The communities of utopian socialism

The English communities between 1820 and 1845 are the product of a rich mixture of ideas and action. Their theoretical origins are to be found within what was later termed 'utopian socialism' whilst, for their practical source, it is hard to disentangle the communities from the wider cooperative movement that took root in this period. There were also important links between the English communities and comparable schemes elsewhere in Europe and the United States. These three aspects – the model of utopian socialism, the practical context of the cooperative movement, and the overseas links will be considered in turn, before looking at the details of the communities themselves.

2.1 Utopian socialism and community

The term 'utopian socialism' refers to the form of early socialism that emerged, in France and Britain especially, in the second quarter of the nineteenth century. At its very heart is a commitment to community – both in the broad sense of a harmonious society and in the more specific sense of restructuring society in the form of small, voluntary communities. Indeed, the term 'communitarianism' stems from this period to denote the particular method of social change that was involved.

In France, important theorists of this form of socialism include Noel Babeuf and Filippo Buonarroti, Claude-Henri de Saint Simon, Charles Fourier, Etienne Cabet, Auguste Blanqui, Pierre Leroux, Victor Considerant, Louis Blanc and Constantin Pecqueur; and in Britain, while Robert Owen was the most important figure, William Thompson and Goodwyn Barmby also made significant contributions. The ideas of these latter three can all be shown to have close and direct links with the English community movement and will be reviewed in more detail than those of their French contemporaries. However, before concentrating on the British theorists, a broader view will be taken of the nature of utopian socialism, the philosophical foundation for this particular phase of communities.

From the period of the French Revolution to the collapse of the 1848 revolutionary attempts in Europe, utopian thought (and, as part of that, the community ideal) can be represented as an antithesis to the reality of contemporary political and socio-economic conditions. In political terms, the French Revolution could be seen after the event as a political and symbolic achievement for the bourgeoisie, that left the greater part of society little better off than before. Noel Babeuf was the first of the utopian socialists to expose the vital difference between the achievement of political equality (as a liberal achievement of political rights) and the achievement of material equality, without which the pre-revolutionary injustices of society would remain. The significance of Babeuf's ideas was understood less at the time than after his death, when Filippo Buonarroti published and embellished his ideas in 1828 [1]. Less dramatically, the 1832 Parliamentary Reform Act in England served to illustrate the same point of a distinction between political and material equality, contributing to a comparable split in a middle- and working-class alliance.

In exposing the relative worthlessness of political equality on its own, yet at the same time lacking an effective strategy to achieve material equality, the utopian socialists occupy a bridging point between the critical writings of Rousseau and other eighteenth-century political theorists, and the subsequent 'scientific socialists' from the middle of the nineteenth century. Like Rousseau the utopian socialists shared the belief that Man in his wretchedness was the victim of society, and that freedom was impossible except in a community of equals. They also shared a belief in the political basis of morality, in that an improvement in the human condition was only possible through changes in social organisation. But they went further than Rousseau and other eighteenth-century political philosophers in relating these notions of progress to the new conditions of industrial society. By the nineteenth century, 'State of Nature' theories (which had been presented as a way of measuring Man in society against an idealised precedent), gave way to an assessment of human potential in relation to actual circumstances. The utopian socialists were concerned, not with hypothetical conditions, but with what was immediately possible within a new form of society with industrial resources at its disposal. At the same time, in their assessment of the historical situation and the material basis for a changing balance of power, they fell short of the economic and historical analysis contained in the subsequent form of socialist theory developed by Marx and Engels.

Utopian socialism took shape in the context of a rapidly developing capitalist industrial system. In the early years of the nineteenth century both France and Britain were still primarily agricultural nations, and towns and factories as they were then emerging were essentially new phenomena. The relationship between production, wealth and the physical infrastructure of towns and transportation was complex and poorly understood. It is true that Adam Smith had provided an early rationale for what was happening, but this was overtly in support of the pattern of bourgeois ownership, with little consideration of alternatives. Forty years later, Malthus and Ricardo tackled some of the technical weaknesses in Smith's theories, strengthening classical liberalism as the political ideology of the ascendant manufacturing class [2].

But there were contradictions in the contrasting living and working conditions of early nineteenth-century society, and in the immense inequalities in the distribution of wealth and income, which liberalism could not satisfactorily answer. However inadequate in hindsight, the utopian socialists performed a role of stepping into the breach and of providing alternative answers and portrayals of how society might be organised in the future. It will be shown that their advocacy of communities was an integral part of this broader strategy of social and historical change.

The ultimate goal of the utopian socialists was a harmonious society, governed by cooperation rather than competition – a society where true freedom would be possible. It is the clarity of this goal which distinguishes their ideas most sharply from competing ideologies.

There was little that was novel, for instance, in their underlying belief in progress (to this extent they were on common ground with the liberals). The utopian socialist belief was based, however, on an evolutionary sense of history, where society was sufficiently mature to receive their ideas. Society had been 'guided' through various stages from barbarism to capitalism and, with the help of their prophetic leadership, was poised for the final step to a state of utopia (to a large extent, synonymous with a society of communities). It is a theory of history which was based more on divine guidance than on material reality. Only St Simon presented an historical analysis which offered reasons as to why his ideas were in the 'true' interests of the working class.

But for all their differences and uncertainties in historical perspective, the utopian socialists were at one in deploring the degradation of labour and human life that was part and parcel of the competitive, industrial system. They reacted against a system which accounted for humans as simply marketable units in the chain of production, a means for profit-making regardless of individual suffering. Their analysis was by no means a fully-developed concept of alienation; in many ways it was rather simplistic, resting on the removal of certain obstacles (in particular, ignorance) as the way towards the restoration of Man's lost soul. But as an antidote to liberalism's cold rationalisation of bourgeois control, and, in compensation for the logical weaknesses in their own thinking, the sincerity of their concern was a powerful influence.

As a way out of these conditions, it was not that the utopian socialists believed either in a non-industrial system or in a society of leisure; nor were they apprehensive that wants might be created which either could not be satisfied or would not satisfy even if attained (a fear that Rousseau had expressed in the previous century). On the contrary, a belief prevailed that Man's future lay in the full development of a new industrial system, with human labour at the centre. It was not industrialisation as such that was at fault, but the way that it had been organised so far. What they wanted, in place of the existing system, was to organise production more rationally, to ensure that Man would earn the full product of his labour; and, from that, a just society would emerge.

At the root of their belief in progress and the emergence of a just system, was their faith in the power of education to liberate Man from the state of ignorance that society had imposed on him. In the current of the Enlightenment it was believed that 'reason' and 'rationality' were qualities that could be nurtured and that, through Man's higher understanding, the way would then be open towards a better society [3]. Educational theories figure consistently in the formulations of the utopian socialists and, understandably, schools are a vital component in community experiments.

It is understandable too, given their belief in the potential for human development once artificial barriers had been removed, that a number of the utopian socialists were also active feminists. Fourier and Owen, for instance, were both concerned to create a form of community where women could be freed from their traditional roles. The theme is an important one, not simply in terms of nineteenth-century social theory, but in relation to communities in particular which, in many cases, afforded new opportunities for experiment in marriage and family structure, in work roles, and forms of dress. This is a function which communities have continued to perform in the twentieth century, challenging established patterns of sex roles and family life.

The relationship between town and country was also of considerable importance to the utopian socialists. It was not simply the new physical pattern of towns to be railed against, but the underlying process of urban domination which had been increasing from the late-mediaeval period. The appearance of the new towns was only the manifestation of a more pervasive economic process associated with the rise of capitalism. Faced with this situation the utopian socialists anticipated a continuing theme in socialist theory, in seeking ways to reconcile the conflict between town and country. There were plans for both farming and industry in the communities, in contrast to some of the schemes later in the century which were much more in the nature of escape routes from industrial capitalism.

Attitudes towards the State are ambivalent, yet tend towards a belief that centralised control of society would lessen in the future with the removal of those conditions which fostered competition and struggle. Communities figure prominently as ways of implementing a decentralist philosophy. Yet there is also a contradiction in that the utopian socialists envisaged a strong leadership role for themselves in guiding society from the 'old' to the 'new'; in Owen's case this assumed messianic proportions:

the mission of my life appears to be to prepare the population of the world to understand the vast importance of the second creation of humanity, from the birth of each individual, through the agency of man, by creating entirely new surroundings in which to place all through life, and by which a new human nature would appear to arise from the new surroundings [4].

Owen was not alone in thinking in this way. There is, generally, amongst the utopian socialists, little faith in the ability of the working class to create their own future [5]. This was a fundamental point of difference with later socialists, and an important indication of how the community experiments were invariably managed.

2.2 Ideas for the new society

Of the British theorists, Robert Owen, William Thompson and Goodwyn Barmby each developed the general ideas of utopian socialism in relation to particular models of community.

'Villages of cooperation'

In the case of Robert Owen, while it would be superfluous, in the light of the excellent works already available, to repeat the details of his life and beliefs, it remains important for the purpose in hand to direct attention to his particular approach to communities [6]. Whatever the merits or otherwise of his proposals there is no doubt that his notion of the 'ideal community' was of considerable influence both on schemes at that time, and as a physical blueprint for a variety of planned schemes later in the century.   Owen's activities extended over most of the first half of the nineteenth century to embrace, in turn, a variety of roles – philanthropic factory reformer, theoretician of the new society and practical community builder, early Trade Unionist and pioneer of the cooperative movement. Yet the ideas which underlie all his activities were remarkably consistent. They amount to a simple doctrine that rested on the initial belief that character is not innate and that, instead, human beings are moulded by their cultural and physical environment; that as a result of an adverse, irrational environment (and at various times he singled out the principle of competition, the hold of established religion, and the intolerable living and working conditions), the human species had itself become both irrational and selfish; but that with 'reason' it was within their earthly power to improve these external conditions and, in turn, the condition of humanity itself. Only ignorance stood in the way of universal progress. The logical outcome was therefore to remove ignorance – to undertake a 'revolution of reason'.

Far from being novel, Owen's ideas were located firmly within a tradition of Enlightenment thought. Locke, for instance, had argued in the seventeenth century that ideas are not innate, but are derived from one's experience of the external environment. And in the eighteenth century both Rousseau and Godwin had fostered the belief that equality was a natural condition of Man, and that it was society (in the way that it had evolved) which was responsible for inequality [7]. At the same time as Owen, the French utopian socialists were more explicit in exposing the limitations of political change to date, and in pledging their faith in the potential for unlimited human progress. Yet, although his ideas were not original, the strength of Owen lies in his attempts to apply them, a judgement that is nowhere more true than in the case of the communities. It is a measure of his influence that there were some sixteen communities in America, and another ten in Britain, associated either directly or indirectly with Owen [8].

Owen's practical experience in community formation started with his reformist activities at the industrial village of New Lanark (where he assumed effective control of the spinning works in 1800 and remained until 1824). It was during this period that he presented his essay *A New View of Society* (1813), which provided a statement of his views on the environmental determination of character. At the same time he introduced immediate improvements in all aspects of the living and working conditions of his workforce. 'What are the best arrangements under which these men and their families can be well and economically lodged, fed, clothed, trained, educated, employed, and governed?', asked Owen while at New Lanark [9]. His various innovations reflected his constant search to find the answer in a better environment.

His educational ventures at New Lanark attracted particular attention, not least of all his explicitly-termed 'Institution for the Formation of Character'. It was an ambitious scheme by any standards, the epitome of his golden principle that human progress would be impossible without first eliminating ignorance. In the many rooms of the Institution the children of New Lanark learnt reading, writing, arithmetic, sewing and knitting and, when their day had finished, the rooms were 'cleaned, ventilated and in winter lighted and heated, and in all respects made comfortable' [10] for the evening session for older

Fig. 2.1 New Lanark: Early nineteenth-century view of the model village.

Fig. 2.2 New Lanark: Current view in the village (which is now a conservation area) showing part of Caithness Row (1792) on the left, and Robert Owen's store (with bow windows), the original nursery building, and New Buildings (with bell tower) on the right.

children and adults. There was no less attention paid to dancing, exercises, music and singing, and in the summer months there were excursions into the surrounding countryside. It was a progressive model of education that was widely acknowledged at the time, and one that was to reappear, in varying form, in later community experiments. New Lanark was a formative period in Owen's own development. Even at the time he recognised it as only the start of something bigger, and later looked back on it as 'the first commencement of practical measures with a view to change the fundamental principle on which society has heretofore been based from the beginning' [11]. It was from this experience, and in reaction to the rebuttal of his more radical ambitions by fellow members of the ruling class, that he turned away from the path of philanthropic model villages and towards an emerging socialist conception of what he termed 'villages of cooperation'.

Widely referred to as 'Mr Owen's Plan', it was first presented, as a way of relieving unemployment and of taking the strain off the collapsing system of Poor Law Relief in the period following the Napoleonic Wars. He later extended the concept to one of a national network of communities for all categories of the population [12].

What he envisaged was a form of small community, involved in both farming and manufacturing. For social and economic reasons population would be restricted to between 300 and 2,000, but ideally 800 to 1,200. The amount of land around the village would vary according to its fertility but would generally provide for the needs of the indigenous

Fig. 2.3 A model of Robert Owen's ideal community – from a design prepared by his architect, Stedman Whitwell, before Owen left for America in 1824.

population, with a surplus for trade elsewhere. Owen expressed a preference for the use of the spade rather than the plough, not only because he considered it to be a superior technique, but also as a way of keeping labour gainfully employed.

The villages would be located in the centre of the farmland, and a layout was envisaged to maximise the communal way of life and minimise the threat to health that was symptomatic of the disorderly towns. A parallelogram was preferred for the new communities, with an absence of the traditional streets and alleys that were believed to be damaging to health and a source of crime.

Owen's belief in rationality and persuasion extended to the conviction that these communities would be brought into being with the aid of capital from landowners and industrialists, parishes and counties, and groups of farmers, mechanics and tradesmen who would each be attracted by a mixture of motives – capital gain, benevolence, economy of rates, belief in cooperation.

Each of the communities would produce a surplus of whatever it was best suited for, and exchange would take place between them to provide for other needs. Within the communities all would receive what they needed, so that motives of selfishness and competition would disappear. Moreover, labour was to be the standard of value, with the community's own bank notes to represent labour inputs. With an increasing population and productivity, the demand for goods would also increase, so that 'bad times' and unemployment would become a thing of the past.

While the 'old society' would continue for the time being alongside the new communities, Owen was at pains to point out that far from being a subversive element, the communities would return taxes and support the country in times of war (though he included a half-hearted attack on the irrationality of war). Moreover, there would be no need for the institutions of law – courts, prisons and punishments – within the new communities, as cooperation would provide a new standard. Outsiders would be so impressed with the new communities that, in time, they would naturally choose to follow the example.

Whatever the deficiencies of 'Mr Owen's Plan' it demonstrates a number of important characteristics of utopian socialism, many of which are picked up in subsequent community schemes. For a start he was challenging the basic assumptions of classical liberalism, founded as they were on the idea of harmony arising out of unchecked competition. He refuted Malthus' popular belief that unemployment was both an inevitable and even desirable check on the over-use of resources, arguing instead that 'manual labour, properly directed, is the source of all wealth. and of national prosperity' [13]. Each of his communities was likened to a small, efficient 'machine' that would gainfully employ their population at all times, and generate an ever-increasing demand for goods. What is more, with spade cultivation instead of the plough the land (of Great Britain and Ireland) would support a population of up to 100 million so there was no immediate prospect of running short of food. To Owen, through manual labour, production and consumption would keep pace – a direct inversion of the doctrine of Malthus. He also digressed from Ricardo when he argued that it was low wages which were the source of low consumption and consequent unemployment. Although it was not fully formulated he pointed towards a redistribution of surplus value as a basis of the new society.

He shared with other utopian socialists a firm belief in material progress, and in the power of Man over Nature. It was not the new machines which were seen to be at fault, but the capitalist system of production and distribution. The 2,500 employees at New Lanark were producing as much as 600,000 fifty years before, and 'I asked myself, what became of the difference between the wealth consumed by 2,500 persons and that which would have been consumed by 600,000' [14].

Progress would only be just when everyone acted rationally, and this was dependent on the spread of education. In turn, this amounted to a rejection of violent revolutionary change; society would change with guidance and because it was ready to do so. But while Owen purports to a sense of history, arguing that society was then prepared to receive his views he failed to provide objective reasons why this should be so – why the working class should at that particular time be ready to respond to his call.

Although the concept of alienation is not fully developed, Owen was centrally concerned with finding ways to overcome the degradation associated with the new industrial system and to 'restore' the dignity of human labour. Owen envisaged a society based on production with Man as a worker, but, instead of the 'unhealthy pointer of a pin'(an attack on Adam Smith's division of labour), he looked forward to a 'working class full of activity and useful knowledge, with habits, information, manners and dipositions that would place the lowest in the scale many degrees above the best of any class which has yet been formed by the circumstances of past or present society'[15]. But it was still, in general, a simplistic notion of alienation which relied more on the removal of the barriers of poverty and ignorance and associated environmental improvements; and less on an understanding of Man transforming himself in the course of transforming society.

Although he did not go as far as some of the utopian socialists, Owen reacted against centralised State control in favour of a redistribution of power to the small community, as a prerequisite for a harmonious society. His plan would have created a new balance between town and country, with farming and industry existing side by side.

Finally, Owen cast a new (though still limited) role for women, tackling the related issues of marriage, the family and the status of women in a new, rational society. With many of the traditional tasks of child-rearing, cooking and washing transferred to the community, women would undertake work in the factories and vegetable gardens, or share in other communal tasks on an equal basis. He adopted a reformist attitude towards marriage – attacking, for instance meaningless legal contracts and impediments to divorce – which attracted widespread opposition.

Although the ideas of Robert Owen had the greatest influence on the community movement over a long period, they were by no means the only source of inspiration. In the latter half of the 1820s (when Owen was for much of the time in the United States) the ideas of William Thompson gained a ready following in Owenite circles and, particularly, in the emerging cooperative movement.

'Common exertion and common benefit'

It is generally acknowledged that Thompson provides a sharper critique than Owen against the classical economists, in defence of an alternative system where community would emerge as the basic form in society. Like Owen he shied away from the use of force to achieve change, arguing that the appropriation of existing property and wealth would in any case be a meaningless gesture, since the new wealth to be created would greatly outweigh all that had accumulated so far. But he showed greater sensitivity than Owen in the need for the exploited class to create their own future. He doubted, for instance, the likelihood that capital for new communities would be forthcoming from the manufacturing class and looked, instead, to the potential of workers' organisations to sponsor their own schemes. 'If done without any aid from the rich and idle, how animating to the industrious classes! – to the rich, the selfish, what a humiliating reproach!' [16].

It was Thompson's belief that only through community would it be possible to reconcile 'security' (used in the sense of the ability of labour to secure for each worker their full entitlement) with 'equality'. For Thompson, the worker could not have security unless he received his full entitlement, and all workers could not receive their full entitlement unless all were treated equally – if some were given greater rewards, then others would necessarily receive less than their due. Under the prevailing system of competition, in which inequality was reinforced, it was inevitable that a disparity between security and equality would continue. In its place, Thompson advocated a system of communities (each with a population of about 2,000) that would operate on the basis of mutual cooperation. Thompson's notion of community was:

an association of persons, in sufficient numbers, and living on a space of land of sufficient extent to supply by their own exertions all of each other's wants ... Community denotes common exertion and common benefit, common exertion according to the capabilities of each individual directed in the way most conducive to the common good, and common benefit according to the varying states and wants of each individual so as to produce as nearly as our best directed efforts can accomplish, equal happiness to all [17].

He outlined the advantages of community in more detail:

The obvious benefits of the proposed arrangements seem to be that
1. They would save the waste, at least within the precincts of the association, of mere unproductive consumption.
2. They would save the waste of labour and skill, now unemployed, through mere ignorance or want of market, or now uselessly, or perniciously, directed.
3. They would save the waste, now consumed under the name of profits, of wholesale and retail dealers: every cooperator being himself a joint proprietor and capitalist: production and consumption being shared equally by all.
4. They would save, by means of physical arrangements and the communi-cation of knowledge, the waste of life, of health, and enjoyment, now caused by poverty, ignorance and neglect.
5. They would save the incalculable waste of happiness, now arising from the contentions, animosities and cruelties engendered by the institutions of insecurity, and in some degree inseparable from the most chastened pursuit of individual gain: the social combinations proposed removing the causes of those crimes and vices and, by the education of the understanding, implanting opposite, permanent, dispositions and habits.
6. They would render supply and demand always commensurate and reduce the economy of supply and demand, population, and other contested questions of morals, legislation and political economy, to fixed and easily ascertained data, and principles founded thereon [18].

Thompson does not appear to be personally responsible for initiating a specific community, though the plans of the 'London Cooperative Society' in 1826 for a community within fifty miles of London are identifiable with his own writings [19]. He also (in 1830) produced a set of instructions to make the establishment of cooperative communities as easy as for that of 'any ordinary manufacture', and included a blueprint

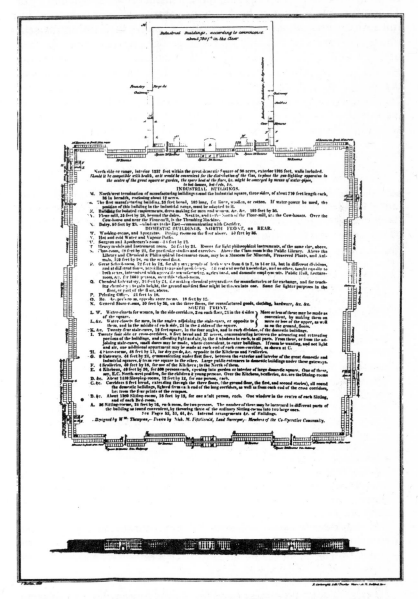

Fig. 2.4 William Thompson's plan for an ideal community: 'Ground Plan and Elevation, of a Community's Domestic, Manufacturing, and Agricultural Buildings, for 2,000 persons of all ages, on 2,000 acres of land' (Thompson, 1830).

for future schemes (Fig. 2.4). It made provision for living accommodation for a population of 2,000, together with ancillary uses, all sited
around a single, central square. Industrial buildings were sited away
from the living quarters. The layout is not inspired, but in its concern for
health, and in the provision for schooling and libraries, the overall plan
shares many of the merits of Owen's scheme, published ten years earlier.

Thompson's main contribution is less one of introducing original
designs, and more one of increasing the credibility of the political
economy of a cooperative system. Additionally, within the cooperative
movement, he was able to provide a more soundly-based antidote to
some of the more extravagant proposals of Owen – a schism between the
two developing into open conflict at the First Cooperative Congress in
1831 [20].

'The ulterior millennium State'

A third proponent of community in this period was Goodwyn Barmby,
born in 1820 and active, first as a Chartist and in the 1840s as a
'Religious Communist'. Barmby developed a vision of an equal society
that was derived from the principles of the early Christian Church where
the disciples of Jesus had 'all things in common'. It was his view not only
that the Bible inferred communism as the divine destiny of society, 'but
also that the mightiest minds of antiquity, among whom I name,
reverently, Plato, More and Campanella, were apostles in theory of the
communitive life' [21]. At the same time he was well versed in the new
technology, and a contemporary collaborator, Thomas Frost, later
described Barmby's utopian romance, *The Book of Platanopolis* as a
description of a place 'where in short, all that has been imagined by
Plato, More, Bacon and Campanella is reproduced and combined with
all that modern science has effected or essayed for lessening human toil
or promoting human enjoyment' [22].

Barmby's early audiences were agricultural workers in his home
county of Suffolk, at the time that Chartism was attracting a large
following. In 1840 he went to Paris, where he made contact with the
'Egalitarians' (disciples of Babeuf) and with Etienne Cabet himself,
with whom he later corresponded. Amongst the claims he made at that
time was to be the first to use the term 'communism' and, in the
following years, he founded a number of organisations and produced a
variety of publications to further his version of communist principles.

As with other utopian socialists Barmby assumed a messianic role.
Having identified private property and bourgeois legislation as the
source of society's problems, he recalled that he had seen it as his 'duty,
not relying on myself, but on true principles and the power of the Most
High, to enter, single-handed, upon the greatest work of reformation to
which the human race have ever been called' [23]. The start of his
crusade, 1841, was renamed as Year 1 of the era of Communization, and
in that year he vowed: 'I have faith in community as the will of God. I

believe in community as the law of love. This is Love, Light and Liberty. This is the Alpha and Omega. Yea! Verily! I believe; I believe' [24].

1^{α}

PARADIZATION

2	3	Early Ages
PASTORALISM	CLANISM	

IV

BARBARIZATION

5	6	Middle Ages
FEUDALITY	MUNICIPALITY	

VII

CIVILIZATION

8	8	Latter Ages
MONOPOLISM	ASSOCIALITY	

X^{ω}

COMMUNIZATION

Fig. 2.5 Goodwyn Barmby's model of 'societarian' change from 'paradization' to an eventual state of 'communization' (*The Promethean*, March 1842).

The attraction of community was consistent with his millennial perspective. Barmby outlined an evolutionary view of human progress, in which there was a progression from 'Paradization' (the original state of nature) to Communization' (the social consequence of positive association) (Fig. 2.5). In this ultimate state:

every societarian and individual interest and instinct will be melodized through the means of common love, industry, and property. The requisite conditions

1. Community of sentiment, labour and property
2. Abbreviation of manual labour by machinery
3. Organisation of industry in general and particular functions
4. Unitary architecture of habitation
5. The marriage of the city and the country
6. Economy through combination in domestics
7. Love through universality in ecclesiastics
8. Order, through justice or abstract mathematics in politics
9. Medicinally prepared diet
10. Common or contemporaneous consumption of food
11. Unity in distinction of domestic, ecclesiastical and political government
12. Absorption of the king and the priest in the patriarch
13. Unitary government of the world
14. Unitary common capital
15. Unitary common law
16. Unitary common language
17. New geographical division and nomination of the globe
18. Succession of electorality by rotation in local government
19. Universal fertilisation of the soil
20. Introduction of medical agriculture
21. Cultivation of the air
22. Amelioration of the climature
23. Fertilisation of the ocean
24. Facility of travelling for all
25. Security of aerial voyaging and the government establishment of balloons
26. Protection in general travel
27. An immediate international congress
28. Universal peace
29. Unity of science
30. Prevention of disease
31. Prevention of thunderstorms, volcanic eruptions and floods
32. Prevention of improper celibacy
33. Increase of population
34. Increase of machinery
35. Increase of intellectual labour
36. Fusion of the variety of human species
37. Fusion of all general and individual interests
38. Unitary common vesture
39. Unitary common calendar
40. Indivisibility of talent, labour and capital
41. Assimilation of characters and conditions of the highest kind
42. Increase of the human capacity in the power of creating circumstances
43. Unity of faith in Love as the real Jehovah, Allah, Law of God
44. Universal establishment of communization

Fig. 2.6 Goodwyn Barmby's table of 'societarian wants' (*The Promethean*, March 1842).

being the republic, and the universal commonwealth. Communization is in fact the ulterior millennium state of the world. It is the prophecy of the poets, the scriptures of the genii, the hope of all people, the destiny of our planet, the future of Humanity [25].

It is a model of evolution – the fall from grace, followed by long years in the wilderness, and the imminent prospect of a return to paradise following the communal reorganisation of society – that is characteristic of the utopian socialist view of history. In true utopian style, Barmby also outlined the basis of the new society through what he claimed as his understanding of forty-four 'societarian wants', ranging from common property to regulations for prospective air travel (Fig. 2.6).

Barmby remained an active propagandist for his utopian communism throughout the 1840s. He maintained links with both Cabet's 'Icarians' and Fourier's 'Phalansterians', and travelled to Paris at the time of the 1848 Revolution to lend the support of his 'Communist Church'. In spite of his continuing belief in the universal establishment of 'communization', his own practical attempts came to little. He initiated a short-lived community, the Moreville Communitorium at Hanwell, Middlesex in 1843 [26]. At about the same time, he made contact with a sect in Ireland, known as 'The Society of White Friends', which Barmby claimed was sympathetic to his ideas [27]. He also contemplated another community, to be known as the 'Caxton Communitorium', on the island of Sark, though it is doubtful that this was ever much more than a publicity venture to stimulate the circulation of his journal, *The Communist Chronicle* [28].

2.3 Communities and the cooperative movement

The communities in this period are the product not only of abstract theories but, equally, of the experience and association of more practical ventures. They are part of an unfolding pattern of working-class organisation and activity, encompassed within the early cooperative movement and the general tide of 'Owenism'. Robert Owen was a dominant figure throughout this period, but there were others who carried the banner and who also made their own distinctive contributions. It was, in fact, the 'Owenites' more than Owen himself who contributed most to the practical development of the cooperative movement [29].

The origins of the cooperative movement are frequently portrayed solely as a trading venture, an interpretation which loses sight of the importance of the underlying process of cooperation as an experience in itself, and of community as the ultimate goal for cooperators. An early exhortation to think of the essence of cooperation is provided in an editorial in *The Economist* in 1821:

the object sought to be obtained is not equality in rank or possessions, is not community of goods, but full, complete, unrestrained cooperation, on the part of all the members, for every purpose of social life, whether as regards the means of subsistence, or of promoting the intellectual and moral improvement and happiness of the whole body [30].

One of the pioneers in cooperative trading, Dr William King, was also aware of the danger of losing sight of what it was all for. 'There are some societies that mistake the means for the end, and from the success attending trading at their store, regard buying and selling as their main object; forgetting that our motto is that labour is the source of wealth. . . . trading is only the ladder' [31]. And in 1830 William Thompson enthused about the spread of cooperative associations 'all with the intention of ultimately forming themselves into complete Cooperative Communities as soon as they shall all have saved out of the profits of their trading fund . . .'[32].

Although industrialists were not above applying some of Owen's ideas to create 'model villages'[33], probably the first attempt to create a cooperative community was that of a London printer, George Mudie. It was Mudie who initiated the 'Cooperative and Economical Society', the ultimate object of which was described as being to establish a 'Village of Unity and Mutual Cooperation, combining Agriculture, Manufactures and Trade, upon the Plan projected by Mr Owen of New Lanark' [34]. In pursuance of this object, a small community was established for a while at Spa Fields in London [35]. Mudie was also responsible for a new journal, *The Economist* (published in 1821 and 1822) which set out to spread Owenite ideas, and which reported on cooperative schemes elsewhere. The dissemination of Owenite ideas was continued by a later group of London cooperators in a subsequent journal, the *Cooperative Magazine and Monthly Herald*, in which were included some notes on a community near Exeter [36].

Owen was more directly involved with a short-lived organisation 'The British and Foreign Philanthropic Society', formed in 1822 to raise funds for a community experiment at Motherwell in Scotland. In spite of the early dissolution of the philanthropic organisation and of Owen's departure for North America in 1824, sufficient interest remained to proceed with plans. Abram Combe (who had earlier been impressed with New Lanark and had developed his own ideas for a cooperative society) and Alexander Hamilton (a local landowner who had sympathetically received Owen's *Report to the County of Lanark*) secured some 300 acres of land at Orbiston at a cost of £20,000.

Ambitious plans were laid for a single building to house 200 families, together with a kitchen, bakehouse, library, drawing rooms, lecture room and dining rooms. Machinery, including an elevator to carry provisions between floors, and apparatus to clean shoes and clothes, were designed to remove drudgery. The economy was to be based on a balance of farming and industry, and in its two years of existence, 1825 to 1827, Orbiston attracted a wide variety of craftsmen to the community. Progress was reported in the *Cooperative Magazine* and some of the craftsmen who arrived were London cooperators. The fundamental issues of communal property and equal distribution were debated, but never resolved before the collapse of the scheme in 1827. In its physical and social form Orbiston made advances, but was far from complete. The death of Combe marked the end of the community, but there were other reasons for its early demise. For a start, Orbiston was desperately short of capital, and its failure gave weight to those who were arguing for smaller, less ambitious schemes – at least until this new form of organisation could be seen to work. Perhaps more significantly, the settlers joined with little or no previous experience in managing their own affairs, and the utopian ideals of the new community were, inevitably, beyond reach in a single leap.

Compared with the rise and decline of Orbiston the cooperative trading societies made steady progress. William King's 'Cooperative Society' in Brighton kept its sights on the ultimate goal of a community, and in 1827 it was reported that 200 members had plans to secure a farm and 'live in community' [37]. There is no evidence that this particular scheme came to anything, but cooperative societies continued to spread, and the next decade is marked by a series of short-lived attempts to centralise the various local movements. One of the first of these was the formation in 1829 of the 'Association for the Promotion of Cooperative Knowledge' which through its journal (*The Magazine of Useful Knowledge and Cooperative Miscellany*) reported the existence of some 500 local societies in 1830. But it was in the agricultural setting of western Ireland that the idea of cooperative communities received its most practical boost.

For two years, between 1831 and 1833, the 'Ralahine Agricultural and Manufacturing Cooperative Association' sought to improve conditions and manage the affairs of a 700 acre estate at Ralahine, County Clare. The ideas were generated by the Owenite, E. T. Craig, who assumed effective management of the venture with the full support of the landowner, John Scott Vandaleur. It was envisaged that farm stock, equipment and land would remain the property of Vandaleur until the society could buy it themselves, and transfer it to a system of joint property between the members. In its two years the record of improvements that were introduced, and the extent of mutual cooperation that was reached, is impressive. Labour notes circulated, and a community building was completed to accommodate single settlers. Although sympathetic, Robert Owen had little to do with the scheme, except to investigate the possibility of selling the produce to labour exchanges in England. The potential seemed considerable until Vandaleur squandered his fortune and his family reclaimed the estate to bring the experiment to an abrupt end. E. T. Craig's own belief in the value of community was not abated, and he reappeared a few years later in the scheme at Manea Fen [38].

Meanwhile, the first of a series of Cooperative Congresses was held in 1831, and it was there that the different views of Owen and Thompson came into the open – the former maintaining that it was essential for communities to be large-scale ventures under strong, central direction, the latter now favouring smaller communities with government by committees. In spite of differences of this nature the underlying idea of community remained firm to the extent, indeed, that Congress could resolve a consolidating motion that it was considered 'highly desirable that a Community, on the principles of mutual cooperation, limited possessions, and equality of exertions and of enjoyments should be established in England as speedily as possible, in order to show the practicability of the cooperative scheme' [39]. It was proposed that such a community could be established through the sponsorship of the 200 cooperative societies, which could each elect a resident member for the new community and support him with £30 capital.

This simple objective was not to be, and Owenism passed through various phases before returning to the unifying idea of community towards the end of the 1830s. The middle of the decade had already seen the relative collapse of cooperative trading, of the 'Grand National Consolidated Trades Union', and of labour exchanges (centres where cooperative goods could be exchanged at their true value as measured in terms of labour input). There followed a short period after 1836 when subscriptions and capital were directed towards the construction of 'Halls of Science' where workers could prepare for a more rational society. In the course of its meanderings, with hopes repeatedly raised and lost, many of Owen's followers left to joint the Chartists, while some of the more ardent supporters of community lost patience and set sail for North America.

When Owen redirected attention to community it was on a strongly moralistic basis, to the point of identifying the coming of the first community with the start of the millennium. In 1834 a new Owenite journal, the *New Moral World*, was launched to spread the gospel: 'The time for man's regeneration is come! The hour of the deliverance from sin and misery is at hand! Behold the coming of that new life, when the world shall be so changed that every man shall sit under his own vine and his own fig tree, and there shall be none to make him afraid' [40].

In the latter half of the 1830s a succession of societies was established (largely at the instigation of Owen) to realise the new order – the 'Association of All Classes of All Nations' in 1835, the 'Community Friendly Society' in 1836, the 'National Community Friendly Society' in 1837, the 'Universal Community Society of Rational Religionists' in 1839, and the 'Home Colonisation Society' in 1840. Debate ranged over a wide range of community issues from the millennial prospects of community, to more practical matters such as whether subscriptions to benefit societies and other bodies were delaying the establishment of full communities. Owenites like Harry Howells Horton toured the northern lecture halls, spreading the message that: 'Communities (will) be the result of circumstances, which are now spreading their genial influence abroad, and which will cause them to rise like a phoenix from the ashes of the old immoral world' [41].

And as the possibility of establishing a community grew stronger, more attention was paid to the practicalities of social composition and ideal location. Owen believed that there should be a middle-class leadership, 'until our system shall create a new class of very superior directors as well as operators' [42]. He also believed that hired agricultural labour would be needed in the early stages of community, until members themselves were able to take over. Although Owen himself saw agriculture as the main activity, a fellow Owenite, John Finch (known as 'Deputy John'), advocated a community in one of the manufacturing districts, with engineering as the main occupation to reflect the skills of many of their members. On the question of size the orthodox Owenites retained an inflexible belief in large communities, and were quick to criticise the smaller scheme that was started at Manea Fen in 1838 [43].

While most of the debates and issues surrounding community still remained unresolved, matters were brought to a head when, as a result of the investigations of an estates sub-committee of the central Owenite body (what had then become the 'Universal Community Society of Rational Religionists') a decision was made to acquire land at East Tytherley in Hampshire. A ninety-nine year lease was negotiated and possession dated from the 1 October 1839. Robert Owen disclaimed responsibility for the experiment (subsequently known as 'Harmony Hall') [44], which he regarded as premature, though he was closely involved with its progress over most of its six years duration.

The eventual collapse of Harmony Hall in 1845 marked the effective end of the Owenite period of community building that had started at Spa Fields nearly a quarter of a century earlier. What is most striking throughout this period is the way that attempts to establish communities were inseparable from parallel examples of working-class organisation. The end of this particular phase of communities, no less than the collapse of related ventures, is as much a reflection of the immaturity of the working class as a consciously organised body at that time, as of the practical deficiencies of the schemes themselves.

2.4 New frontiers

What was happening in England at this time was not unique. It reflected a particular stage in the historical development of capitalism, and there is evidence of community schemes fired by the same general philosophy in other countries. Understandably, France, with its prominent early socialists, was amongst these, though the community experiments were by no means as noteworthy as the theoretical contributions [45]. There were also utopian experiments in Eastern Europe, but it appears that these were also of very limited success [46]. Instead, it was westwards to the new lands of the United States that the main hopes of the communitarians were turned.

The attractions of establishing communities on new ground were both philosophical and practical. As a philosophical venture, emigration to the United States at that time could be seen to symbolise the breaking of ties with the Old World, offering liberty in place of the oppressive restrictions of established European society:

Land of the West, we come to thee,
Far over the desert of the sea;
Under thy white-winged canopy,
Land of the West, we fly to thee;
Sick of the Old World's sophistry;
Haste then across the dark, blue sea,
Land of the West, we rush to thee!
Home of the brave: soil of the tree, –
Huzza! She rises o'er the sea [47]

In purely practical terms, also, there were advantages in community formation in the New World as opposed to the Old. Something of the appeal in sailing westwards is conveyed by Thomas Hunt, an Owenite who was closely involved with Harmony Hall, but who argued that the same effort that was expended in Hampshire would have yielded considerably greater results in North America. In 1843 he outlined his own proposals for an Owenite Community, and presented arguments as to why others should leave England and follow him to the 'North-Western Territories' of the United States:

How is it, that after such an expenditure of time and money, our society has not succeeded in making 100 persons independent of external aid; while the Rappites, in America, with little more than £3,000 to begin with, made themselves independent of the outward world after the first harvest, and at the end of eight years they numbered 800 persons, whose property was estimated at upwards of £45,000? I could hardly conceive that it would be contended that these persons were either more skilful, more industrious, or more economical than an equal number of persons professing the social principles, and was consequently led to inquire whether this discrepancy might not arise from national causes, and whether America was more favourably circumstanced for such an undertaking [48].

Hunt went on to demonstrate (through a hypothetical example) that it was indeed these 'natural causes' which accounted for the difference. In addition to what he regarded as the more liberal institutions to be found in the United States, new settlers would find taxation less onerous, land was productive yet very much cheaper, and it was quick and easy to transact. As a result the:

expense of locating a single family of five persons in the north-western part of America I calculated to be about £72, including travelling, share of purchase money of estate, etc. The cost of locating twenty families, comprising 100 persons, would therefore be £1,440. The sum expended upon the estate in Hampshire is £30,000, by means of which, in three years, about seventy persons have been admitted. This £30,000 expended in America instead of England, would have established twenty-one sections of a community similar to the one I propose, these sections comprising in all 2,100 persons, possessing freehold land to the extent of 4,200 acres [49].

But Hunt was merely reiterating the advantages that had been recognised by Robert Owen and others some twenty years earlier. To Owen, the prospect of community formation in a new nation, receptive to his ideas, took on millennial proportions. In contrast to the offhand way he had been treated by the British Parliament, Owen found a ready audience in the American Congress and in the personal interest of the President himself. Presenting the President of the United States with a 6-foot square model of his ideal community, Owen could envisage the whole nation evolving according to his blueprint. In consequence, it is of little surprise that Owen saw fit to invest the greater part of his fortune in buying the estate and existing community buildings of 'Harmony' from the Rappites in 1825. Although it did not accord to his own design Owen declared that:

It will enable us to form immediately a preliminary society in which to receive the new population, to collect, prepare and arrange material for erecting several such combinations as the model represents, and of forming several independent, yet united associations, having common property and one common interest. This new establishment will be erected on the high lands of Harmony, from two to four miles from the river and its island, of which the inhabitants will have a beautiful and extensive view, there being several thousands of acres of cultivated land on the rich second bottom lying between the highlands and the river. And here it is, in the heart of the United States, and almost in the center of its unequalled internal navigation, that Power which governs and directs the universe and every action of man has arranged circumstances which were far beyond my control, and permits me to commence a new empire of peace and good-will to men, founded on other principles and leading to other practices than those of present or past, and which principles in due season, and in the allotted time, will lead to that state of virtue, intelligence, enjoyment, and happiness which it has been foretold by the sages of the past would at some time become the lot of the human race [50].

Nearly a thousand settlers came to what was renamed 'New Harmony'. Yet in spite of its promising start (due in large measure to Owen's financial support and enthusiasm) the early ideals of the community proved hard to put into practice, and within a few years it disintegrated into a number of factions. There were lessons, though, from the experience which, of all people, Owen seemed least willing to acknowledge. At New Harmony he saw the value of using existing buildings in order to accommodate a high number of communitarians from the outset, and to allow them to concentrate on earning a livelihood and organising their new way of life. Yet, fifteen years later, at Harmony Hall it was Owen who discounted the short-term use of existing buildings on the site, and was responsible for the construction of what amounted to a palace – in advance of social and economic foundations which could support it. And at Harmony Hall, in trying again to start the millennium single-handed, Owen also showed that he had forgotten his American venture:

I had hoped that fifty years of political liberty had prepared the American people to govern themselves advantageously. I supplied land, houses, and the use of capital, and I tried, each in their own way, the different parties who collected here; and experience proved that the attempt was premature, to unite a number of strangers not previously educated for the purpose [51].

In spite of the relative failure of New Harmony to achieve all that was expected of it – a community of equality to set the pattern for the settlement of the whole of America – and in spite of the lessons lost, it is still credited with supporting a variety of experiments in education that persisted long after the community itself declined. And it proved to be a stimulus to further Owenite communities in the 1820s – at Wanborough, Illinois; the Blue Spring Community, near Bloomington, Indiana; the Friendly Association for Mutual Interests at Kendal, Ohio; the Franklin Community at Haverstraw, Rockland County, New York; the Community of Forestville, also in New York; Yellow Springs, Greene County, Ohio; the Friendly Association for Mutual Interests at Valley Forge, Pennsylvania; and a community at Nashoba, Tennessee [52].

The French utopian socialists were no less interested in the idea of establishing communities in North America, particularly during the 1840s. Charles Fourier failed in attempts to establish his ideal form of community, the 'Phalanstery', in France, but after his death it is estimated that there were at least forty-one Fourierist communities in the United States between 1840 and 1850. And Etienne Cabet, with his followers the 'Icarians', assumed a personal role in trying to pioneer his own model of Utopia, 'Icaria'. Starting in 1848 with a site of over a million acres in Texas, modified versions of Icarian schemes persisted until the end of the century. The 1840s also saw a regeneration of Owenite activity, with the establishment in 1843 of four new communities – Promisewell and Goosepond, both in Pennsylvania; Skaneateles, New York; and Equality, Wisconsin, the last being the brainchild of Thomas Hunt, fresh from his experiences at Harmony Hall in Hampshire [53].

2.5 Community profiles

In comparison with the United States the communities in England were few in number during this period – there was the Cooperative and Economical Society at Spa Fields in London (1821), the Devon and Exeter Cooperative Society at Rockbeare (1826), the Hodsonian Community at Manea Fen in Cambridgeshire (1838), Harmony Hall near East Tytherley in Hampshire (1839), Concordium at Ham Common in Surrey (1842), and Moreville Communitorium at Hanwell in Middlesex (1843).

In spite of this small number they occupy an important place in the mainstream of early socialist developments. Both Spa Fields and the Devon community exemplify the communitarian tendency of the early cooperative movement; the Hodsonian Community and Harmony Hall were caught up in the Owenite fervour at the end of the 1830s; Concordium furthered the cause of educational reform and, at the same time, sought to widen the spiritual basis of socialism; while at Hanwell, Goodwyn Barmby like Owen saw a new community as the start of the millennium. In the remainder of this chapter the various characteristics and relationships between these communities will be explored.

The Cooperative and Economical Society, Spa Fields, Clerkenwell, London

It is certainly time that something should now be done beside talking.... Could a community be commenced in town, or in the immediate vicinity of town, doubtless, if conducted with prudence and spirit, it would give a greater impetus to the cause of co-operative fellowship than half a dozen villages established at three or four hundred miles from the metropolis. It would be like a pebble thrown into the centre of a pool, village would succeed village, till the circle would at last embrace the whole country. Besides being near to or within the focus of all that is great, and immediately under the inspection of men of talent and the oracles of the times; when it was discovered that all that Mr Owen had advanced in favour of the system was verified in the face of hundreds of thousands of human beings, all capable of judging for themselves, such an institution within or near to London would do more to remove the prejudices of the public, than the publishing of twenty volumes could do [54].

The note of urgency was answered in the form of a little community which lasted for three years, from 1821 to 1824, at Spa Fields in London. The experiment is of interest for a number of reasons. For a start it is probably the first attempt to create a community in accordance with the ideas of Robert Owen (though Owen himself was not involved, and was even accused, later, of decrying the experiment as it did not agree, in every respect, with his own ideas) [55]. Secondly, in establishing the pattern of cooperative trading as a means by which the working class could accumulate their own capital as a prelude to more ambitious schemes of community, Spa Fields is an important step in the development of the cooperative movement. Thirdly, in its short life, it made interesting inroads into the main areas of utopian socialist concern – a more equitable system of production and consumption, educational innovation, a revaluation of the place of women, communal patterns of leisure and eating, and the sharing of tasks. Fourthly, Spa Fields transpired to be one of the few communities in the nineteenth century to be located in an urban area – not by chance, but because they thought there was good reason for doing so. Finally, it set a familiar pattern of accommodating a printing press and letting the world know, not only of their own fortunes, but also of the wider prospects for an alternative system to capitalism. It did this through a weekly publication *The Economist: A Periodic Paper – Explanatory of the New System of Society, Projected by Robert Owen, Esq.; and of a Plan of Association for Improving the Condition of the Working Classes, During their Continuance at their Present Employment.*

✻ THE COOPERATIVE AND ECONOMICAL SOCIETY

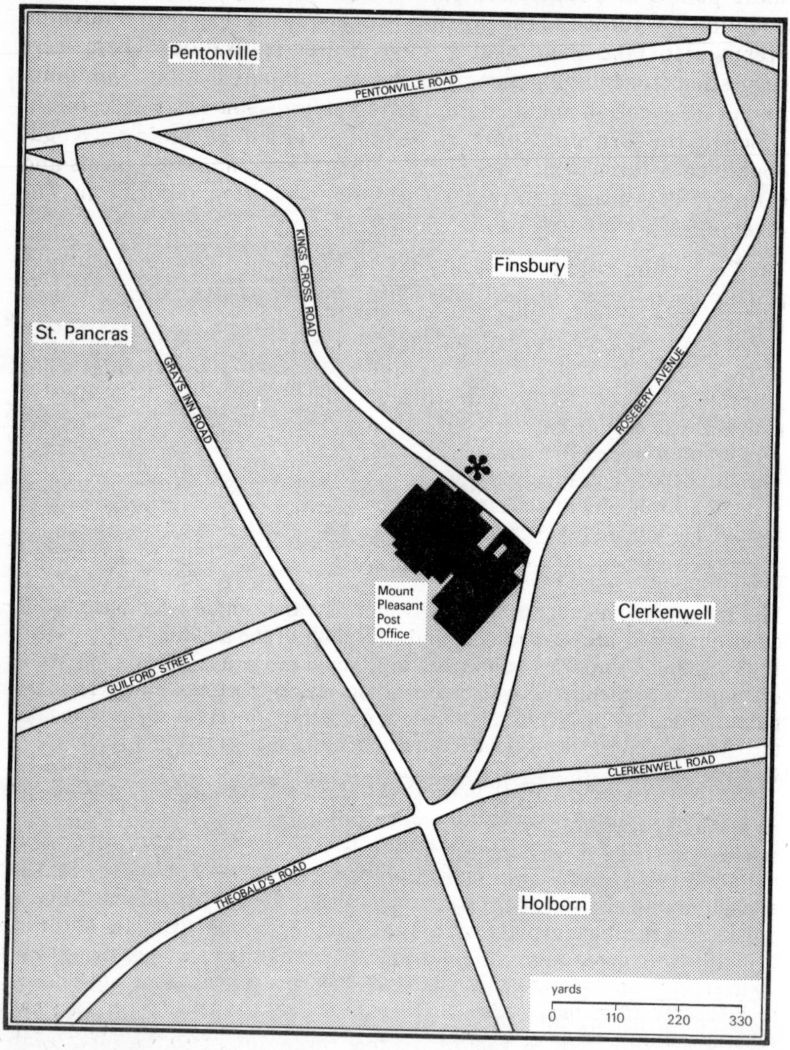

Fig. 2.7 Location of the Cooperative and Economical Society.

The prime mover behind the community, and editor of *The Economist*, was a printer, George Mudie. He was responsible for the formation of the 'Cooperative and Economical Society' in January 1821, and outlined its objective as being to create a community for 250 families[56]. The scheme bore many of the features contained in Owen's blueprint for 'villages of cooperation' (published in the previous year), though Mudie considered it would be necessary for most of the men to retain their existing jobs, at least in the early stages. After a relatively short period of cooperative purchasing by members of the society, attention was turned to the possibility of acquiring their own residential premises to take their plan a stage nearer realisation. There were suggestions for building a completely new complex for the community but, in the event, they settled for a group of houses in Spa Fields, one of which (at the corner of Guildford Street East and Bagnigge Wells Road) contained a room which was large enough for communal meals and eating [57]. An account of their progress was soon reported in *The Economist:*

The Cooperative and Economical Society of London ... have now reduced to practice the principles of their association, and are making very satisfactory progress towards their complete accomplishment.

The means by which the Society effects its objectives are as follows:
I. The families contribute to a common fund for providing the necessities of life, at wholesale prices and at the best markets, in proportion to the number of individuals in each family respectively, according to the following scales:

A man, his wife and five children	£1. 2. 6 per week
A man, his wife and four children	£1. 0. 3 per week
A man, his wife and three children	£ 18. 0½ per week
A man, his wife and two children	£ 17. 1 per week
A man, his wife and one child	£ 16. 3½ per week
A man, his wife and no children	£ 14. 5 per week

The above scale of expenses is exclusive of rent and clothing; but includes all other outgoings, and the training and education of the children.
II. The families breakfast, dine, etc., together at the general tables; and in the evenings amuse themselves with conversation, reading, lectures, music etc. in the public room. The individuals, however, are at perfect liberty at all times, to take their meals, and to spend their leisure hours, in their private apartments.
III. The domestic duties of the females are performed under a system of combination, which greatly lessens the labour, and enables the females either to be profitably employed, or to command a considerable portion of leisure for rational pursuits and innocent recreations. Thus, the cooking for the whole of the families being performed at once, and at one fire, occupies comparatively but a small portion of time, and is done in a much superior manner to what is possible for small individual families; and a proportionate advantage is gained in all the other departments of housewifery, such as cleaning, washing, getting up linen, etc., etc. This economy of time also enables a proper number of females to be spared from their usual avocations, and to take under their constant superintendance, *without a moment's intermission*, in and out of doors, the whole of the children – securing for them the best possible attention to their health, comfort and morals.
IV. Such of the females as are not required for the discharge of the duties of housewifery, and for the care of the children, are employed during a moderate portion of the day, in such profitable work as can be obtained for the benefit of the Society at large. The elder children are also employed during six hours daily, for the common benefit, and will be carefully instructed in the principles of Christianity, and in one or more branches of useful industry. The remainder of their time is occupied with their education, and such sports, under the care of their superintendants, as are suitable to their age. When a child is employed six

hours daily, the parents of that child are reduced on the scale of expenses for living in the proportion of one child less than the actual number of their family.
V. The fund to be accumulated from the profitable employment of the females and children from the surplus accruing from the scale of expenses of living, and from the dealings of the Society, will be employed in providing profitable work for the Members on their own and the Society's account – in trade, – and, as soon as possible, a sufficient sum will be invested in buildings, for the residence of Members. The whole of the congregated Society, by means of the capital acquired from the various sources of accumulation, will be gradually employed on its own account, in the proceeds of which each congregated family will have an equal interest; and by means of which the Society will be enabled to insure its Members against the consequences of loss of employment from sickness or any other cause, and their families from the usual distress and wretchedness consequent upon the death of the parents. The orphans of the Society will be in all respects treated in the same manner as the children of the surviving Members. The profits of the Society will also enable the expenses for living to be gradually reduced, or the clothing and rent of the Members to be provided for out of the funds.
VI. The Society already employs its own shoemakers and tailors, and will speedily be enabled to perform all its own work within itself. The Society also can now promptly execute, for the Public, in the best and cheapest manner, orders for carving and gilding, transparent landscape window blinds, paintings on velvet, boot and shoemaking, gentlemen's clothing, and dressmaking and millinery [58].

George Mudie claimed that nothing could now prevent the rapid spread of 'the system' [59]. Only the following week, though, in March 1822, *The Economist* ceased publication, and an important record of the community's further development was lost. It appears that the group (sometimes referred to as the 'Congregational Families') stayed together for another two years, until Mudie left for Orbiston in 1824. The physical record of Spa Fields is no more helpful as a guide to what the community did between 1822 and 1824. The area has long changed out of all recognition, and today not even the streets where the properties were leased remain as they were to mark the pioneer venture [60].

Devon and Exeter Cooperative Society, Rockbeare, Exeter, Devon

Another short-lived cooperative community is that which was established near Exeter in 1826, as an offshoot of the Devon and Exeter Cooperative Society. There were plans for a population of 2,000 in line with Owen's recommendations but, in the very year of its inception, the chief sponsor Jasper Veysey withdrew his support. The initial community rapidly dispersed, but some of the communitarians moved on to another farm nearby, forming themselves into the Dowlands Devon Community. This second attempt extended the experiment for, at most, another year.

Jasper Veysey was a linen draper and hosier in Exeter, and gained some renown in the local cooperative movement through the publication of a pamphlet *The proper study of mankind is Man*, which

❋ DEVON AND EXETER COOPERATIVE SOCIETY

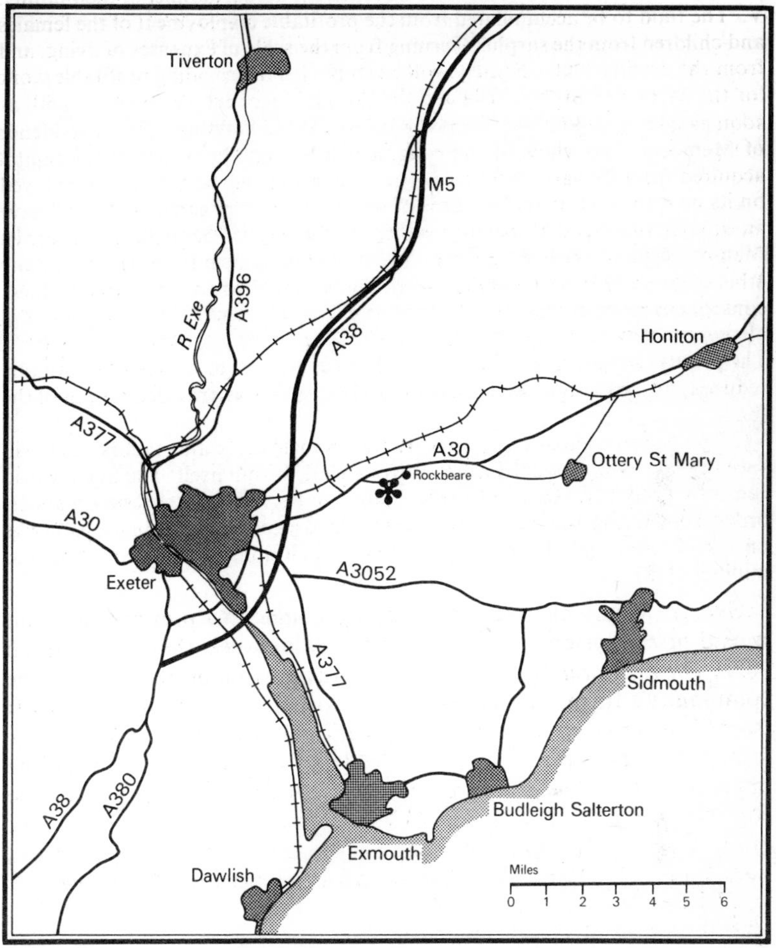

Fig. 2.8 Location of the Devon and Exeter Cooperative Society.

claimed to put forward a 'practical and easy method of immediately banishing poverty from the world, and within a short period ignorance and misery, vice and crime' [61]. At the same time as its publication, he took another step towards saving mankind, when he advertised in the *Exeter Flying Post* for land of between 100 and 1,000 acres, within 10 miles of Exeter. Although he had to settle for only 37 acres, Veysey lost little time in making a start on the community [62]. By July of that year the first communitarians were already at work:

The friends of the system of mutual cooperation and equal distribution will rejoice to hear, that some gentlemen belonging to the Devon and Exeter Cooperative Society have purchased a small estate, and commenced arrangements for the formation of a community, about six miles and a half from that city. The estate consists of thirty-seven acres of excellent land, possession of the whole of which will be given at Lady-day next; but the purchasers are allowed to have immediate possession of as much of it as they choose, on paying for the crops now on the land. They have accordingly taken possession of six acres, and thirteen Cooperators, consisting of a Gardener, Carpenter, Quarrier, (there being a stone quarry on the estate), Drainer, Well-sinker, Clay Temperer, Moulder, etc. etc., have been set to work, and scores, it is said, are waiting anxious to join them, as the funds of the society will enable them to purchase more of the crops, and take possession of the land. Plenty more land it is said may be purchased, or rented near this estate: now therefore is the time for those who are really desirous of carrying our principles into practice to come forward.

They have at Exeter nearly one hundred members with their families who are desirous of being amongst the first to commence operations; but accommodation could be afforded for a few Masons, Bricklayers, and Machinists, particularly Steam Engine Makers [63].

Fears that the community would pose a threat to the rest of society were eagerly allayed; in time all would see the wisdom of their ways:

Capitalists who are friendly to the system, have here we think an opportunity for the safe investment of their funds. It is proposed to erect a boarding house detached from the other buildings, for the reception of ten or twelve genteel families of independent income, which will form a market for the productions of, and be a source of revenue to the community. By this means those who are unwilling to enter immediately upon an equality in every respect with the cooperative classes, may avail themselves of some of the advantages of the system, and at the same time contribute to its success [64].

The rate of progress was impressive. Only a month later, in August 1826, it was reported that:

The members who have located themselves on the land purchased, are proceeding with alacrity in raising temporary buildings for the reception of a considerable number of operative mechanics and others, who are expected to join them as soon as they can be accommodated. There are already twelve cottages finished: and Mr Veysey calculated, that by a new method of building, dwellings can be raised adequate to the accommodation of four hundred families for one thousand pounds. It is the opinion of Mr Veysey that Mr Owen and most of the advocates of the Cooperative system have laboured under great error, in supposing that the commencement of a community required the enormous funds of from fifty thousand to two hundred thousand pounds, he being confident that he could, on his economical plan, carry an establishment of two thousand persons into complete operation, and furnish it with all the machinery requisite to produce every article essential to the comfortable or abundant subsistence of all the members for five thousand pounds [65].

Within weeks of this report, however, Jasper Veysey withdrew his support – for domestic reasons – and the community collapsed. Those of the communitarians who moved on to form the Dowlands Devon Community stayed together through the summer of 1827. A report showed that the crops were good, the few trades in operation were paying their way, and there were plans to provide schooling for local children. But there was also a dearth of newcomers, and a desperate plea for more capital [66]. There is no evidence to suggest that it was able to continue beyond the end of 1827.

Hodsonian Community,
Manea Fen, Cambridgeshire

Over a decade after the cooperative communities in London and Devon, the establishment of communities at Manea Fen in Cambridgeshire in 1838, and at East Tytherley in Hampshire in the following year, mark a different stage in the development of socialism. Gone was the caution which marked the early schemes – accumulating capital through their own efforts, and gradually convincing others of the merits of their ways. Instead, both the Hodsonian Community at Manea Fen and Harmony Hall at East Tytherley were caught up in the urgency and expectancy of

✱ **HODSONIAN COMMUNITY**

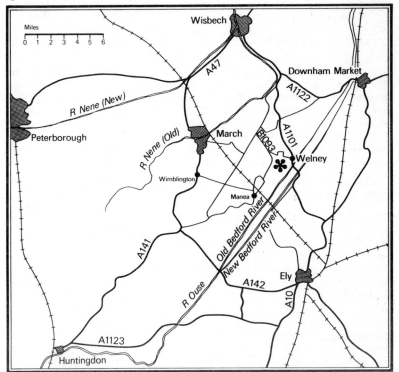

Fig. 2.9 Location of the Hodsonian Community.

the socialist debate at the end of the 1830s. There is no lack of evidence of solid ground work in the communities, but they were unable to escape the surrounding mood of a new age that was about to dawn – a mood that was fostered by the ubiquitous Robert Owen, still the dominant figure in the socialist movement. There is little, though, today in the flat and open landscape of Manea Fen to reveal the colourful history of the Hodsonian Community and the turbulent debates in which it featured.

A farmstead that bears the name 'Colony Farm', evidence of the claypit that was used at the time, and the last remains of a landing stage to the Old Bedford River are all that mark its former presence. The 200 acres of fenland, that over the three-year period between 1838 and 1841 supported a vigorous community of between 100 and 200 socialists, has long been converted to extensive agriculture. And the Old Bedford River, where the communitarians carried goods in their cutter *The Morning Star*, and the banks along which they promenaded on summer evenings, are now infrequently used. But, if it is hard from the ground to envisage a venture in community, one can look, instead, to the detailed record provided by the community newspaper *The Working Bee and Herald of the Hodsonian Community Society*, and the 'official' Owenite publication *The New Moral World* [67].

The sponsor of the scheme and owner of the estate was a farmer, William Hodson. He made it clear from the outset that he intended to challenge the class divisions of society through the practical example of a socialist community:

I will endeavour to show, as early as possible, the great benefit which will arise from a union of the working classes, upon two hundred acres of land belonging to me. . . . It is a well known fact, that the present distinctions in society are the cause of more envy and strife than any thing which has ever been produced in the world. In order to avoid this calamity, there will be no distinction – no individual property – the motto will be 'each for all'. All will labour for the benefit of the whole. That which is found to be best for one, will be adopted by all. The clothing will be the same, so will the provisions. All will be taken from the general stock. The food will be cooked by a scientific apparatus; thus saving an immense labour to the females; a spacious dining-room will be erected for all to dine in, etc.; a large school-room will be established, and sleeping rooms for the children from the age of two-years to twelve and upwards. The best masters will be selected to teach the families at the commencement; and I am certain by this union, the children will be educated far superior to the present nobility. Machinery, which has hitherto been for the benefit of the rich, will be adopted in the colony for lesssening labour. A steam engine will be erected for thrashing and grinding corn, as well as steaming food for cattle, and many other purposes. . . . The average time for work will be about four hours per day, and, as the colonists will have been accustomed to more hours, they will, undoubtedly, find it advantageous to employ themselves to some other work for three to four more hours, in order to redeem the houses and land as soon as possible: the remainder of the day will be spent in delightful recreations. None will spoil their hat in bowing to superiors, all will be equal, consequently envy, strife, and all uncharitableness, will find but little food under such arrangements [68].

In its three years the community went some way to realising these early socialist ideals. Hodson's belief in technology (so characteristic of his contemporaries) was reflected not only in the construction of well-ventilated and heated homes, but also in more fanciful excursions, like the observatory with its Union Jack at the top, 'indicative of conquered tyranny cowering below it', and a platform 'of sufficient dimensions to allow forty persons to sit down to tea' [69]. Agriculture was successful but the community also ventured into the manufacture and sale of farm machinery, taking advantage of the navigable river along its boundary and the large local market. There were also advertisements for the sale of bricks and tiles made in their own works, and 'good Worsted and other Stockings'. For a time, money was replaced by labour notes issued for work done, and exchangeable at the community store.

A library was installed, and the school enlisted the services of the experienced communitarian, William Craig, who had left Ireland with the collapse of Ralahine. Although the communitarians worked for much longer than the four hours a day that Hodson had anticipated, leisure pursuits were not forgotten. In the summer there were games of cricket and river trips, while in winter the 'evenings are spent by some with a book, by the cottage fireside; by others at classes. ... The latter are, on the whole, well attended, with one exception, the one for Metaphysics' [70]. Even the question of clothing was tackled and, to the amusement of local villagers, the men wore a 'green habit . . . presenting an appearance like the representation of Robin Hood and his foresters, or of the Swiss mountaineers. The dress of the females is much the same as the usual fashion, with trousers, and the hair worn in ringlets' [71].

The whole mood during the first two years was one of optimism, and the pages of *The Working Bee* record their many achievements. There

Fig. 2.10 Hodsonian Community: View of the original community (looking from the south across the Old Bedford River), included in the first edition of *The Working Bee* in 1840.

was more land available nearby, and though in the early days of 1840 the community numbered about fifty there was talk of an eventual population of 700. A layout was envisaged that would develop beyond the first square, through the addition of further squares, 'six or eight as future circumstances may determine, in which we shall be enabled to

Fig. 2.11 Hodsonian Community: Current view of the reclaimed fenland (looking from the north towards the Old Bedford River) with 'Colony Farm' in the middle ground.

classify our members according to time of membership, congeniality of mind, knowledge of our principles and amiability of disposition, preparatory to the erection of a final community' [72].

The orthodox Owenite body – the 'Universal Community Society of Rational Religionists' – had been sceptical about some of the features of the Fenland community. Owen had himself taken issue with the fact that it started with such small numbers and inadequate capital, while others questioned the dominant role played by William Hodson. But this initial source of conflict gave way to a measure of reconciliation, and even to talk of an amalgamation. Hodson became increasingly attracted by the idea of a union, based on the complementary nature of their two communities – his own and that sponsored by the Owenites at East Tytherley. 'By uniting then, the body of Socialists will be in possession of two estates – one adapted for an educational, and the other as a manufacturing and commercial establishment; a union of such advantages cannot fail to give a new impetus to our common cause'[73]. In a new spirit of cooperation further communities would follow from those already in existence, with Hodson defining a role for the 'Universal Community Society' to control and encourage this process. There seemed no limit to what might be done. But as with many other examples, the shaky foundations of this type of community was liable to collapse at any time. In the case of Manea Fen the optimism of 1840 turned sour by the end of the year, with increasing quarrels between Hodson and his associates. It was (as the Owenite critics had warned) a highly centralised system with too much dependence on Hodson. And when, as eventually happened, Hodson withdrew his financial support, there was nothing to hold the community together.

In its three years the Hodsonian Community had achieved an extraordinary amount, both in terms of its own development, and through its newspaper, in spreading the example and promise of socialism to a wider population. At the same time, based as it was on such a charismatic notion of social change, and with little regard for the workings of the economy outside its own boundaries, its downfall was inevitable. As it transpired, the orthodox Owenites, who were not slow to criticise the community, failed to appreciate the true nature of its contradictions, and themselves made comparable mistakes in their own experiment in Hampshire.

Harmony Hall,
East Tytherley, Hampshire

Harmony Hall, on the site of Queenwood Farm near East Tytherley, Hampshire was in the hands of the Owenites for six years from 1839 to 1845. It was the only community to be sponsored directly by the Central Board of Owenites, and was Robert Owen's best opportunity to create his ideal form of settlement on British soil. Paradoxically, the direct involvement of both the Central Board and of Robert Owen, in themselves, contributed to the community's relative failure.

�֍ HARMONY HALL

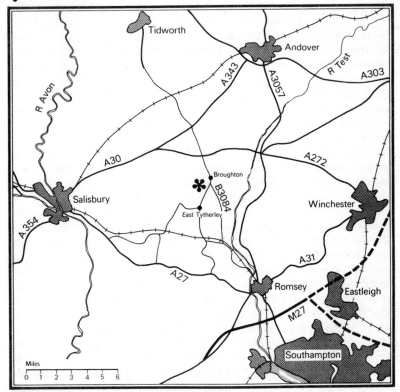

Fig. 2.12 Location of Harmony Hall.

In the first place, the Central Board saw itself with the clear role of uniting the efforts of the working class in their struggle for socialism. It was not simply a question of communicating Owenite principles and of raising funds on a national basis, but also a matter of standardising patterns of behaviour, of dress and furniture, and even of approving each and every applicant to join a community (even though they were already sponsored by their own branch organisation). In consequence, one of the persisting problems at Harmony Hall was the tension and conflict between centralised control and a constant desire for local autonomy. In the second place, Robert Owen's own role presented problems. He wavered between ecstatic support for the community as the start of a new era, and dissatisfaction that it did not embrace all his ideals from the outset. He declined to act as Governor of the community and went to see his family in America when his presence was most needed in England, yet he interfered constantly in the affairs of the community to the point of its eventual bankruptcy. In assessing the part played by Owen in community experiments the view has been put that Owen's unique contribution lay more in raising hopes than in the practical side of implementing a plan – 'Owen made theatrical appearances, but not always with a due sense of timing'[74]. It is a view that was nowhere more true than in the case of Harmony Hall.

The first settlers arrived in the early winter of 1839, mainly from Owenite branches in northern industrial towns. By May 1843 there were forty-five adults and twenty-five children, and plans were in hand to increase this number to 300, together with an industrial school for 1,000 pupils. The total acreage of the estate was well in excess of 1,000 acres – 'a day is insufficient to walk around it'[75] – and as most of the land was in leasehold, the rents incurred were substantial. It was to be the vast outlay of capital required for new buildings, though, which aroused most concern. Instead of making use of existing farm buildings in the early stages, Owen was determined to construct a centre for the community at no expense spared. The result was 'Harmony Hall', a three-storey red-brick building to accommodate the colonists and the various ancillary uses, including a school. It was more in the style of a Fourierist 'phalanstery' (a community in a single building) than Owen's original notion of buildings around a square. In 1841 Owen laid the foundation stone, with a selection of his writings encased in a copper box for posterity. Above the main door the carved letters 'C.M.' signified the commencement of the millennium, dating from the acquisition of the estate. In addition to the spacious layout the architects were briefed to include an advanced heating and ventilating system, a mains water supply to each room, and various contraptions including a miniature railway to carry dishes into the kitchen. Around the building were wide promenades and landscaped gardens. Even in a half-finished state the cost was in the order of £30,000. Yet Owen had his sights on still greater things – a £600,000 community from whose towers 'would be reflected at night, by powerful apparatus, the new koniophostic light,

Fig. 2.13 Harmony Hall (afterwards Queenwood College) – which the Owenite, G. J. Holyoake, condemned as 'a monument of ill-timed magnificence'.

which would brilliantly illuminate its whole square' [76].

Such extravagance (although it did not extend to the colonists themselves who, for most of the period, endured little more than subsistence and were widely praised for their industriousness) was soon to attract criticism. The view of one observer was that a village of cottages, each with a garden, would have been more appropriate for a working community, and much cheaper too [77]. G. J. Holyoake was less restrained:

The Hall itself more resembles Drayton Manor, the residence of Sir Robert Peel, then the home of pioneers. Everything has been provided in the most expensive way. Economy appears to have been laughed at in its erection. During that panic of pride, a pretty infants' school, erected under Mr Joseph Smith's superintendence, was contemptuously termed a 'shed'. The cellar of the Hall, now used as a dining room has a costly range of windows, tastefully panelled, the sides of the whole room ribbed with mahogany, and all the tables, neither few nor small, of the same costly material. Of the kitchen, it has been reported, that there are few in London so completely and expensively fitted up, and with 'one who has whistled at the plough', I am sorry to say, that such is to all appearance the case. No objection can be held against having every thing that is really useful and of good quality. It is the profusion of contrivances and vessels that strike the observer as being only necessary in the higher stage of epicureanism. The ball room and classrooms, on the basement storey, have ceilings richly finished, and everywhere are elegance and splendour. The Hall is a monument of ill-timed magnificence . . . With us communities are but experiments, and we can't too cheaply try to show whether cooperative life can be made to accord with the genius of the English people, and the communities at the same time be self-supporting establishments. When this has been proved it will be time enough for Socialists to engage the architect of the Birmingham Town Hall to erect their farm house [78].

There was more support for the workman-like way in which the community tackled the previously infertile Hampshire soil – the criticism that was levelled at communities for employing industrial workers on the land being ill-founded at Tytherley. Farming was the main activity of the community, though there is evidence of other occupations, including watchmaking [79]. Compared with the surrounding farms the socialists were able to extract good yields from the shallow, flinty soil. One of the reasons for their higher yields was the systematic manuring they practised. An agricultural observer at the time noted that they had constructed a reservoir to store liquid manure, and in the woodlands on the estate the vegetable mould had been carefully gathered into heaps and mixed with lime for use in the fields. There was also some experimentation with spade cultivation, a long-standing hobby-horse of Robert Owen. In fact, to outsiders, it was the success of socialist farming rather than the allure of socialist principles which posed the greater threat to established society:

Those noblemen, gentlemen, clergy and others who dislike the Socialists would do well to show the working population that good farming is not necessarily an adjunct of Socialism; else, perhaps, the working population will think the doctrines of those who pay best, employ the most, and produce the greatest abundance of crops, are the best doctrines. This is no light subject. Missionaries of all religions in all parts of the world, in all ages have succeeded in proselytising more by introducing arts and sciences, by teaching new means of acquiring wealth, than by preaching abstract theories . . . unless the landed gentry take a step in advance, or at least side by side in the same road with the Socialists, they will find the labourers of Hampshire voluntarily converted to the new doctrine. Again I say this no light subject. Let the gentry and clergy look to it [80].

Although there were many Owenites who wanted to see an industrial community, the inaccessibility of Queenwood at the time ruled this out. Indeed, its remoteness was rarely overlooked by visitors in their accounts of the community. G. J. Holyoake described at great length how he set out one morning from Nine Elms Station in London and was given a ticket to Farnborough where (after a confrontation with some attendants of Louis Philippe, who was returning from a visit to Windsor) he was then directed on to Winchester. From there he walked nine miles to Stockbridge and took overnight accommodation at a cost of 1s. 6d. After another half-day's walk he arrived at the village of Broughton and subsequently to his destination. He did not miss the therapeutic value of his ordeal: 'It is a perfect pilgrimage to visit Harmony, so remotely is it situated from any of the Socialist Branches. Really, those who have the hardihood to make the journey ought to be enabled thereby to ensure their social salvation. Catholic redemption has often been purchased on easier terms' [81].

The more serious point is that at that time, Harmony Hall was, in spite of its firm links with the Owenite movement, in practical terms very remote from the mainstream of socialist activity. If it was to serve as an example to others or, at the very least, as a meeting place for conferences and rallies a more favourable location could surely have been chosen:

Yes reader! in a remote part of Britain, down in Hampshire's very heart, as far as possible from any seat of manufacture or commerce, and out of the way of every body concerned, is situated the famous Socialist experiment. Had it been near Manchester, or Birmingham, it would have commanded, in its own friends, without expense of conveyance, a ready and unfailing market for all its produce. Had it been near some coal district, and contiguous to some river, manufactures might have formed, as was always intended, a part of its operations. But it has neither natural nor artificial advantages as a trading community. As an agricultural colony only can it, for a long time, succeed [82].

Particularly because of Owen's direct association with the community and as a symbol of socialism its remoteness did not save it from a constant barrage of external abuse and criticism. A great deal of this was, characteristically, the product of myth and ignorance. Socialism was fostered in the public imagination as the Devil himself, a race apart from ordinary folk. Even a tolerant observer (with a less tolerant

NEW HARMONY — All Owin' - No payin'

Fig. 2.14 George Cruikshank's cartoon (in *The Comic Almanack*, 1843) was accompanied by a lyrical indictment of Harmony Hall:
'Oh, Socialism is a pretty thing
For bards to sing:
And Harmony's a title worth some guineas,
To take in ninnies. . . .'

companion) on a visit to Harmony Hall could not resist the comment, on his first view of the estate: 'When we reached the turnip field I remarked to my friend that if these were Socialist turnips they promised well. They *were* Socialist turnips, and we soon after found seven hundred Socialist sheep, which made my friend exclaim, "Lord bless me! who would have thought it!" ' [83].

The Established Church, notably in the personage of the Bishop of

Exeter, and of John Brindley, a clergyman from Chester and one of Owen's most persistent opponents, ensured that the affairs of Harmony Hall were kept clearly in the eye of both Houses of Parliament. Local magistrates were alerted to suppress any sign of wayward behaviour, such as that of the colonists who were reported to have returned from an inn at Broughton shouting 'Queenwood Socialists for ever!'. Criticism was intense and sustained, but it was not public outcry which eventually broke up the community. Overtly it was the constant problems of finance and threat of bankruptcy which led to its abandonment in 1845.

Fig. 2.15 Queenwood Farm, opposite the site of Harmony Hall – the buildings which originally housed a laundry room and chapel for Queenwood College.

The main building, Harmony Hall, was to enjoy a distinguished future as an experimental school [84], but was eventually destroyed by fire in 1920. Its foundations and cellars can still be traced, and there are other remnants such as a sawn-off lamp standard and the gateposts that once marked the way to the great house. Adjoining the site of Harmony Hall, the former masters' cottages still remain (now converted as a private house), and opposite are some farm cottages which originally housed a laundry room and chapel.

Concordium,
Ham Common, Surrey
Some fifty miles from Harmony Hall another community, generally known as 'Concordium' [85], was taking shape around a school that had been started in 1838. The school itself, Alcott House, was closely bound up with the educational ideas of Pestalozzi, and was also a renowned centre for health reform. Its progressive ideas had already attracted a variety of sympathisers before there was any talk of extending the

✱ CONCORDIUM

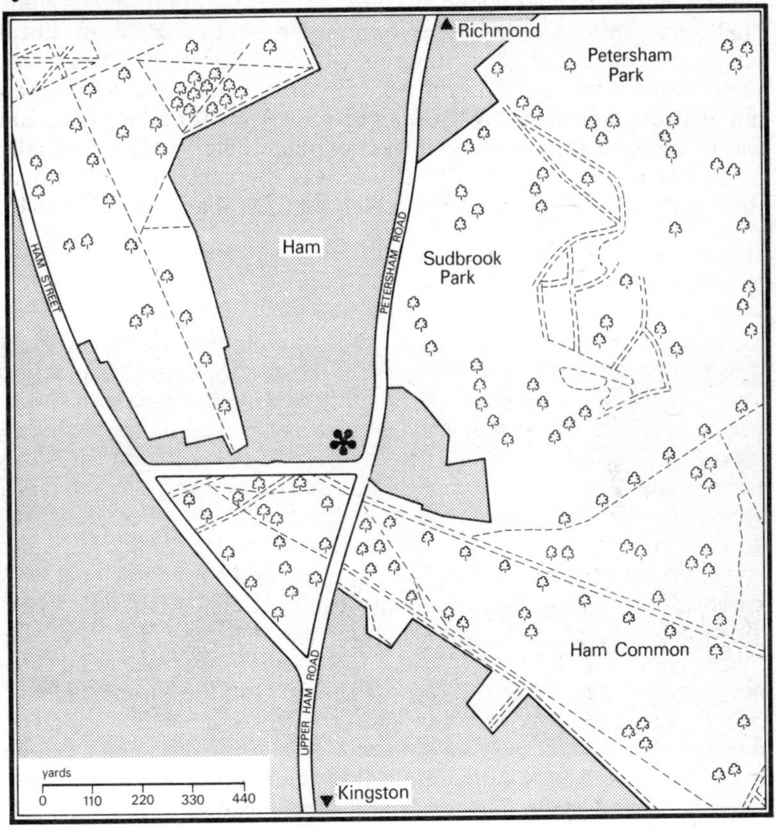

Fig. 2.16 Location of Concordium.

experiment [86]. It was in 1841, three years after the start of the school, that a prospectus was issued for a community. In the following year, in 1842, the proposals were put into practice, some months after the death of its major proponent, James Pierrepont Greaves.

The two communities, Harmony Hall and Concordium, were well known to each other, with the latter attracting some of the Owenites on the collapse of the Hampshire experiment. Generally, though, the Owenites considered the methods of Concordium to be too extreme to be practical, 'at all events, as far as the amelioration of the masses was concerned' [87]. The austerity of Concordium seldom escaped the comment of observers. Thomas Frost (1880) (B), who had tried unsuccessfully to join the community at Harmony Hall, moved on to Concordium, but decided that it was not for him when he found that he was expected to remain celibate until his soul was regenerated. And George Holyoake [88] recalled that salt, sugar and tea were all prohibited and that when his wife, on a visit, asked for some salt with her breakfast of raw cabbage it had to be hidden under the plate so as not to deprave the weaker brethren.

But the point of issue with the Owenites was not simply one of austerity. There were also more fundamental differences between the unique blend of socialism and mysticism enshrined in the philosophy of Greaves (the 'Sacred Socialist') and the material basis of Owen's. While Greaves shared with Owen and others of his period a firm belief in the importance of a new form of education as a first step to improvement, he differed in his explanation as to how the changes would come about. After a period of working with Pestalozzi, and subsequently applying Pestalozzian educational principles in London, Greaves developed his own mystical theory of social change. It rested on the belief that there are three dimensions to Man's existence – the external (or physical), the inward (or intellectual) and the spiritual (or moral), and that salvation lay in living in the third of these, the spiritual. He took issue with Owen for concentrating on the first level, the physical, and for failing to appeal to the 'Love Spirit' to change society. Instead of relying on the prior reorganisation of external conditions as the key to social change, Greaves looked to immediate ways of releasing Man's inner goodness. He believed that association and refinement of habit in communal living would provide the conditions in which this inner goodness could be liberated. Once that occurred, the beneficial effects would spread outwards, first to other communities and then to the rest of society [89].

In spite of differences with Owen, Concordium attracted a number of Owenites who were agreed on the importance of education and the need for educational reform; who were drawn in by the intangible appeal of mysticism; or who, already within a web of millennialism and a cult of leadership, found little difficulty in transferring their allegiance from Owen to another paternal system, at a time when the influence of the former was already waning. 'The period has fully arrived when parties should begin to act out the good that is in them', was the cry at

THE NEW AGE,

AND

CONCORDIUM GAZETTE.

A Journal of Human Physiology, Education, and Association.

"Erect a standard of distinction, and let all those who, by useful labours, contribute to the support and maintainance of society, gather round it, and you will discover the enemy that preys on your vitals."
Volney's Ruins of Empires.

No. 1. Vol. I.   SATURDAY, MAY 6, 1843.   PRICE 1*d.*

Fig. 2.17 *The New Age* was published at Ham Common between 1843 and 1844.

Concordium [90] – and the millennial tones were not unfamiliar in Owenite circles.

The ideas which sustained Concordium were transmitted to a wider audience through their own periodical, *The New Age, and Concordium Gazette: A Journal of Human Physiology, Education, and Association.* *The New Age* represented the section which carried articles on general principles (such as mysticism, vegetarianism and reviews of books on mesmerism, anti-smoking and hints for railway travellers), while the *Concordium Gazette* dealt specifically with the affairs of the community. It was the latter which, in its first edition, included an account of Concordium:

Its origin, we dare to affirm, is of divine generation. However low it may descend in its application, and although the instruments of its introduction to the world are frail and defective, we can acknowledge no lower primitive parentage. Our institution, however, is established; it is to be seen, examined, and investigated by every friendly and rational means. All persons are freely invited to visit and test the truth of our assertions respecting it. The locality is most salubrious and picturesque, nearly adjoining Richmond and Kingston, about two miles from each, and the same from Hampton Court and Bushy Park. It was originally called 'Alcott House School', after a benevolent educator of that name in New England – it is now also called 'Concordium'.

Its basis being high, the principles, of course are in accordance with it; and emanating from Love, as exhibited in the triune law of goodness, wisdom, and power, it aims to present the most loveful, intelligent, and efficient conditions for divine progress in humanity. Its members unite, for the purpose of submitting to this universal law until they accord or concord with it, and are, therefore, denominated Concordists, and the place of their residence is Concordium. Love is the infallible standard to which all are called to submit; submission to this immutable standard is the one concentrated discipline of the Concordists. Of course the daily practice occasions the needful diversity of occupation, and unites usefulness and pleasure.

The purpose of the College is to furnish the most ample conditions for the evolution of benevolent, affectionate feeling, the clearest and most truthful perception and expression, and the most powerful and efficient practice in all goodness – to offer the conveniences of a home, the advantages of a school or college for instruction and education, with the comforts and affections of the domestic circle, and all variety of industrial occupation for the practical operator. It cannot be expected that any great degree of completeness in these purposes is at present attained, but certainly something towards it is effected. About twenty persons are in friendly and progressive association. Removed from the bustle and care of the outward world, they carry on their designs in quiet and unmolested conditions – they are unannoyed by the competition and struggles of worldly traffic. Food, clothing, lodging, education, etc., are provided for them without anxious concern: they have no laws to fetter or punish them, but only such as they voluntarily submit to for their own well-being and happiness. Their food is simple and wholesome, and free from slaughter and blood-shedding; Their table is never polluted by the mangled limbs of the innocent animal – the flesh and blood of animals constitute no part of their simple fare; they therefore escape the innumerable filthy necessities of those who indulge their vitiated appetites in such unseemly aliment, as well as avoid many diseases to which the flesh-eater is subject. The Garden is much improved and well stocked with vegetables, fruit trees, and bushes. Printing, shoemaking and tailoring are carried on in the best manner on the premises. Orders in any of these works will have the best attention, at very moderate prices. At present they are deficient of a Matron, an efficient Educator, and an experienced gardener – these persons are still wanted. We make this announcement to the progressive world, in the faith that we shall shortly be well supplied with these needful officials [91].

There were calls for new communities elsewhere [92], and plans at Concordium to extend the community on a new site where it could be made self-sufficient. An appeal was made for more land:

Should any of our readers know of a good freehold estate for sale, of from thirty to sixty acres, situated in an open part of the country, with pure air, good water, and average quality of land, with or without a good house, gardens, and orchards, we shall be obliged to them for any information they can give us respecting it [93].

But by the time the periodical ceased publication a few months later there had been no land forthcoming. In 1848 the community disbanded, and the building was used from 1849 as a cholera orphanage for girls, later known as 'The National Orphan Home'. The building was replaced in 1862, and its use was subsequently changed to a private residence, 'South Lodge' and, more recently, into luxury flats. It is unlikely that those who lived on 'raw carrots and cold water . . . when the snow lay thick upon the ground' [94] would have condoned these recent changes.

Fig. 2.18 Site of the former Concordium. The present building dates from 1862, when it was used as an orphanage, and has more recently been converted into luxury flats.

Moreville Communitorium,
Hanwell, Middlesex

At the same time as both Concordium and Harmony Hall, Goodwyn Barmby started his own community experiment. He was sustained by a fanatical belief that communities were the only acceptable form of advanced social organisation, and that the time had come for him to usher in a new era with his own example. Even more than Robert Owen, though, Goodwyn Barmby had more success in spreading ideas than in overcoming practical difficulties, and his modest attempt to form a community at his home at Hanwell, Middlesex belied his grandiose expectations.

The prospectus was first issued in *The Promethean* in 1842:

It is hereby announced that it is the intention of those being affiliated to the Communist School, who are desirious of becoming practicians, to organise an Association or Joint Stock Company for the particular object of the establishment of the first Communitorium or Educational–Industrial–College, founded upon the Communitive basis.

The projected Communitorium is intended to be organised in accordance with the Communitive Educational, Industrial idea of Goodwyn Barmby, as expressed in the *Promethean*, the *Educational Circular*, the *New Moral World*, the *Cheltenham Free Press*, and other publications. To what extent the Communitive idea will be carried out in the proposed establishment, will be determined by a select and capacitated convocation of the friends of that measure and will be hereafter stated.

It is intended however, that the idea of a Total Industrial Development, or of the appliance at stated intervals of the heart, head, and hand, of every commoner or member of the Communitorium, to labour, shall be fully carried out, as a most necessary condition, of sentimental, intellectual, and physical health to the human being and as the only industrial means of founding and conserving that spiritual melody without which no communitive attempt will ever succeed.

Although however, in accordance with his views, Goodwyn Barmby, notwithstanding his intended residence in the projected Communitorium, will not undertake its actual governance. The direction of the establishment will be conducted by a universally elected and removeable archon and archoness, assisted by a rotational council of seniors. The house intended for the Communitorium will be taken upon a lease of ninety-nine years, with certain powers of purchase. It will be required that there should be attached to it from twelve to twenty acres of land to be cultivable by the commoners. It will unite all the advantages of country and town, villa and city mansion. In it each commoner will take his meals either at the common board or in private, at will, and in it each commoner will be provided either with a mixed animal and vegetable or with a pure vegetable diet. It will contain a library, orrery, and museum, and in time afford as many as possible of the requisite conditions for the existence of the loving, the thinking, and the working.

It is also projected not only to make the first Communitorium an adult educational industrial establishment or normal school for the community, the commune, the republic, and the universal commonwealth, but it is also proposed to constitute in it a juvenile school for both sexes, conducted upon communal or universal principles, throughout which the greatest care would be taken to produce a total educational development of the children [95].

In the event, Barmby used his own house at Hanwell for what he termed the 'Moreville Communitorium' [96]. An advertisement in *Communist Miscellany* in 1843 showed that the experiment was already under way. Whatever his ultimate design for a more democratic structure, it is his name and that of Catherine Barmby that appear as Patron and Matron of the community. His house was described as a small villa with a beautiful flower garden, and excellent kitchen garden and a pleasant meadow, with the prospect of extending the grounds if numbers made it necessary. There was an aviary and piggery, a baptistry was projected, and a library with four-hundred books.

The community was open to all who wanted to put into practice the 'Religion of Communism'. An emphasis was put on both the educational and industrial opportunities. The aim of the 'Educational Compartment' was to provide an education to prepare children for the 'Communitive Life'. In the 'Industrial Compartment' there was an immediate need for a gardener, a shoemaker, a tailor, and a young woman to assist in the domestics. A note was added that those 'Believers in Communism' who already possessed property that they would be prepared to add to the common stock would 'be treated with'.

Hanwell is only a few miles from Ham Common, and Barmby was familiar with the Concordium – for some years he even parted his hair down the middle and wore a chocolate-coloured blouse in the style of the Concordists. James Pierrepont Greaves had regarded him (according to Barmby) as 'a most wonderful young man ... creative and facultative' [97]. The praise did not, extend, however, to the dietary habits at Moreville, which the vegetarians at Ham Common thought were not 'a very great forwardness in progress' [98]. Undeterred by such criticism, Barmby was already comtemplating a project for forming the whole of the British Isles into a 'Communarchy', and later even envisaged a world of 'communisteries' [99].

But in Barmby's own admission, Moreville did not turn out to be the success for which he had hoped. Looking back on the venture he noted that few had availed themselves of the opportunity:

and these were minds who were unprepared for the practice of the principles. . . . At the Moreville Communitorium I saw from practical results the importance of the religious basis, of the idea of duty, as the foundation of the Communitive state. It was there that . . . I saw the necessity of more largely diffusing its principles among the public, before continuing further practical proceedings [100].

Chapter 3

The communities of agrarian socialism

The issue of the land looms large for all the communitarians. For the utopian socialists, control of the land and return to a village scale of operations was part of a wider strategy of property reorganisation; for the sectarians, land, at times, assumed a sacred quality as the location for the millennium; while for the anarchists, a return to the land was bound up with the broader pursuit of a spiritual purification and simpler way of life. But for others, the 'agrarian socialists', the land was treated not as a secondary but as a primary means for the fulfilment of their wider aspirations – control of the land was the key to all else to which they aspired. The first two sections of this chapter will develop this explanation and will show the historical origins of this commitment; the third section will indicate the context of land movements for the nineteenth-century communities; and the final section will look at the communities themselves.

3.1 Land and community

In essence, agrarian socialism is seen as a challenge to prevailing land relationships – to inequalities in land ownership, and the social hierarchy that reflects these divisions. In turn, it carries with it the presumption of a more equal alternative – in a 'return' of the land to its rightful inheritors, the common people.

It is of more than semantic interest that the words 'agrarian' and 'agrarianism' have, in themselves, an explicitly radical meaning [1]. In the late eighteenth and early nineteenth century they were used alongside the terms 'radical' and 'radicalism', though in a more restricted sense. 'Agrarianism' was applied to any movement that proposed to interfere with established property customs, though it came to stand, specifically, for the equal division of landed property. Its topicality can be found in the debate of the eighteenth-century American and French revolutionaries, where landed interests were themselves central to a wider discussion of political rights and justice. There was a presumption that land was the source, not only of all wealth but also of all power, and that, if land were to be more equitably divided, then it would follow that all other relationships would be similarly reformed. Economic theories, which claimed that land was indeed the source of all wealth, and philosophical arguments to establish the natural rights to a free distribution of land, gained a ready following in England as well as in France and America in the latter half of the century.

But by the middle of the nineteenth century the focus of radical debate had shifted to the rightful value of labour and, to some extent, away from land. Reflecting this shift, in 1848 the relatively new term 'socialism' was described as 'a social state in which there is a community of property among all the citizens; a new term for agrarianism'[2]. The new term was required because of the limitations of 'agrarianism', partly because of its continuing connection with landed property to the exclusion of other forms of property, and partly because agrarianism still suggested an individualistic 'division' of property, in contrast to the aims of those who wanted to 'socialise' it as the common, undivided property of all.

However, the urge for land as a rightful inheritance did not disappear, and its survival can be traced amidst a broader socialist response. For all its preindustrial roots, 'agrarian socialism'[3] persisted in the new urban conditions of nineteenth-century England, and those who were attracted to its various manifestations were more likely to have been factory workers than farm labourers. Its appeal was based on a strong mixture of myth and reality. It drew on a popular version of history whereby the peasant had been reduced from an individual with rights in land and a measure of control over their means of production, to that of an alienated wage labourer. Far from eradicating its appeal, the growth of an industrial system marked the ultimate in a long and continuing process of alienation; for the industrial worker to regain both dignity and material well-being, it was necessary to regain control of the land – the symbol and reality of lost rights.

The process of restoration was generally assumed to amount to a confiscation of all large estates, and the reallocation of land in small parcels. The new pattern of ownership was, in one sense, individualistic but, in another sense, was modified by cooperative ideals. It was not envisaged that one would own more than another and, beyond one's own plot, there was ample scope for cooperation. An image of the independent peasant, yet bound together in an inextricable network of social and economic support, was repeatedly recalled. Where communities were established it was because a collective scheme provided the best means of wresting land from large owners, and because they could most effectively pursue the cooperative side of agrarian life. They complemented the individual occupation of plots with their own schools, and with cooperative ventures in production and distribution.

In appealing to alienated workers in town as well as country, agrarian socialism was not apart from alternative forms of socialism. Where it differed fundamentally was in its limited explanation of how alienation had come about, and in restricting its area of solution to the land. It was regressive because it attempted, not to reconcile the differences between town and country, but to widen them. It went some distance towards recognising the common existence of alienated labour, and then drew back, transferring attention to geographical location rather than to the underlying process of capitalist production. By implication, it ruled out the possibility that freedom could be won in the towns as well as in the country. The suggestion that to depart from the towns and to take control of a few acres would bring about a material transformation was of obvious appeal, but its simplicity was illusory.

Town and country were inseparably linked in a capitalist network of production and distribution, yet the agrarian socialists pursued a separatist approach. Their communities were specific attempts to reorganise rural life and when they foundered, what was revealed was not simply their localised difficulties but the broader contradictions on which they were based. They expressed a deep historical search for a lost idyll of peasant fulfilment and village cooperation, but they showed less appreciation of the nature of historical change and of the realities of a new industrial workforce.

At the same time, the agrarian socialists made one important contribution to socialist thought and practice. In drawing attention to the real materialist dilemma of dispossession and separation from the land, they went some way towards correcting an urban bias that was, in its own way, no less contradictory. It is, perhaps, for helping to keep alive, if not adding to an awareness of the labourers' dilemma, that the communities of agrarian socialism have a significance beyond the boundaries of their own experiments.

3.2 The roots of agrarian socialism

The story of the English agricultural labourers is one of the saddest in our history ... no pen can exaggerate their sufferings and the lowness of their condition. There were numbers of rural labourers in every country, but in no country but ours were they a class apart, a caste, a permanent part of a land system composed of landlords, tenants and labourers. Our landless peasantry became a unique class, and their counterparts could be found in no other country in Europe [4].

In its English context, the roots of agrarian socialism are embedded in a long history of growing alienation from the land – a process where the yeoman farmer was reduced to the position of a dependent tenant, and the peasant proprietor to that of a landless man. The Norman Conquest is commonly portrayed as marking a break with an earlier Saxon world of free peasant landholders, subject to no lord below the king. But even the reallocation of land and servitude imposed by the Normans was only a stopping-point in what continued as a relentless process of deteriorating conditions and contracting rights to land. Historical facts are, at times, lost beneath a cloud of popular imagination. But history and imagination are never far apart, and from their intercourse, the memory that the common folk had been torn from the land was kept alive. The memory kept its hold over many centuries and, from time to time, erupted into political action. Peasant revolts, revolutionary writings, local riots and national campaigns, and direct attempts to resettle the land, are recurring signs of its persistence. The land issue is itself part of a wider theory of lost rights, already referred to as the 'Norman Yoke'[5] – the theory that people did not forget the rights that they had lost, and regarded their separation from the land not simply as something to be regretted, but also as a condition that could be rightfully reversed. It is this deeply-rooted dream that provides a means of understanding the motivation behind the agrarian socialist communities of the nineteenth century.

The process of dispossession has been marked by dramatic incidents (of which the Norman Conquest was the most far-reaching), but it has also been enacted through an unending application of varied techniques that have together secured the capitalisation of the land. Enclosures and improvement schemes (where people were physically moved from the land), the intricate and extortionate systems of rents and feudal payments, and the repressive laws to protect the game, crops and wood of the propertied classes have achieved this transition.

Enclosures have been a source of particular hardship and bitterness, over a 600-year period from the thirteenth century. It was in 1235 that the 'Statute of Merton' gave the barons increasing rights over all land and, in so doing, extinguished rights of access for the descendants of existing freeholders and commoners. The process of enclosure was continuous from that date, though it was not until 1710 that it was sanctioned by Act of Parliament rather than by private action. Between 1710 and 1867 no less than one-third of all existing cultivated land in England and Wales was enclosed. The statistical record of enclosures in this period is, in itself, a sufficient story but, in earlier times there were more literary indictments of the system. Writing of England in the early sixteenth century, for instance, Thomas More describes the realities of giving up land in favour of sheep:

Each greedy individual preys on his native land like a malignant growth, absorbing field after field, and enclosing thousands of acres with a single fence. Result – hundreds of farmers are evicted. They're either cheated or bullied into giving up their property, or systematically ill-treated until they're finally forced to sell. Whichever way it's done, out the poor creatures have to go, men and women, husbands and wives, widows and orphans, mothers and tiny children, together with all their employees – whose great numbers are not a sign of wealth, but simply of the fact that you can't run a farm without plenty of manpower. Out they have to go from the homes that they know so well, and they can't find anywhere else to live [6].

Reversing this process of eviction, More's solution was to bring everyone back into contact with the land:

There's one job they all do, irrespective of sex, and that's farming. It's part of every child's education. They learn the principles of agriculture at school, and

R. *Johnson, del.*   T. *Bewick, sculp.*

THE DEPARTURE.

Published January 1, 1795, by William Bulmer, at the
Shakspeare Printing Office, Cleveland Row.

Fig. 3.1 'The Departure': Engraving by Thomas Bewick for Oliver Goldsmith's *The Deserted Village* (1769):
'A time there was, 'ere England's griefs began,
When ev'ry rood of land maintain'd its man;
. . . . But times are alter'd; trade's unfeeling train
Usurp the land, and dispossess the swain;
Along the lawn, where scatter'd hamlets rose,
Unwieldly wealth and cumbrous pomp repose . . .'

they're taken for regular outings into the fields near the town, where they not only watch farm-work being done, but also do some themselves, as a form of exercise. Besides farming which, as I say, is everybody's job, each person is taught a special trade of his own [7].

More was expressing the extremes of suffering and ideals that, both before and after his writings, also surfaced in the form of direct action on the part of those who were most aggrieved. Inevitably, conditions on the land were at the heart of the peasant revolts that date from the aftermath of the Black Death and the iniquitous laws that were passed at that time in order to retain a cheap labour force on the land. Prior to the first major uprising in 1381, John Ball travelled through the countryside, awakening the peasants to their relentless drift into slavery, and Wat Tyler subsequently channelled their discontent into specific demands. The episode is frequently returned to as a landmark in the fight to regain what land had been lost; as in Robert Southey's *Wat Tyler*, 1794, where John Ball's egalitarianism rang a topical note for its eighteenth-century readers:

Ye are all equal: nature made ye so.
Equality is your birthright . . .
Boldly demand your long-forgotten rights,
Your sacred, your inalienable freedom.

Later peasant revolts – commonly portrayed as spontaneous and irresponsible riots – were even more specific and conscious in their attempts to regain rights of ownership and access to land. The 1450 uprisings led by Jack Cade, the 1549 uprisings (repressed only with the aid of foreign mercenaries), the 1607 revolt in the Midlands, and disturbances in the western counties in the late 1620s and 1630s – all occurred against a background of increasing enclosure of land, and severely enforced laws to protect the interests of the propertied class.

Yet, by the middle of the seventeenth century, with a high demand for both wool and corn, there was renewed incentive on the part of the landowners and merchants to appropriate further common and waste lands, to farm the royal forests, and to drain the fens and marshes. In Gerrard Winstanley's estimate, from a half to two-thirds of England was not properly cultivated [8]. Of the urgent need to improve the yield from the land, both rulers and ruled were agreed; where they disagreed – and where the overthrow of the monarchy failed to settle the conflict – was over who should effect the changes. For as much as a century before the height of the radical political claims to land in the 1640s and 1650s, there had been a steady encroachment upon the forests and wastes by squatters and local commoners, spurred on by land shortage and pressure of population. The Digger movement and the ideas of Gerrard Winstanley were significant, not least of all because they gave form to what had previously been a myriad of separate acts. But, also, they went beyond mere individualism and portrayed a vision of possessing land, not as isolated fragments, but in association [9].

For a brief period, in the few years around 1650 the prospect of a peasants' republic aroused the deepest of hopes. Returning to the theme of the Norman Yoke, with the execution of Charles I it was argued that so, too, had disappeared the rights of land ownership that had stemmed from the favours of William the Conqueror. Three verses from what was known as a Diggers' Christmas carol capture the essence of popular rhetoric at that time:

The Lords of Manors, I say,
Do bear a mighty sway;
The Common Lands they hold,
Herein they are too bold:
They will not suffer men to till
The common lands, by their goodwill.

But Lords of Manors must know,
Their title to common is low;
For why their title came in
By William the Norman King.
But now the Norman successor is dead,
Their Royalty to th' Commons is fled.

Therefore let me advise
All those which Freedom prise,
To Till each Heath and Plain,
For this will Freedom gain:
Heriots and Fines this will expel,
A bondage great men know full well [10].

It is probable that these words were written in the Digger community in Surrey, though not necessarily by Winstanley himself. They are of the same order, however, as Winstanley's own writings – a clear and simple message in the language of the people. What could have had greater appeal than the sight and experience of those endless acres of untended land, and the call for their possession by those who, not only had most need, but also historical rights? There was nothing mysterious or complex in urging common people to work upon and improve the common lands. Such an action would harm no one and be of benefit to all and, what was more, with the end of the Norman lineage, it could no longer be regarded as illegal. It was without ambiguity, and so easy to achieve, and yet, beneath its simplicity, was a far deeper vision of a communist society. The appropriation of land was essential, not simply as a means of improving yields, but as a means of achieving freedom. 'True freedom lies where a man receives his nourishment and preservation, and that is in the use of the earth . . . [11].

In his own attempt to form a community, Winstanley explained this link between land and freedom – 'I took my spade and went and broke the ground upon George Hill in Surrey, thereby declaring freedom to the creation, and that the earth must be set free from entanglements of lords and landlords, and that it shall become a common treasury to all, as it was first made and given to the sons of men' [12].

"England is not a free people, till the poor that have no land, have a free allowance to dig and labour the commons..."
Gerrard Winstanley, 1649

Fig. 3.2 The illustration (designed by Oscar Zarate) is from a poster for the film *Winstanley*.

With the removal of the Norman-derived system of land allocation, Winstanley looked, instead, to a theory of natural rights where no individual had claim to more than that of any other. And he looked forward to a new system, where the land would be worked in common, and where there would be common store-houses to which all would have access according to their needs:

The earth is to be planted, and the fruits reaped, and carried into barns and store-houses by the assistance of every family; and if any man or family want corn, or other provision, they may go to the store-houses, and fetch without money. If they want a horse to ride, go into the fields in summer, or to the common stables in winter, and receive one from the keepers, and when your journey is performed, bring him where you had him without money. If any want food or victuals, they may either go to the butchers shops, and receive what they want without money; or else go to the flocks of sheep, or herds of cattle, and take and kill what meat is needful for their families, without buying and selling. And the reason why all the riches of the earth are a common stock is this, because the earth, and the labours thereupon, are managed by common assistance of every family, without buying and selling ... [13].

Winstanley urged the common people to follow his example, and also, in vain, he appealed to Cromwell to complete the revolution – 'to see that the free possession of the land and liberties be put into the hands of the oppressed commoners of England' [14]. The fact that neither the people nor Cromwell responded does not, in itself, invalidate the essence of Winstanley's ideas. In the event, the English Revolution was a triumph for the bourgeoisie, but the note which Winstanley had struck was one which had been heard before and which was yet to be heard again. Above all, perhaps, Winstanley defined a notion of 'true freedom' – based not simply on the appropriation of land, but on its communal working and enjoyment – which contrasted sharply with the succeeding liberal notion of freedom based on individualistic effort and property. In the mainstream of dominant ideas, the bourgeois revolution was to transform property from its place in a monarchical hierarchy to a system of competitive individualism. The role of the State was effectively redefined to protect what was individually owned. In contrast, against the main current, Winstanley forged a vital link between a mediaeval impulse towards equality and the development of a socialised version of property in the growth of nineteenth-century socialism.

For a century after the restoration of the monarchy, alternative ideas on property lay dormant. They surfaced again at the time of the American and French Revolutions, revived amidst the wider debate over human rights. Was it natural or was it a product of society that land and wealth were distributed unevenly, and that some exerted power over others? Was it indeed natural that there should be property at all? In a situation of colonial authority in America, and one of monarchical rule in France, the political sense of these questions is apparent. The fact that they were no less challenging in the English context is evidence of an uncompleted revolution, where the monarchy had been contained but the common people had gained little. The old issues resurfaced, now in the hands of radicals like Thomas Spence and Thomas Paine. With others in the latter years of the eighteenth century, they reminded Man of his natural rights, they sought to expose the injustice and artificiality of the existing arrangements of property and land allocation, and went on to propose how the situation might be remedied [15].

In an early pamphlet *The Real Rights of Man* (1775), Thomas Spence was already clear that the land problem was not an isolated issue, and that a meaningful solution had to encompass fundamental changes in the rest of society, particularly in the way it was governed. He was in favour of the appropriation of all existing ownership claims, and the reallocation of land on an equal basis (on the authority of 'long-lost rights'), under the administration of parishes. The parishes would have extensive responsibilities, though they would be linked together in a loose form of federation. All revenue would be derived from rent payable to the parish:

Let it be supposed, then, that the whole people in some country, after much reasoning and deliberation, should conclude that every man has an equal property in the land in the neighbourhood where he resides. They therefore resolve that if they live in society together, it shall only be with a view that everyone may reap all the benefits from their natural rights and privilege possible.

Therefore a day is appointed on which the inhabitants of each parish meet, in their respective parishes, to take their long-lost rights into possession, and to form themselves into corporations. So then each parish becomes a corporation ... The land with all that appertains to it, is in every parish made the property of the corporation or parish, with as ample power to let; repair, or alter all or any part thereof, as a lord of the manor enjoys over his lands, houses, etc; but the power of alienating the least morsel, in any manner, from the parish either at this or any time hereafter is denied. ... Thus there are no more nor other lands in the whole country than the parishes; and each of them is sovereign lord of its own territories ...

Government does not meddle in every trifle; but on the contrary allows each parish the power of putting the laws in force in all cases ... A certain number of neighbouring parishes, as those in a town or county, have each an equal vote in the election of persons to represent them in Parliament, Senate or Congress [16].

'There is much that is significant in Spence's contribution to the land debate. For a start, it represents an early scheme for land nationalisation, but one where control would be vested, not in the State as a centralised body but in local parishes. In this way Spence was able to appeal both to a sense of justice in restoring lost rights, and to the lingering dream of reviving the village commune. The decentralist philosophy is substantiated by his scheme for a simplified system of taxation (a century in advance of Henry George's 'single tax' [17]).

Spence later described a utopian country, 'Spensonia: A Country in Fairyland situated between Utopia and Oceana', where these ideas were applied and defended in the light of their seeming impossibility: 'But how,' said an Indian to a Spensonian, 'How is it that you have no Landlords? We never heard that men could be civilised or be Christians, without giving up their common right to the earth, and its natural produce to tyrants, called Landlords' [18].

Spence was not alone in defending his vision of a world without 'tyrants called Landlords'. A close associate was Thomas Evans, who contended that 'all the land, the waters, the mines, the houses, and all permanent feudal property, must return to the people, the whole people, to be administered in partnership' [19]. Like Spence he believed that this partnership could best be administered at parish level.

In the historical context of the French Revolution the 'Jacobin' ideas for land reallocation could not be divorced from the wider issue of republicanism. Thomas Paine demonstrated, through the French example, that constitutions that were unacceptable to the people could indeed be overthrown to accord more closely to popular will. And he raised again the spectre of an illegitimate Norman lineage as a continuing impediment to human rights. 'If the succession runs in the line of the Conqueror, the Nation runs in the line of being conquered, and ought to rescue itself from this approach ... May then the example of France contribute to regenerate the freedom which a province of it destroyed' [20].

Inevitably, to continue this logic, Paine argued that a constitution which did not reflect the popular will was hardly the basis for legitimating the uneven distribution of land. What is more, the only natural system was one where every man was born to property:

It is a position, not to be controverted, that the earth, in its natural uncultivated state, was, and ever would have continued to be, the 'common property of the human race'. In that state every man would have been born to property. He would have been a joint life-proprietor with the rest in the property of the soil, and in all its natural productions, vegetable and animal [21].

At the same time he accepted that, over the years, the land had been improved and that, in looking towards a new system of allocation, a distinction should be made between the earth in its natural state, which is rightly the common property of all, and improvements made to it which should be credited to individuals. Arising from this distinction Paine proposed that all landowners should pay a 'ground rent' to the community for the natural element of their land. The fund so accumulated could then be used to make a payment of £15 to everyone when they reached the age of twenty-one and £10 per annum from the age of fifty-five. These payments would be seen 'as compensation in part for the loss of his or her natural inheritance by the introduction of the system of landed property' [22].

The land schemes of Spence and Paine were challenging, not simply because of what they proposed, but because they exposed, once again, the link between land and authority – and at a time when authority seemed particularly vulnerable. Once again, though, the challenge passed, and when in the nineteenth century fresh claims were made for land, they were far more on the margins rather than at the core of revolutionary debate.

3.3 Nineteenth-century land movements

There is no single ideology or political movement to explain the varied communities of agrarian socialism. What holds them together as a type was a common commitment to the land, and their generally egalitarian objectives – but, beyond that, their source is threefold [23]. In the first place there was the phase of Chartist communities in the late 1840s, emerging from the frustrations and disappointments of popular radicalism and working-class action in the preceding years. Secondly, there was the romantic revival of mediaevalism, associated with, among others, John Ruskin. And, finally, there was the continuing tradition of 'home colonies', culminating in a 'back to the land' movement towards the end of the century.

'The land belongs to the people'
In the period after 1815 the long-standing sense of grievance among the

farm labourers was revealed, yet again, by a worsening of their material conditions. The contraction of the food market with the ending of the Napoleonic Wars, coupled with the steady introduction of new farm machinery and methods, posed a dual threat to agricultural employment. At the same time, the severity of the Game Laws and the inadequacy of parish relief contributed to considerable suffering among those with little or no work. As a result, there were periodic instances of machine-breaking and threats to farm property, generally of a localised nature but widespread in their incidence, culminating in the 'labourers' revolt' of 1830.

It was in this atmosphere that the Radicals of the 1820s – Cobbett, Hunt, Oastler and others – found a ready audience in country districts. And after the 1830 revolt there was a noticeable increase in political organisation in these areas, with early pockets of trade unionism in the 1830s, and the establishment of Chartist branches in country towns and villages towards the end of the decade. The true revolutionary potential of a scattered rural population may well have been limited, but there was deep-rooted anger and material suffering – and it was with this that the Chartist leader, Feargus O'Connor, made contact. Numerically, the greater support for O'Connor was to come from the towns, but it is a measure of what was achieved that the appeal of 'the restoration of the land to its natural legitimate and original purposes' [24] was answered by working-class supporters from all areas [25].

Between 1846 and 1851 the attempts to establish communities on the land were effectively the result of the practical and theoretical efforts of O'Connor. In the wake of the failure to secure the implementation of 'The People's Charter' (first presented in 1838), and with an existing body of national support and organisation, O'Connor veered away from the parliamentary route of mainstream Chartism and sought instead to realise their objectives through small working-class communities.

From as early as 1842 O'Connor outlined (in his own newspaper, *The Northern Star*) his plans for the settlement of large numbers on the land, as a way of securing political power for the working class. Each colonist would receive freehold possession of his property, at a minimum annual value of forty shillings – the amount that was required to qualify a householder for a county vote. In this way, universal suffrage and with it a change in the political prospects of the working class would gradually be achieved. More than that, O'Connor portrayed a cottage and smallholding in itself as a quick route to freedom, free from landlords and the wage slavery of the industrial system.

In a series of letters and articles in *The Northern Star*, O'Connor's plans unfolded. What he envisaged was the spread of communities, each of about 125 families, with a cottage and about 4 acres per family, and with a school, library and hospital in each community. He designed a standard type of cottage himself and presented this, too, in *The Northern Star*. He also wrote a book called *A Practical Work on the Management of Small Farms* (1843) (C), with details on crops and management, and from time to time in *The Northern Star* supplemented this with anecdotes and hints on what to keep and grow on a smallholding.

The economic basis of his scheme was simple, though as it materialised, over-optimistic. In essence, the idea was to raise capital through a large number of small subscriptions collected on a national basis, and then to use that capital to buy estates and build cottages and community buildings. Subscribers would be eligible to enter a lottery, through which the property would be allocated. Capital with interest would be recovered in the form of rent from the colonists, and then used to purchase more land for others. O'Connor envisaged that he could settle 24,000 families on the land within five years and that, ultimately, his system of intensive farming could support a national population of 300 million.

The viability of the scheme rested on whether or not a family could support itself on a maximum of 4 acres (most of the plots being of 2 or 3 acres). O'Connor argued that they could, but his critics were scornful. The view that 'the plan of buying farms, and dividing them into 3 and 4 acre allotments, to be cultivated by the spade by artisans and weavers from the manufacturing towns, is about as hopeful as would be a scheme for buying large power-loom factories, pulling down the steam machinery, and appropriating each of the looms to be worked by a farm labourer' [26] was harsh criticism but not isolated. Experience suggested that some form of additional income was usually necessary.

O'Connor chose the Chartist Conference of April, 1845 to launch the 'Chartist Land Company' (subsequently changing its name to the 'Chartist Cooperative Land Company' and, again, to the 'National Land Company') as the first stage of his scheme. In spite of its grand-sounding title the legal basis of their operations was always in doubt and under public scrutiny. In 1848 the operations of the Land Company were the subject of a Parliamentary Inquiry, and in 1851 the company was closed by Act of Parliament. The five communities that it established in its six years of existence were, from 1851 administered by Chancery, and then dispersed in private ownership over another seventy years.

The eventual collapse of the Land Company was always, for economic and legal reasons, an inevitability yet, while it lasted, O'Connor revived the now faint but still tantalising image of a peasants' republic. He echoed the call that 'the Land belongs to the people. It is the people's heritage. Kings, princes, lords and citizens have stolen it from the people. Usurpation is the work of the rich and powerful' [27]. And on the ground the image took shape.

While the main Chartist movement subsided, the Land Company attracted 70,000 subscriptions from all parts of the country. There were over 600 local branches, and sales of *The Northern Star* increased with the wave of widespread enthusiasm for the scheme. O'Connor himself acted with a single-minded, if not quite single-handed, commitment – as the company's 'bailiff, contractor, architect, engineer, surveyor, farmer, dung-maker, cow and pig jobber, milkman, horse jobber and Member of Parliament' [28]. On behalf of the company he purchased five substantial estates, and supervised the construction of nearly 280 cottages and four schools, quite apart from new roads, wells, and preparation of the ground for intensive agriculture. Two of the communities, O'Connorville and Lowbands, were started in 1846; two more, Charterville and Snigs End, in 1847; and Great Dodford in 1848.

The political wisdom of what he did, and how he personally set about it, was endorsed less enthusiastically by the major figures in the Chartist movement than by those who subscribed to the scheme. O'Connor's vigorous personality itself presented a problem. The more restrained Chartist leaders saw him as a threat to the image of sobre, working-class respectability that was being fostered to justify a share of parliamentary power. But also the very cult of leadership and manipulation of mass support was recognised as an obstacle to the longer term development of working-class consciousness and responsibility. In terms of the objectives of the Chartist movement, O'Connor's land policy met with resistance on the grounds that it was diverting energies and attention away from the main issues of legislative reform. From 1842, disagreements between O'Connor and the main Chartist movement grew more pronounced, culminating in a final split towards the end of 1845. After then, the issue surrounding the communities was less one of internal tactics – whether it would weaken or strengthen the Chartist cause in itself – but rather one of whether or not the communities could even be regarded as socialist.

There were those who viewed the process of company formation, with shares and profits, and the subsequent settlement of working-class families on their own plot of land, as the very antithesis of land nationalisation in particular, and of socialism in general. The editor of a rival paper (the *National Reformer*) in 1847 warned his readers that for working men to support the Land Company was tantamount to enlisting on the side of the Government against their own order. What O'Connor had done was to reverse the Chartist strategy of securing political equality in advance of meaningful social advancement. The appeal of his communities lay in the immediate prospect, through a lucky draw at a lottery, of transformation from the wage slavery of the factory system to a life of independence and fresh air on England's lost acres. O'Connor maintained that he was always loyal to the Charter, but that it was worthless unless the ground was prepared with a 'solid social system to take the place of the artificial one we mean to destroy' [29]. The rhetoric was sound, but in the communities themselves the way ahead was less than clear.

'The Guild of St George'

Some twenty years after O'Connor the banner of the land was taken up again, this time by John Ruskin [30]. In their methods the two could not have been more dissimilar – O'Connor the orator, arousing mass support for the cause; Ruskin, instead, relying on his own personal connections, and explaining his cause in terms which few of those who would benefit from his schemes would understand. And in their aims, O'Connor the land republican, as opposed to Ruskin's notion of 'feudal socialism', communal but also hierarchical. Both recalled the past but O'Connor in the tradition of working-class radicalism, and Ruskin in the mainstream of nineteenth-century romanticism.

What Ruskin envisaged was a restoration of 'lost-values' through a return to a form of economy based on agriculture and crafts. He formulated his proposals in relation to a mediaeval ideal, where companionship and social order was possible, though within a rigid hierarchy of control. Towards this end he created the 'Guild of St George', an organisation that would accept a 'tithe' from each and everyone to be used to accumulate a 'National Store' for the common good. The first use for the fund was 'to begin, and gradually – no matter how slowly – to increase, the buying and securing of land in England, which shall not be built upon, but cultivated by Englishmen, with their own hands and such help of force, as they can find in wind and wave' [31].

The process would secure a twofold transformation – the land would be improved to yield its full potential, and the workers would escape from the alienation of industrial society. Because common effort and individual contact with the soil – 'the highest possible education, namely, of English men and women living by agriculture in their native land' [32] – mattered more than the immediate need for food, the poorer the quality of the land the greater the challenge. 'Whatever piece of land we begin work upon we shall treat thoroughly at once, putting unlimited labour on it, until we have every foot of it under as strict care as a flower garden' [33].

The world of which Ruskin dreamed was one of aesthetic perfection, a world of feudal community where even liberty would not disturb the tranquillity:

We will try to make some small piece of English ground, beautiful, peaceful, and fruitful. We will have no steam-engines upon it, and no railroads; we will have no untended or unthought-of creatures on it; none wretched, but the sick; none idle, but the dead. We will have no liberty upon it; but instant obedience to known law, and appointed persons: no equality upon it; but recognition of every betterness that we can find, and reprobation of every worseness. When we want to go anywhere, we will go there quietly and safely, not at forty miles an hour in the risk of our lives; when we want to carry anything anywhere, we will carry it either on the backs of beasts, or on our own, or in carts, or boats; we will have plenty of flowers and vegetables in our gardens, plenty of corn and grass in our fields – and few bricks ... Every household will have its library, given it from the fund, and consisting of a fixed number of volumes – some constant, the others chosen by each family out of a list of permitted books, from which they afterwards may increase their library if they choose. The formation of this library for choice, by a republication of classical authors in standard forms, has long been a main object with me. No newspapers, nor any books but those named in the annually renewed lists, are to be allowed in any household. In time I hope to get a journal published, containing notice of any really important matters taking place in this or other countries, in the closely sifted truth of them [34].

Like O'Connor, Ruskin was frustrated in his vision by constant legal harassments, concerning the right of the Guild to collect and use subscriptions to this end. But, unlike O'Connor, Ruskin lacked the energy and single-minded commitment that had led to five Chartist land colonies in the space of a few short years. Over a ten-year period from the inception of the Guild in 1871, only four estates were pursued. The first was in the form of a gift of 7 acres of woodland in Worcestershire, which Ruskin appears to have taken no steps to 'transform'. The second, in 1874, was also in the form a gift, this time an acre of rocky ground together with some cottages at Barmouth in West Wales. In spite of the arrival of Auguste Guyard (the exiled French social reformer) who cultivated rare herbs and trees on the hostile soil, and went some way towards achieving Ruskin's vision of restoration, a combination of legal difficulties and Ruskin's deteriorating health left the small estate under the effective management of the donor rather than the Guild.

At Totley, on the outskirts of Sheffield, where Ruskin bought the land from the Guild's own funds, there was more involvement. It was also at Totley that Ruskin enlisted the support of William Harrison Riley, an avowed socialist whose writings included a draft 'British Constitution' with the following clause on land: 'The Land of Great Britain is the national inheritance of the Commonwealth, and all buildings on the land of Great Britain, and all the crops or produce of the land and the water of Great Britain are the property of the Commonwealth, to be used for the good of the Commonwealth' [35]. For all his high ideals, he proved to be an unpopular choice at Totley.

The fourth and final land venture of the Guild was the purchase of a small plot of land at Cloughton, near Scarborough. It was bought specifically for a Companion of the Guild, John Guy, whom Ruskin admired for refusing to work a steam-driven machine in his previous employment. Guy proceeded to work the difficult ground for a period of five years, as a tenant of the Guild, with little guidance from Ruskin.

The practical achievements of the Guild fell far short of Ruskin's vision. It was a romantic dream which did little more than contemplate that a world composed of fourteenth-century communes would be a better place than one that was driven by the new technology of rational minds. Ruskin abhorred capitalism because it had shattered something that was aesthetically purer, but the Guild of St George was ill-equipped to fight the dragon.

What is of wider interest for its bearing on community formation is to consider whether romanticism is necessarily conservative in its effect, or whether it was simply this particular interpretation of its potential. There was undoubtedly much in the nineteenth-century romantic revival that was both creative and progressive. It was a challenge to the established, scientific view of progress that had gained ascendancy in the Enlightenment, and posed an alternative world of simpler, purer relationships. The distance between humans and Nature would be narrowed, and imagination released from the bonds of a disciplined society so that individuals could reach their true potential. Romanticism was passionate and emotional, and inevitably antagonistic towards the emerging form of modern, industrial society. In all the arts it was manifested in themes of Nature and love, in the cult of youth, in the cause of young nations, in a fascination for the subsconscious world of dream, and in attempts to recapture the wholeness of a lost order.

There are elements of romanticism in all the nineteenth-century communities – consciously or sub-consciously looking back for reassurance or inspiration. But in Ruskin's case there is little attempt to reconcile this image with the realities of historical change. He stands apart from the masses for whom he feels undoubted pain, believing that the fulfilment of their capabilities will come only when the new order is already achieved. The possibility that consciousness is itself a prerequisite for revolutionary change is not admitted. It is for this reason that Ruskin's version of community – while far-reaching in itself – is, in another sense, incapable of realisation. Romanticism is capable of a more dynamic context, as William Morris later demonstrated in his belief that romance meant the capacity for a true conception of history, a power of making the past a part of the present [36]. But this belief was itself shaped in a situation of sharper political confrontation, and drew heavily upon the experience of Ruskin and the earlier romantics, for all their limitations at the time.

'Back to the land'
In the last quarter of the nineteenth century the question of possession of the land as a people's right was revived, this time under the general theme of 'back to the land'. It embraced a variety of schemes and organisations, a number of them proposing only marginal reforms, but others committed to the idea of land nationalisation and the dispersal of the urban population. Much of their rhetoric was not unfamiliar – as, for instance, in the writings of Robert Blatchford:

You will find that the original title to all the land possessed by private owners is the title of conquest or theft ... You may say, of course, that the law of the land has confirmed the old nobility in the possession of their stolen property. That is quite true. But it is equally true that the law was made by the landowners themselves. In the eighteenth century the big landowners robbed the small landowners in a shameful and wholesale way. Within a space of about eighty years no less than 7,000,000 acres were 'enclosed' [37].

Blatchford was writing in the 1890s, but for twenty years previously there had been an upsurge in movements to restructure the inherited system of land allocation. Many of the ideas from this period were synthesised in a series of articles which Blatchford wrote for the socialist newspaper *The Clarion*, under the collective heading of 'Merrie

England' [38]. In essence, what he proposed amounted to a rejection of urban-centred capitalism in favour of an agrarian life based on the public ownership of land.

Like others at this time, Blatchford acknowledged the enormous influence of Henry George in furthering the cause of land nationalisation. One-hundred-thousand copies of George's major work, *Progress and Poverty*, were sold in England in the ten years following its publication in 1879, and various organisations were formed to promote his ideas. In essence, he asked why it was that alongside unparalleled technological and economic progress there were still recessions and widespread poverty. His own answer was that it was the artificially high price of land which most interfered with production, keeping prices high and wages low. In consequence, to 'extirpate poverty, to make wages what justice commands they should be, the full earnings of the labourer, we must substitute for the individual ownership of land a common ownership. Nothing else will go to the cause of the evil, in nothing else is there the slightest hope' [39].

But, in spite of the obvious challenge to the whole basis of capitalism that was inherent in his analysis, George was led to a reformist solution. What he preferred was a means of achieving common ownership, while leaving the existing fabric of society intact. The means could be found, not in the appropriation of private property, but in the introduction of a new tax on land values which, because it tapped the very source of wealth would replace all other taxes. 'I do not propose either the purchase or the confiscation of private property in land. The first would be unjust; the second, needless . . . what I propose is to appropriate rent by taxation' [40].

There were others who shared an understanding of the inequities of the existing land system, but who also drew back from revolutionary alternatives. In the wake of Henry George, A. Russell Wallace promoted a modified scheme through the 'Land Nationalisation Society'; H. M. Hyndman agreed on the need for nationalisation while settling for reformist 'stepping stones to further development'; Joseph Fels sponsored a number of smallholding schemes; and Jesse Collings promoted the cause of land reform from the Liberal benches in Parliament. In tangible terms, the 'dispossessed' won little more from these sources than localised smallholdings granted by the more progressive county councils [41], and resettlement in a limited number of charitable 'home colonies' [42].

Examples of more radical resettlement schemes were few – those to be considered being the Methwold Fruit Farm Colony (1889), Starnthwaite Home Colony (1892) and Mayland Colony (1896). In each of these cases the motives went further than either the alleviation of immediate pockets of distress, or a 'petit bourgeois' preference for one's own parcel of land. There is evidence, in each case, of wider cooperative ideals and of the belief that through their actions the colonists were taking practical steps towards a more just and egalitarian society. The debate on the merits of leaving the towns as a counter to alienation features in each of the three communities, and again there was talk of regaining 'lost rights'.

The old tradition of reclaiming lost rights was still not exhausted. It was taking an 'unconscionable time dying. Its ghost haunted the labour movement long after the reality had disappeared. From the earliest writings of Owen to the last disintegration of Chartism, and beyond, men thought they could escape from capitalism by building rural cooperative or communist communities' [43]. At the end of the nineteenth century most of the working population lived in towns, but the memory of a rural inheritance persisted.

3.4 Community profiles

Each of the three movements considered in the previous section produced its own communities. The main contribution was that of the Chartists, with their five communities in the 1840s – O'Connorville in Hertfordshire (1846), Lowbands in Worcestershire (1846), Charterville in Oxfordshire (1847), Snigs End in Gloucestershire (1847), and Great Dodford in Worcestershire (1848). Their location, in a triangle to the west of London, enabled O'Connor (with the assistance of the Great Western Railway) to maintain easy contact with them all. The Chartist

�֍ THE CHARTIST COMMUNITIES

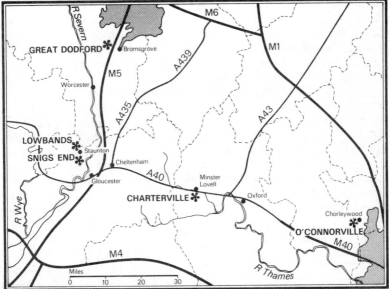

Fig. 3.3 Location of the five Chartist communities.

settlements were all divided into smallholdings, in contrast with Ruskin's communal experiment, the Totley Colony near Sheffield (1876). Finally, towards the end of the century, there were the three 'back-to-the-land' communities – the Methwold Fruit Farm Colony in Norfolk (1889), the Starnthwaite Home Colony in Cumbria (1892), and the Mayland Colony in Essex (1896).

O'Connorville,
Heronsgate, Hertfordshire

Herringsgate Farm was the first estate to be bought by the Chartist Land Company. It was to be the smallest and cheapest of all the estates – 103 acres in extent, and costing £2,344 – and the purchase was completed in May, 1846. A lottery was held in Manchester a month before the completion date, and thirty-five plots were allocated to the winners (thirteen of 4 acres, five of 3 acres, and seventeen of 2 acres). The estate was formally renamed O'Connorville [44].

It was the policy of the Land Company to build the cottages, to lay out the roads and paths, and even to plant the first crops before the colonists could take up their land. Many of the lottery winners came from northern industrial towns, few of them with previous agricultural experience, and O'Connor was determined that they should have every chance to succeed in their new lives. When they arrived a year later they found the buildings complete, including a school, and in each plot a stack of manure and a fuel supply to last for two years.

Another feature, to be repeated in the later developments, was the direct involvement of O'Connor in the building process. Rejecting contractors' prices of £230 for each house, O'Connor with his overseer, Henry Cullingham, took up residence in the existing farmhouse and supervised their own building operations. They hired labour, bought materials at wholesale prices, and from the estate took their own sand, dug deep wells, and made use of available timber. As a result, they kept costs down to £100 for each house.

In the summer of 1846 there were 200 men working on the site, and the first two houses were completed with a ceremonial raising of flags from the chimneys. Ceremony was an important part of the history of each of the estates, but in O'Connorville, in terms of setting an example, especially so. Through the columns of *The Northern Star*, O'Connor lost little opportunity to recount their progress, and to point to the hope that was embodied with every new brick. Each act had symbolic meaning – the first Chartist cow was named after the Rebecca Riots in South Wales, and her milk yields were avidly monitored as proof of the better life to be had.

An open day was held in August so that visitors could see for themselves what working men could do. As many as 20,000 arrived at O'Connorville from all parts of the country; the London branch of the company arranged for horse-drawn omnibuses to leave from Marble Arch, and this formed the largest contingent. Against the background of the partially-completed buildings it was a day of bands and Chartist

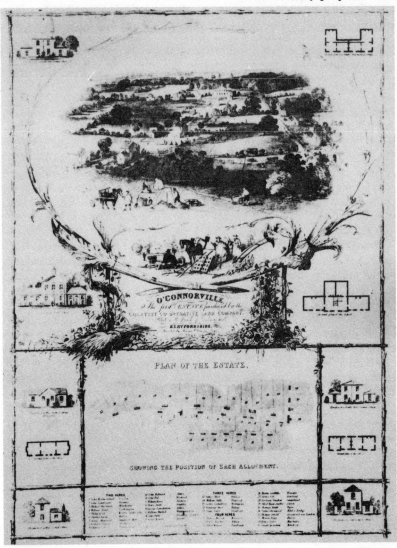

Fig. 3.4 O'Connorville: from a steel engraving issued by Feargus O'Connor to commemorate the settlement of Herringsgate Farm in 1846.

songs (like *The People's First Estate*), of flags and bunting, of food and drink in tents erected for the occasion, of donkey racing and fireworks, and of speeches from leading members in the movement. It was there that O'Connor proclaimed he was an 'elevator' not a 'leveller', wanting to see 'the cottage the castle of the freeman, instead of the den of the slave'. The arrival of the first settlers on 1 May 1847 (when 'never was such a merry May-Day seen in Hertfordshire or in England before') and a visiting day three weeks later were, equally, occasions to report. The possibility of working-class progress, built upon such peaceful and cooperative foundations, was a message for those who read *The Northern Star* as well as for more sceptical onlookers.

In the following winter a visitor to O'Connorville drew a pleasing prospect of what he saw:

Among the residents I found all classes and trades – weavers, one of whom came from Nottingham, direct from the Union House, to his estate; and, although he is taunted with having little else but potatoes to eat in the first year of his residence, he was healthy and happy, and the appearance of the young wheat on his land intimated that something better awaited him for the next. Another weaver, from Manchester, whose wife was putting down a large pig they had just killed, and who told me she would not live in a town again upon any

Figs. 3.5, 3.6 3.7 and **3.8** Current views of O'Connorville.

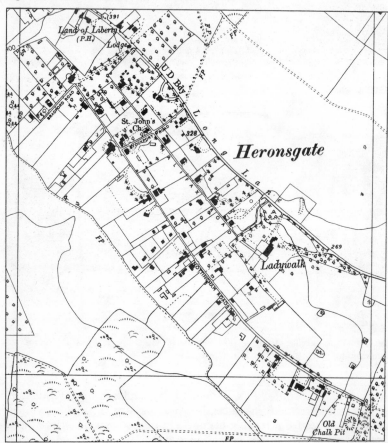

Fig. 3.5 The name of the settlement has changed, but the Chartist layout remains largely as it was.

Fig. 3.6 A modern conversion of one of the Chartist houses – built at an original cost of £100 for each unit.

Fig. 3.7 The former Chartist school, now a private house, 'The Grange'.

consideration. There was a shoemaker from Northampton, a toll-collector from Worcester, a chairmaker, a mariner, a cutler, a tailor from Reading, who told me he worked twenty years and had nothing else but the Union House staring him in the face in his old age . . . As far as I saw and conversed with the occupants, they expressed themselves contented and happy [45].

But visitors drew what conclusions they wanted, and there were others who picked, instead, on the growing discontent among the settlers. The bare facts are that, within a decade, all but three of the original lottery winners, had left the settlement. Understandably, for many the challenge of a new way of life proved too great, and there were few who could pay their rents. From its origins as a refuge from industrial servitude – remote to the extent that there were complaints in the early years that the nearest outlet for their produce was three to four miles away – the estate has now become an exclusive retreat for Metroland commuters and a retired population. The narrow lanes are jealously guarded as part of the quasi-rural setting, and deep hedges and tree belts divide the previously open plots. Instead of the odd pig or cow, each so vital to a marginal livelihood, the ground has given way to tennis courts and swimming pools, with double garages larger than O'Connor's cottages that won such wide acclaim at the time.

The striking social changes have not eradicated a number of visual reminders of the original settlement. The layout with its narrow roads is

Fig. 3.8 The name and siting of the public house (immediately beyond the boundaries of the estate) sought to expose what some saw as a contradiction between 'temperance' and 'liberty'.

largely unchanged, and their names (Bradford Road, Halifax Road, Stockport Road and Nottingham Road) mark the origins of the first settlers. There has been infilling between the Chartist cottages, and most of the buildings have been extended and refaced beyond recognition. In a number of cases, though, the distinctive gable insignia remains, and the plots are still generally large. One wing of the school building was replaced with a later Victorian extension, but the rest remains intact as a private property, 'The Grange'. O'Connor's warnings on the evils of drink led at the time to a beer house on a piece of ground just beyond the estate, and this has been converted to a public house, the 'Land of Liberty, Peace and Plenty'. His advice to keep religion from the estate has not been so heeded, as there is now a church in Stockport Road.

Lowbands, Worcestershire
In December, 1846, with the buildings at O'Connorville well under way,

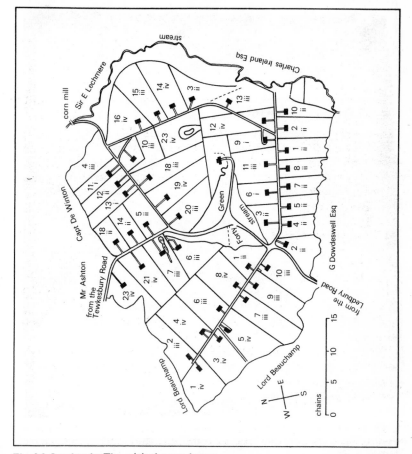

Fig. 3.9 Lowbands: The original estate layout.

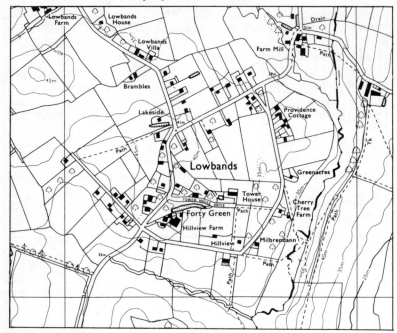

Fig. 3.10 Lowbands: Current layout.

possession was secured on a second estate, that of Lowbands in Worcestershire. It took the form of two farms (Lowbands and Applehurst) with a total area of 170 acres, and costing £8,560. With the Chartist cow, Rebecca, O'Connor moved to the new site to take charge of the building work. Enjoying a plentiful supply of water (without the need to dig deep wells) and with cheaper local building materials than he had found in Hertfordshire, the estate was ready for the first colonists in August 1847.

The Chartist cottages were models in working-class housing improvement and, though there were ready critics of their farming methods and the economic rationale behind the schemes, the quality of what was built won little but admiration [46]. The lottery winners for a plot at Lowbands were asked whether they would prefer a three-roomed house with outbuildings, or a four-roomed house without. A plan of the former was published in *The Northern Star* (13 February 1847), reflecting O'Connor's own preference for the one which offered superior working space. All the allottees shared O'Connor's choice, and the estate was laid out on that basis.

It followed a similar pattern to that of O'Connorville, with the cottages arranged around a simple network of 9-feet lanes. Twenty-three of the plots were of 4 acres, eight of 3 acres, and fifteen of 2 acres. Additionally, there was a large school-house, and 10 acres of open land left as a water meadow. Fruit trees were expensive but popular, and a

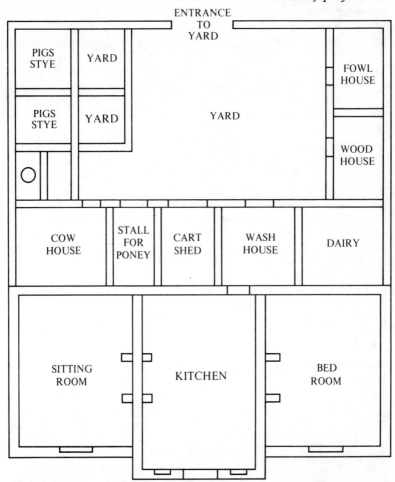

Fig. 3.11 Plan of O'Connor's model cottage, showing the importance he attached to outbuildings (*The Northern Star*, 13 Feb. 1847).

double row of pear trees was planted on each side of the road in front of all the cottages. Taking advantage of the easy access to fresh water, each of the cottages had its own pump which, together with its own privy, amounted to something of a sanitary revolution in the year before the first Public Health Act.

Whether the Chartist farming methods, contrasting with those of neighbouring farmers, represented a comparable advance was always more debatable. The twenty-two horses which O'Connor brought to the estate for labour and manure were a dramatic gesture, but attracted heavy criticism on account of the costs they incurred. In place of ploughing, O'Connor advocated the use of a long fork to break up the ground. Seeds were planted systematically in trenches rather than broadcast in the way of local farmers – and this was claimed both to save on seeds and also to improve the quality of the crop. In supporting what amounted to a traditional system of organic farming some visitors pointed to record crops of wheat and potatoes. Even the sceptical John Revans, collecting evidence for the Poor Law Commissioners (who were concerned that the failed colonists would soon be calling for relief), could find individual cases of success. Generally, though, he thought the small plots compared unfavourably with larger units cultivated by plough [47].

After the initial exuberance when the first settlers arrived, the story of Lowbands follows what became a familiar pattern of rent disputes, of individuals returning to the towns, and of a core staying on after the Land Company was legally disbanded. It has remained an area of smallholdings, still in a quiet, rural setting with an exceptional view across open country to the Malverns. The thick blossom of the orchards along the narrow lanes is a reminder of what was claimed to be no less than 8 miles of pear trees planted in its early years. Across the fields one can see the familiar design of the school-house, now a private house, 'The Towers'.

Lowbands was always recognised as a beautiful site, and there was symbolism to be found in that too, green and hopeful in contrast with the blackness of the outside world. Thomas Martin Wheeler made a tour of the Chartist estates and 'could not help remarking on the extreme abundance of the mistletoe ... its white berries and verdant boughs strangely contrasting with their sombre and decayed appearance; it

Fig. 3.12 Current view of Lowbands: Orchards surrounding the Chartist cottages have always been a distinctive feature of Lowbands.

Fig. 3.13 Current view of Lowbands: The former school building, now a private house.

seemed like hope, ever green and flourishing, clinging to the human heart, when all within was dark and ruined, or like sunny childhood laughing in the arms of age' [48].

Charterville,
Minster Lovell, Oxfordshire
The third of the Chartist estates was an area of exposed downland, immediately to the south of the village of Minster Lovell. In the heady days of its inception it was named Charterville, and because of its persistent use for smallholdings long after the original allottees had left, it has since been known as Charterville Allotments. It was the largest of the estates, nearly 300 acres in extent, and costing £10,878. Possession was secured in August 1847 and building proceeded at a remarkable rate through the winter, so that it was ready for occupation in the following March. Readers of *The Northern Star* were kept informed of O'Connor's Herculean efforts, ever more personalised in style – O'Connor now portrayed as fighting the revolution single-handed:

Here, in the depth of winter, I have all but completed 80 cottages, a quantity of road-making, and have ploughed the whole once, and a large portion a second time, and shall have shortly completed the draining of a portion of the ground that required it; making this farm – that was before a wilderness – an object of admiration to every passer-by. And on Friday next I start with my troop of 40 horses to erect 90 houses upon the Snig's End Estate . . . and every one of which, together with roads, ploughings, etc., I shall have completed before the 1st of April [49].

The sense of challenge was evident in all he did. For years he had advocated the intensive application of manure as an act of good husbandry. At O'Connorville he had ordered ten barge-loads of dung

Fig. 3.14 An engraving of Charterville, that was included in a report on the settlement, in the *Illustrated London News*, 12 Oct. 1850.

from London, and at Lowbands had brought in his twenty-two horses. To Charterville he introduced forty oxen and eighteen pigs, and spoke of transforming the wastes that had resulted from centuries of mismanagement and neglect by the upper classes in their large estates.

Figs. 3.15, 3.16 and **3.17** Current views of Charterville.

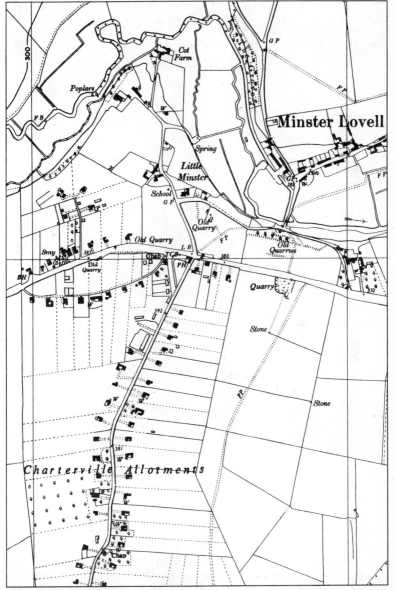

Fig. 3.15 In spite of recent infilling the original layout remains easily distinguishable.

Fig. 3.16 An example of the infilling that has taken place on the large plots. The design of the Chartist cottage (on the right) was repeated with little variation from one estate to another.

Fig. 3.17 The former Chartist school – built several years in advance of the first school in neighbouring Minster Lovell.

He lambasted the Press that persistently criticised his extravagant use of stock, accusing it of sheer ignorance in such lowly issues as farm manure. The land at Charterville was poor, but O'Connor would convert it from 'a wilderness into a paradise'. He promised new occupants 40 tons 'of the very best description of dung' for each 4-acre plot, and together they would expose the surrounding farmers for what they were.

Charterville started well enough, with the plots taken up amidst ceremony. The new school, such a prominent feature of working-class improvement, contrasted sharply with the absence of one in the adjoining village of Minster Lovell. The houses were sound, and the first crops compared favourably with what the land had yielded in the past. Yet by 1852 the Chartist colonists had left, every one of them. What had happened in the intervening period was bitter, though not without comparable incidents at Lowbands and Snigs End. Against the national background of legal uncertainty and final winding-up of the company, and the severe realities of a new way of life that was experienced at the local level, O'Connor personalised the issues into a battle between himself and the colonists. On the surface, it was a question of paying rents and of submitting themselves to a landlord–tenant relationship that the colonists found unacceptable, but this was itself a conjuncture of the wider stresses that all parties experienced after the heyday of the movement. The situation was exacerbated at Charterville because O'Connor desperately needed money to pay interest on a £5,000 mortgage on the estate. In the event, from 1849 there followed an unhappy sequence of court cases, a premature attempt to sell the estate and, worst of all, a series of evictions from the land that had been offered as salvation. In its five years, the heights and depths of the Chartist land movement were experienced in sharp and immediate contrast.

Gradually, the plots of the original colonists were occupied by new smallholders, and the settlement acquired a local reputation for its potato crop. Many of the seventy-eight cottages still remain, sometimes in their own spacious plots, but more often alongside recent infilling and modern estate development on backland. The school-house is in good condition, though not used for its original purpose. On four of the estates O'Connor built schools of sound construction, investments in long-term regeneration, but in no case was the life of the community long enough even to approach this objective.

Snigs End,
Staunton, Gloucestershire
Snigs End is a large and rambling layout, only three miles from Lowbands. A number of the plots are still used as smallholdings – a few pigs and sheep, with potatoes (the favourite crop of the original tenants) and other vegetables, and in high summer a profusion of country flowers. The cottages are generally in sound condition, and the school-building has been preserved as the 'Prince of Wales' public house.

In surveying such a large area (268 acres) it is hard to believe that so much was built in such a short time. True to his word, O'Connor left Charterville in January 1848, making the most of the journey to Snigs End by leading his team of horses and building carts in procession through the streets of Cheltenham. By June, about seventy houses had been completed, the ground prepared and crops sown, and the settlers moved in. It had not, in any case, been an easy period. In April O'Connor was actively involved in presenting the Charter to Parliament,

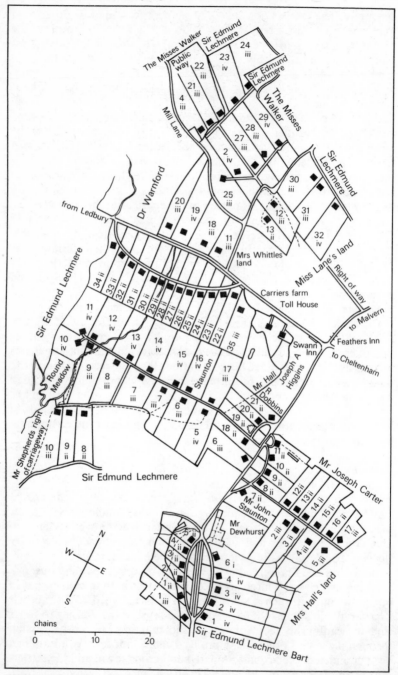

Fig. 3.18 Snigs End: original estate layout.

SNIG'S-END —(FROM THE ROAD.)

Fig. 3.19 An engraving of Snigs End that was included in a report on the settlement, in the *Illustrated London News*, 23 Feb. 1850.

and what he described as three months of incessant downpour had delayed planting. Moreover, prejudice by local contractors and farmers was blamed for the high prices that were paid for materials; and the smallholders later complained of discrimination when they tried to sell their products at Gloucester market.

O'Connor's vision of leading the way towards a peasants' republic was becoming ever more messianic. He wrote in *The Northern Star* of 'the paradise that I have prepared for you' and his description of its opening, when his feelings were heightened by the rain, was ecstatic:

the pleasurable spectacle of 80 families, heretofore slaves, and living in underground cellars, taking possession of their own castles and their own labour fields. Delight is no term to describe their feelings – it was one of pride, of independence, and thanksgiving. All – strangers, and all – confessed that the eye had never beheld such a sight, nor has it. . . . The day was wet, for it poured showers of gold, and I was pleased to be wet to the skin, because it went to the roots of the seed, which will yield my children their harvest. The concourse was immense, and all was harmony [50].

Figs. 3.20 and **3.21** Original and current views of housing at Snigs End.

Fig. 3.20 The front and back of a cottage, as shown in the *Illustrated London News*, 23 Feb. 1850.

But descriptions of what followed are shadowed by the bitter conflict between O'Connor and the colonists over the issue of rent and tenure. Although there were no evictions it was comparable in intensity to that of Charterville, and drew in the neighbouring colonists at Lowbands. At the end of 1849 the half-yearly rents were requested, with the clear ultimatum that anyone not paying would be evicted. Henry Cullingham (O'Connor's former overseer) was now resident at Snigs End, and encouraged resistance to payment, arguing that if they paid rent it would make them tenants of O'Connor, without leases. Some of the colonists did eventually pay, but others threatened they would defend their land with their lives if O'Connor made any move to evict them. The dispute is not to be underrated, bitter in itself, and revealing the deeper weaknesses of the scheme, but nor should it obscure the less dramatic history of the community.

While many of the original colonists left, there were others who stayed

Fig. 3.21 An example of the outbuildings which have now lost many of their functions – but which O'Connor once insisted were worth the loss of a living room.

– sixteen of the original colonists were still there in 1851, and others who had since joined were committed to the new way of life. The land was generally fertile and visitors were impressed with what they saw. It was not easy to support a family on from 2 or 3 acres, but nor was it in the towns from where many of them had come. The urban diseases resulting from congested and insanitary conditions were still rife at this time, but there was no cholera at Snigs End.

In his tour of the Chartist estates, Thomas Wheeler thought highly of Snigs End and neighbouring Lowbands: 'decidedly the most eligible the

Company has yet purchased', and he left them 'with mingled feelings of joy and regret; joy that many of labour's sons would soon be placed in a position to achieve their own independence; and regret that vile laws and class prejudices should continue to keep the bulk of the nation in ignorance and poverty' [51].

Great Dodford,
Bromsgrove, Worcestershire

And yet again the scene is changed,
'Location Day' arrives,
O'Connor's boys come settling here
Like bees from busy hives.
The gay procession wends its way,
The waggons and the gigs,
'Fergus and Freedom' flaunts aloft,
'Less parsons and more pigs' [52].

This time it was more likely that 'O'Connor's boys' were artisans and lower middle class, with a little capital set aside, rather than the 'blistered hands, fustian jackets, and unshorn chins' that he had addressed in *The Northern Star*. For Great Dodford, the last of the Chartist estates, was planned almost in defiance of falling local subscriptions, growing criticism in the national Press, and the impending report of the Parliamentary Select Committee. Even when the report was published, in July 1848, critical of the company's workings, O'Connor thought it might still be possible to salvage the scheme. A particular bone of contention had been the method of allocating plots through a lottery and, now that it was established that this transgressed the Lottery Acts, O'Connor reluctantly agreed to the more conventional procedure of an auction for the land at Great Dodford. Although it was only open to members who had subscribed to the Company, bids for a plot now had to be backed by large deposits or 'bonuses' paid in advance. It was a method which, inevitably, discriminated against those who had previously been eligible for a plot simply on the basis of their regular subscriptions [53].

This compromise apart, and in spite of the growing uncertainty over the future of the Company, O'Connor's enthusiasm and energies were unabated. The estate was a large one, 280 acres, and cost the company £10,350. In the fourteen months between its purchase in May 1848 and Location Day in July 1849, forty plots were laid out and planted, with cottages identical to those at Snigs End. But there were also signs of the shortage of capital – the original scheme to lay out seventy plots was trimmed and some land was sold to help finance the smaller scheme, there was no school (which had been a central feature in the earlier estates), and the summer planting of crops for the new settlers was delayed until bills could be met. When the colonists arrived there were complaints that a miserable crop lay ahead.

Some of the original colonists had already left before the 'National

Figs. 3.22 and **3.23** Great Dodford.

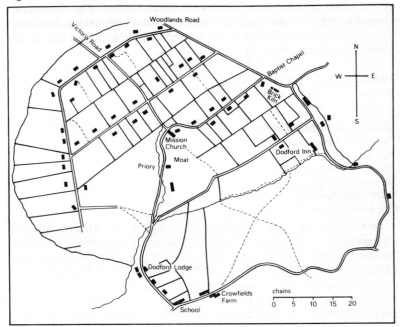

Fig. 3.22 The original estate layout.

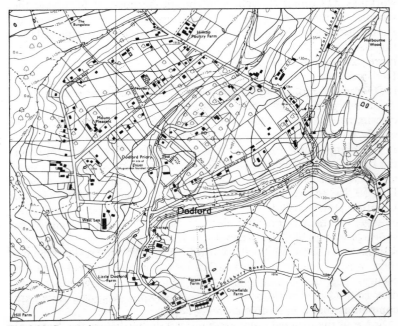

Fig. 3.23 Current layout.

Land Company' was wound up in 1851, but twenty-five stayed on. They payed lower ground rents than on the other estates, as a result of the 'bonuses' which were set against the capital value of the land. In spite of this marginal advantage the record in the 1850s was generally one of bare subsistence, with poor crops of wheat and potatoes. From the 1860s, however, as a result of a new concentration on strawberries and other fruits, flowers and vegetables for the Birmingham market, their fortunes increased. So much so, that Jesse Collings – the Liberal politican campaigning for more smallholdings – wished that there were

Figs. 3.24 and **3.25** Current views of Great Dodford.

Fig. 3.24 Many of the cottages remain in spacious smallholdings – of the type that Jesse Collings idealised in his slogan 'three acres and a cow'.

Fig. 3.25 Sub-division and conversion of one of the cottages.

'three or four thousand Great Dodfords in England'. Although all the original plots were of 4 acres – and although it was becoming more common to earn a supplementary income – Collings looked to Great Dodford as a model for his ideal of 'three acres and a cow'.

The pattern of smallholdings is still the dominant form of the village, and the narrow estate lanes, with thick hedges and orchards on either side, belie the proximity and influence of Birmingham. For most the order has now reversed, with jobs taken outside the village (Longbridge motor works are only 9 miles away), and the large plots used as little more than gardens. It is an attractive setting, but for a life-style with strong roots in the towns of which O'Connor had urged rejection.

Totley Colony,
Totley, Sheffield
Ruskin's most persistent attempt 'to make some small piece of English ground, beautiful, peaceful and fruitful' was that at Totley, 6 miles from Sheffield. It was a 13-acre farm, and was variously referred to as Abbeyfield, the Mickley Estate, or simply as Totley. It stayed under the direct control of the Guild of St George from the time of its purchase in 1876 until the mid 1880s, after which it was leased to a tenant farmer and the name was changed to St George's Farm.

❋ TOTLEY COLONY

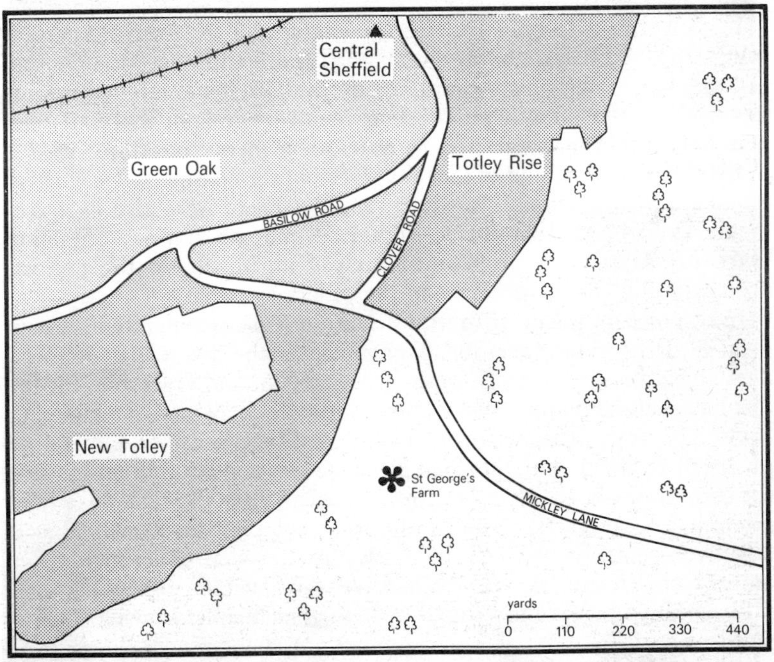

Fig. 3.26 Location of Totley Colony.

From the outset Ruskin (working in Venice at the time) showed more appreciation of its broader ideals than of its practical details:

A few of the Sheffield working-men who admit the possibility of St George's notions being just, have asked me to let them rent some ground from the Company, whereupon to spend what spare hours they have, of morning or evening, in useful labour. I have accordingly authorized the sale of £1,200 worth of our stock, to be re-invested on a little estate near Sheffield, of thirteen acres, with good water supply. The workmen undertake to St George for his three per cent; and if they get tired of the bargain, the land will be always worth our stock. I have no knowledge yet of the men's plans in detail; nor, as I have said in the text, shall I much interfere with them, until I see how they develop themselves. But here is at last a little piece of England given into the English workman's hand, and heaven's [54].

But there was dissent from both the Guild's trustees, who resigned when Ruskin insisted that the purchase should go ahead. Nor was Ruskin vindicated by his action, and he was soon to incur further criticism for his poor choice of land, and his inability to ascertain the suitability of the colonists for the task in hand. As with his other land ventures, the Totley community never approached the attainment of Ruskin's loftier ideals. His exhortation to the colonists that the land had been given to them so 'that you may do the best you can for *all* men' and that they were a fellowship 'more in the spirit of a body of monks gathered for missionary service' [55], was matched by disappointing results on the ground.

Early attempts to grow fruit and vegetables for the Sheffield market foundered, and Ruskin himself was soon to complain of constant outlay of capital and low yields. Admittedly the land itself was reputedly poor, described at the time of purchase as being waste land that had been exhausted and then neglected by previous owners. Averting criticism of his own selection, and of the inexpertise of the colonists, Ruskin also blamed a hostile climate for crop failures. There were also disagreements as to how it should be organised and the arrival of William Harrison Riley, who proclaimed himself as Master of the project, aroused bitter resentment among the others.

In response to the deteriorating situation Ruskin appointed his own head gardener to take over the management of the land, and announced new objectives. Instead of simply growing fruit and vegetables for the local market, he thought that Totley should be developed as a model to show 'the best methods of managing fruit-trees in the climate of northern England, with attached green-houses and botanic gardens for the orderly display of all interesting European plants' [56]. It was a final attempt to salvage the Guild's esteem if not their investment, but it effectively marked the end of Totley as a social experiment. The 'bootmakers, ironworkers and opticians' who had left Sheffield to create a cooperative community found little further interest in what Ruskin had to offer.

Edward Carpenter (who was well acquainted with practical schemes in the Sheffield district, and the wider current of radical ideas at the time) [57], looked back, with some scepticism, at the 'would-be Garden of Eden':

A small body – about a dozen – of men calling themselves Communists, mostly great talkers, had joined together with the idea of establishing themselves on the land somewhere; and I have understood that it was at their insistence that John Ruskin bought the small farm (of thirteen acres or so) at Totley near Sheffield, which he afterwards made over to St George's Guild, and which now, under the name of St George's Farm, has been put in the hands of another, less voluble and more practical, body of Communists – John Furniss, George Pearson, and Co. However that may be, it is certain that the first-mentioned set of men – of whom William Harrison Riley, formely editor of the *International Herald*, was one of the most active, and among them our friend Joseph Sharpe – did for a short time occupy St George's Farm. Their idea was not (at any rate at first) to abandon their various occupations in and around Sheffield, but to give their spare time to communal work at the farm, and in some way to share its produce – the scheme including as most Communistic schemes seem to do, some project for the establishment of a school on the place. Unfortunately the usual dissensions arose – usual, I would say, wherever work of this kind is ruled by theories instead of by practical human needs and immediate desire of fellowship. The promoters of this scheme knew next to nothing of agriculture – being chiefly bootmakers, ironworkers, opticians, and the like – and naturally were ready to dogmatise in proportion to their ignorance: and in a very short time they were hurling anathemas at each other's heads; peace and fraternity were turned into missiles and malice; the wives entered into the fray; and the would-be garden of Eden became such a scene of confusion that Ruskin had to send down an ancient retainer of his (with a pitchfork instead of a flaming sword) to bar them all out [58].

Figs. 3.27 and **3.28** Current views of Totley Colony.

Fig. 3.27 The Pearson family (involved in the original colony) have worked the land as a nursery since the colony was disbanded in the 1880s.

Fig. 3.28 The main farm building, which Ruskin purchased in 1876.

The built-up area of Sheffield has now spread to the very edge of the former colony. But it has kept the name of St George's, and has been farmed by the Pearson family since it was transferred from the colonists in the 1880s. Ironically, while it never achieved success under the colonists as a model orchard and botanical garden, it has for many years since flourished as a commercial nursery.

Methwold Fruit Farm Colony,
Brookville, Norfolk
One of the less pretentious examples of a late nineteenth-century community was that which was initiated by a former London businessman, Mr Goodrich. It amounted to a simple statement in favour of a cooperative life in the country as opposed to competition in the towns. The site of the community, on the road between Stoke Ferry and Methwold in Norfolk, was admired by both colonists and visitors: 'A pleasanter country for a home colony could not anywhere be found. The district is not so flat as to be tame – it is not of the fen type; there are gentle undulations, running streams, and abundant wood – an open, breezy, healthful country, swept by the fresh air of the German Ocean, which is but a few miles distant' [59].

Mr Goodrich had come to know the district for some ten years before he left London in 1889 to take the first steps towards establishing a colony there and, in the course of that time had expressed a growing concern at the decline of farming and country life generally. It was to him 'an awful thing to see large tracts of waste land about the country, and then to see in the towns so many people shuffling about without enough food and clothing. There is so much wealth lying idle in the land, if only some means could be devised for bringing the two together' [60].

The means he devised rested on the belief that it was possible to live quite comfortably on 2 or 3 acres of land. An account of the colony in 1899 was aptly entitled 'A fruit farm colony in Norfolk – how to live and

❋ METHWOLD FRUIT FARM COLONY

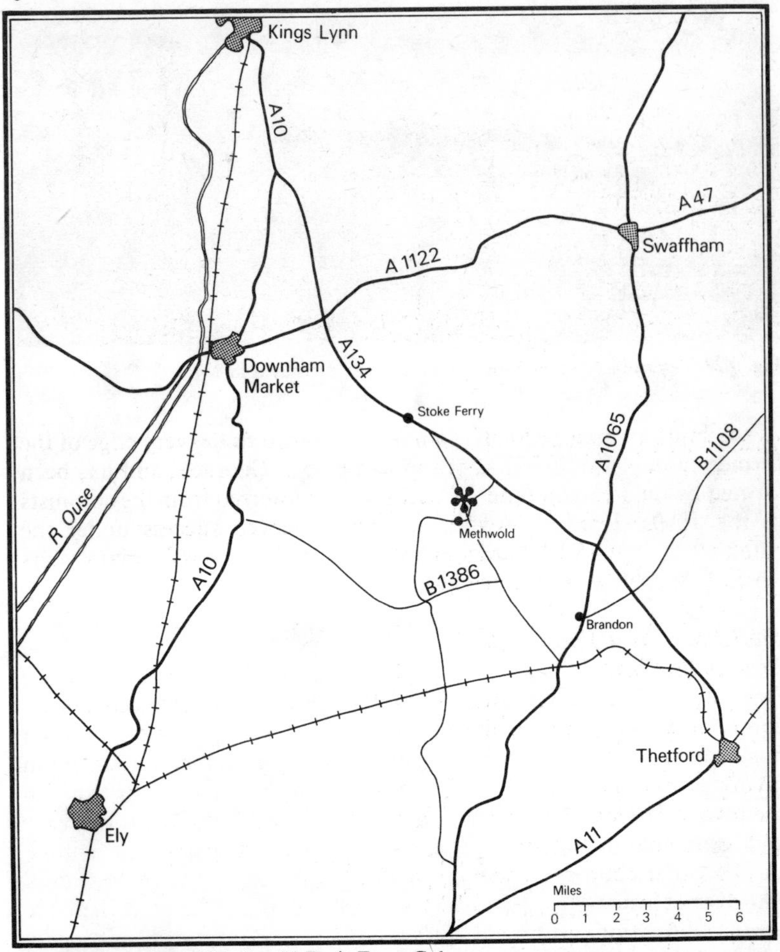

Fig. 3.29 Location of Methwold Fruit Farm Colony.

be happy on two acres'. The reporter explained how the scheme had developed:

For three or four years Mr Goodrich spent his evenings (in Hornsey) in studying books on the land and the various occupations, such as fruit-farming, poultry and bee-keeping, connected with it. Then he worked out a little scheme of his own. It looked so feasible that he began to think he should like to try it himself. His scheme was to colonise a small estate, to bring all possible skill and industry to bear upon its cultivation, and to sell the produce direct to the consumer. He wished to dispense with 'all those forty thieves in London' – that was the phrase Mr Goodrich made use of to me – who took the producers' profit [61].

And, in the tradition of comparable communities, it would be a living example to the rest of society:

Figs. 3.30 and 3.31 'Brook Glen', the house built for Mr Goodrich, in the style of his Hornsey villa.

Fig. 3.30 View which appeared in *The Cable*, 4 March 1899.

Fig. 3.31 Current view of the house, in much the same form.

He was anxious to provide a sort of object lesson, believing that if he could demonstrate to the world at large the possibility of a number of persons settling together upon a small estate, doing the best they could individually, and then cooperating, not on any hard-and-fast lines, but just so far as it might be advantageous to do so, it would be a very great and good thing, not only for the people who came, but for the rural districts. He considered that such a Colony must become a great educational agency, as it would open the eyes of the natives, and show them that it was possible to get very much more out of the land than they had hitherto done by the old system of farming [62].

Goodrich bought for himself a plot of 2 acres (adding a third acre later), and built a house in the same style as his previous villa in Hornsey. The colony grew from these small beginnings, through the purchase and subdivision of adjoining land, to a total area of some 160 acres. The plots averaged 4 acres each, with little brick-built or, in a few cases, wooden cottages.

Goodrich maintained, through his own example, that it was possible to support a family on the produce from this size of plot. As with other communities at that time the diet was primarily vegetarian. Land was used intensively, with a wide variety of fruit, flowers and vegetables, together with chickens and bees. Those goods which were not consumed within the colony were sent directly to consumers in London – a form of transaction that depended both on former contacts who were keen to obtain fresh produce, and on the fast and reliable rail service that existed at that time.

To join the colony Goodrich estimated it was necessary to invest between £400 and £500, enough to buy and plant the land, build a house and outbuildings, and wait until it yielded some return. Once within the colony there was an emphasis on cooperation, with 'the spirit of individual acquisitiveness excluded as much as possible'. So, too, in its decision-making –

although Mr Goodrich is the leading spirit of the Colony, he holds no official position in connection with it. There is no committee, and no form of self-government. Any question affecting the interests of the Colonists generally is discussed amongst themselves in an informal sort of way, as they happen to meet over the labours of the day. This individualistic idea, grafted on to the socialistic system, seems to have been attended with singular success [63].

The Methwold Fruit Farm Colony was a practical example of the 'back to the land' movement at that time. Jesse Collings visited Methwold and commented that if he had worked on a similar scheme in his own village, it might have resulted in more good than ever he had done in Parliament. Like Goodrich himself, most of the new colonists came from London, and it was common to tell visitors what they had gained by leaving the city – 'we live simply, but I would not go back to the town again for anything' [64]. It has a ring of both past and future about it – the old ideal of peasant proprietorship, adapted to a system of cooperative production and distribution, and with a general rejection of capitalist urban life. There are, currently, schemes which bear, at least, some of these characteristics.

Starnthwaite Home Colony,
Crosthwaite, Westmorland
A community with a less harmonious history than that of Methwold is the Starnthwaite Home Colony (commonly referred to as 'The

✽ STARNTHWAITE HOME COLONY

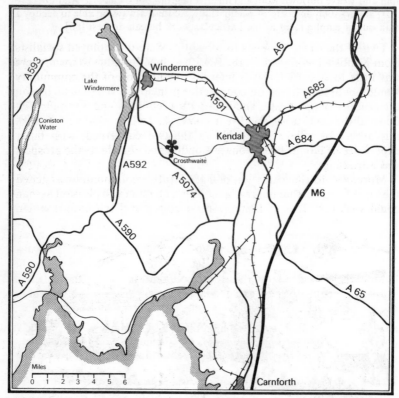

Fig. 3.32 Location of Starnthwaite Home Colony.

Westmorland Commune') [65]. It existed in one form or another for
nine years from its inception in 1892, and was located in the vicinity of
Starnthwaite Mill, near Crosthwaite in the Lake District.

   The conflict that was central to its history arose from the different
aspirations of the socialists who joined the community in the hope of
sharing control of a cooperative venture, and those of the founder,
Herbert V. Mills. For five years before Starnthwaite, Mills had been the
minister of the Unitarian Chapel in Kendal and, in that time, had gained
some renown for a book entitled *Poverty and the State*. In his book, he
proposed self-supporting home colonies as the solution to the problem
of unemployment which, in turn, was the source of poverty. He showed
ample signs of a commitment to radical change:

We must cooperate, not only to produce and distribute, but we must cooperate
also to consume our products. We must lift cooperation out of the rut of selling
groceries and of being a joint-stock company, and must enter upon the era of a
complete cooperation. . . . In other words, we must grow our own wheat and

oats, and potatoes and fruit; we must raise our own cattle, grow our own flax, spin and weave our own wool and linen, and grind our own corn. And I believe that, having such diversity of occupations, we shall always be able to occupy a man out of employment at the particular work he can do best [66].

Two of the early colonists to join Mills were unemployed socialists from Kentish Town, and, in the letter which Mills wrote to them, there was little to suggest that the internal organisation of the community would not also be based on cooperative principles. 'We shall all live on the produce of the village, and in order to secure this end we shall all sit down at the same table, and live in common. Tell me what you think of this aspect of village life' [67]. To the two concerned, with bitter experience of labour conditions in London and elsewhere, the prospect was appealing.

Moreover, to the attraction of a cooperative community was added the lure of a site in the country, 'as convenient, quiet and pleasant as man could wish for'. Robert Blatchford (as editor of *The Clarion*) visited

Fig. 3.33 'A Westmorland Commune': an impression of the setting for the Starnthwaite Home Colony, which Robert Blatchford included in his article in *The Clarion* in June, 1892.

Starnthwaite and found plenty to support his belief that life would be better on the land than in the city. Standing in the warm night air of the Lake District he thought about –

the shirt-makers and the match-vendors; about the sweating dens, the slums, and the slop-shops of murky, sordid, vulgar Modern Athens; and I looked round upon the breezy hills, and upon the silent mill, and upon the old white cottages sleeping in the clean, sweet mountain air, and I felt thankful for these few acres of free England. . . . For the present, suffice it to say that a real Commune does exist, here amid the beautiful Northern hills [68].

There was every hope that Mills's extravagant claim that 'the colony at Starnthwaite Mill will become a small Utopia of great beauty' would be at least partially fulfilled. The original site around the mill was soon extended by the acquisition of 'Browhead', a neighbouring farm of 127 acres. There were orchards in the sheltered valley, and an intensive phase of peat-cutting on the slopes was to be followed by an attempt at arable cultivation. Around a mixed farming base it was intended to introduce various forms of manufacturing to produce a balanced economy.

Yet, within a year, in the spring of 1893, a letter to *The Clarion* entitled 'Trouble at Starnthwaite' opened a sequence of reports and correspondence on the legitimacy of Starnthwaite as a community venture. While the dispute focused on Starnthwaite itself, the underlying issues of leadership, of the sincerity of its declared aims, and of the very effectiveness of this type of community as a means of social change, were of obvious relevance to other comparable experiments of that period. The letter in question was written by one of the colonists, Dan Irving, on behalf of his comrades, to explain their dilemma and to warn others against joining.

It appears that, with the acquisition of the additional land, Mills introduced more stringent rules and, on meeting resistance from the colonists, gave them notice to quit. In Dan Irving's words –

an element of trouble from the first has been the autocratic spirit displayed by Mr Mills continuously coming into conflict with the democratic tendencies of the colonists. . . . We claim that we have been misled and unfairly treated; having been drawn into this place in the belief that it was a commune, whereas it is an outdoor workhouse conducted on more arbitrary lines than any known to Bumbledom [69].

Herbert Mills was unrepentant, claiming that the success of the venture was dependent on his firm direction, and, in due course, three of the colonists (including Dan Irving) were evicted. The colony, in fact, continued to the turn of the century, though gaining a better reputation for its fruit than for its socialism. It still attracted visitors with an interest in land reform, and it was to Starnthwaite that the colonists at Norton in Sheffield looked, shortly before their own community was disbanded in 1900 [70].

When Mills himself left Starnthwaite in 1901, the estate continued to be used as a reformist institution for:

the training of men sent from workhouses by Poor Law Guardians and others. Its aim has been to save youths and men from the listless apathy produced by workhouse life, and to train them to self-respect and self-support, by the healthful influences of a simple country home with the varied and interesting labour on the land, combined with a pleasant social life and a wise and loving discipline [71].

The attraction of the country location for an institutional use persists, as the site is now used as a youth treatment centre.

Mayland Colony,
Althorne, Essex
Robert Blatchford's persistent call for people to return to the land won its own practical response. In 1895 he wrote a series of articles for *The*

Clarion, in which he described the arcadian life of a family that was living beyond their expectations on 3 acres of land in Essex. It was apparently as a result of these articles that a Manchester printer, Thomas Smith, with his wife and two children, came to Essex and bought 11 acres of land – 5 acres of pasture and 6 acres of weed grown and wet arable [72]. He built a house 'Homestead' (which remains today), and subsequently an identical house for his son Bartram.

Advertisements calling for colonists appeared in both the 1897 and 1898 editions of *The Labour Annual* [73]: 'Individualist ownership, tempered by voluntary cooperation. Some more land can be had here, and Socialist settlers would find skilled advice and like-minded comrades.' And, more tersely, in the following year, 'A settlement of Socialists rather than a Socialist settlement.'

Although it was known locally as the 'New Jerusalem' the community achieved little success in its early days, either as an agricultural or as a socialist experiment. Smith himself was new to the land, and most of the early settlers came from urban occupations (clerks, schoolmasters, shop assistants, engineers and warehousemen). For a while Smith returned to Manchester to supplement his income, and from time to time took other jobs locally in Essex. To start with, farming in the colony was mixed, and difficulties were encountered with the heavy clay. But encouraged by the sales of outdoor tomatoes Smith invested increasingly in glasshouses. He gradually went over wholly to glasshouse cultivation, growing tomatoes, lettuces and early strawberries.

Figs. 3.34 and **3.35** Thomas Smith was involved in a number of experiments in intensive farming, on his own colony and in the district.

Fig. 3.34 Taking manure to the hotbeds at Mayland.

Fig. 3.35 Picking early lettuce from under the 'bell cloches'.

The initial aspirations for a socialist community gave way to what was described as a more individualistic scheme of 'peasant proprietors' [74], but Smith's reputation as a horticulturist grew. He practised and later wrote a book on the intensive form of market gardening known as 'French gardening' (the title of his book), and another book *The Profitable Culture of Vegetables*. It was primarily through his practical achievements that he was able to maintain contact with others who supported, to varying degrees, the idea of closer contact with the land, and visitors to the site included Peter Kropotkin, Rider Haggard, Sidney and Beatrice Webb, Keir Hardie and George Lansbury.

Kropotkin was especially interested in the technique of French gardening, with its intensive use of manure and cloches, and looked for examples of its application by English horticulturists. In *Fields, Factories and Workshops* [1899] he recounts the story of some market gardeners in the Vale of Evesham who invited a *maraîcher* from Paris to settle in their area and demonstrate his skills. Having installed his glass-bells, frames and lights his first lesson for the Evesham gardeners was to point to his black trousers and to tell them to 'begin by making the soil as black as these trousers, then everything will be all right'. Smith had shown that even the stiff Essex clay was capable of this conversion.

It was also Smith's reputation which attracted the interest of Joseph Fels, the American owner of the Fels-Naphtha Soap Company. Fels, in collaboration with George Lansbury, had already ventured into land schemes, notably, at Laindon and Hollesley Bay, with the aim, according to Mary Fels, not simply to grow more potatoes or more strawberries but to free the whole human race. He confined his early efforts to partnership with the Boards of Poor Law Guardians, where he wished to alleviate poverty and unemployment. In the case of Mayland

Figs. 3.35 and **3.36** Current views of Mayland.

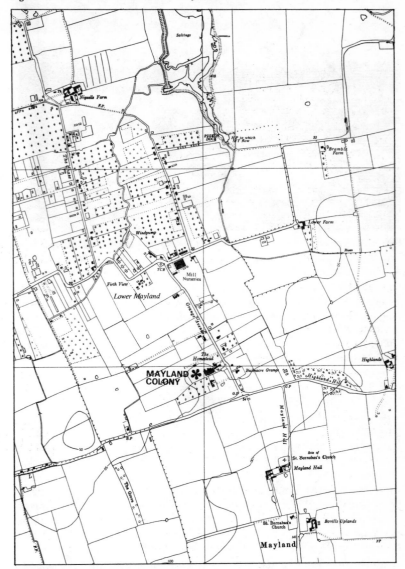

Fig. 3.36 The smallholding character of the area, which took shape in the 1890s, is reflected in the existing layout. Nipsells Farm (with which Smith was also associated) is shown to the north-west of Mayland Colony.

he acquired the 600-acre Nipsells Farm (close to Smith's land), and sought to make it available in the form of smallholdings as a long-term opportunity rather than for short-term relief:

Fig. 3.37 Smith's original house, 'Homestead', with a continued sale of vegetables.

He therefore proceeded to establish upon the farm in question twenty-one holdings of from five to ten acres each equipped with dwelling and out-houses and partly planted with fruit. The larger portion of the estate was carried on as a farm under the management of Mr Thomas Smith, an expert agriculturist and enlightened man, who was willing to give the small holders needful advice and supervise their work until they had learned to find their own way. For the purpose of instruction and also to give a demonstration of the possibilities of intensive culture, a French garden was established which was extended to cover two acres, equipped with frames and bell-glasses, sheds and watering facilities, and a great range of hot-houses. A gardener was secured from Paris and kept for two years to demonstrate the best methods that were being utilised in France [75].

So Thomas Smith became 'supervisor of the Fels Small Holdings, Manager of the Fels Fruit Farm, Windmill Nurseries and French Garden'. He retained his socialist sympathies and contacts – his second book was dedicated to Fels's efforts to break down the monopoly in land – but his comrades in the original venture had long departed. The Tolstoyan journal *The New Order* attributed its failure as a cooperative venture to preoccupation with material circumstances:

With even the small capital and opportunities these colonists have had, and notwithstanding their many difficulties, success might reasonably have been expected, had they possessed the true bond of union. Only the unforced union of lives, abilities and resources, which comes of a common religion (as Jesus understood and taught 'religion'), can create the new community which so many people desire without knowing how to attain [76].

Today the landscape of Mayland is still predominantly one of nurseries and smallholdings with a large number of glasshouses, the legacy of Smith and Fels. There have been few external changes to Smith's house, 'Homestead', and on the roadside can be bought fruit and vegetables from the formerly hostile soil.

Chapter 4

The communities of sectarianism

A third type of community is that which can be located within a dissenting religious tradition. The chapter will start with a view of the general relationship between sectarianism and community, and with an introduction to a wider background of sectarian communities, before examining the English examples in the nineteenth century. It will be shown that although there is a varied tradition of sectarian communities in England, in the nineteenth century their numbers were not large. In part, this was because many of those who might otherwise have turned to sects to express their grievances and aspirations, found alternative outlets in new political organisations and non-conformist chapels. And, in part, it was because others, who did still look to a more radical element in religion, were seduced to sectarian communities overseas.

4.1 Sectarianism and community

A classical explanation of a sect is one that places it in contradistinction to the established Church – the Church embodying the conservative aspects of the teachings of the Early Church, and a sect the radical aspects of the same teachings [1]. Among the characteristics of a sect, is that of its self-conception as an elect group possessing special enlightenment, and displaying a general hostility or indifference to the rest of society [2]. In addition to their radical and separatist nature, sects are typically associated with times of material crisis and political unrest. In the Christian tradition it was the Reformation in sixteenth-century Europe that opened the way for a wide variety of extreme religious dissent that persisted, in varying forms and often subject to persecution, through to the nineteenth century.

Beyond these general characteristics, sects may take a variety of forms, and do not necessarily involve the establishment of alternative communities to fulfil their aims. In some cases, sectarian activity may be directed instead towards, for example, conversion or healing, where a separate community is not required to further their work. In other cases, communities may be formed as an offshoot of some other activity, and may exhibit reformist rather than revolutionary tendencies; this was the case with the Salvation Army colonies and the Quaker settlements in nineteenth-century England, where communities were established as part of a broader reformist programme [3].

Wilson (1970) (D) has distinguished three types of sect which are more likely to lead to alternative communities than others. Firstly, there are 'revolutionist' (or 'adventist') sects which put their faith in the imminent second coming of Christ and have, at times, withdrawn to communities to prepare for the event. Secondly, are the 'introversionist' sects which, in trying to separate themselves from the rest of society, have a strong community tradition. Such sects include the Hutterian Brethren, the Rappites, the Doukhobors, the Amana Society and the Amish Mennonites, all of which have established their own communities as a means of fulfilling a life-style that is in total accordance with the perceived will of God. Thirdly, there are 'utopian' sects which in all cases resort to their own communities, not as an end in itself, but as a way of fulfilling a perfect manifestation of God's will that can then be spread to the rest of society. The social and economic arrangements in their communities, based as they are on divine inspiration, will reflect radical departures from patterns of life accepted elsewhere, and the commitment of the sectarians is characteristically high. Utopian sects – the Shakers, the Perfectionists of Oneida and the Bruderhof – have produced examples of communities which have fulfilled a high measure of their aspirations, and which have persisted over longer periods than other types of sectarian community (and probably all types of political community).

Whitworth (1975) (D) has emphasised the distinction between those sects which are prepared to change the world gradually (though no less radically in the end), and those which live as Mannheim (1960) (A) has put it, 'in tense expectation' of imminent and cataclysmic change. In nineteenth-century England it is this latter type of 'messianic' sect – where there is a leader proclaiming to be a prophet, if not the Messiah, and where there is an overriding belief in the immediacy of the millennium – which characterises the more radical religious communities [4].

The literal source of this type of belief in the millennium is to be found in the biblical writings of the prophets, notably, in the Old Testament Books of Ezekiel and Daniel, and the New Testament Book of Revelation. What is at variance with orthodox Christianity is not the concern with eschatology (the doctrine of the final state of the world), but the particular interpretation that is put on the words of the prophets. Orthodox Christianity has absorbed the issue of the second advent through the notion of the Church as the Kingdom of Heaven where the saints will reign, and through fostering the hope of individual salvation that can be expected after death. In contrast, the messianists look to a collective salvation on earth that can be secured only with the second coming of Christ, and offer precise prophecies as to when this will occur and the form that it will take.

In other words, messianism, used in this sense, refers to a radical belief in the second coming of Christ. It represents an extreme manifestation of orthodox Christian doctrine, substituting a general perspective for a literal interpretation of prophetic literature. The wording and symbolism in the prophetic works allows for a variety of interpretations, but the common view is that the Messiah will return (or, in the case of 'premillennialists', has already returned) to establish the Kingdom of God on Earth. This transformed state will last for a thousand years, the millennium, during which time the saints (variously interpreted as the resurrected Christian martyrs and all faithful Christians who have suffered) will reign with Christ. At the end of the millennium will come the general resurrection of the dead and the Last Judgement, at which point the future lies either in the lake of fire and brimstone or in the eternity of the New Jerusalem, radiated by the presence of God.

Beyond this literal interpretation, messianism has come to assume a more general meaning as a particular form of salvation, and is by no means confined either to Christian sects or even strictly to religious movements [5]. There are frequent cases where the idea of a forthcoming Golden Age is explained in overt political terms, the millennial tendencies of Owenism being a case in point. But, either way, in its literal or more general sense, messianism is forged in a powerful mixture of fear and hope, and is characterised by what amounts to a fanatical level of commitment. Cohn (1970) (D) points to other characteristics, namely, that groups which believe in the millennium always picture salvation as being collective (to be enjoyed by the faithful as a collectivity), terrestrial (to be realised on this earth and not in some other-wordly heaven), imminent (to come both soon and suddenly), total (to transform life on earth to a level of perfection), and miraculous (to be accomplished by or with the help of supernatural agencies).

There is also a close association with charisma – with the spontaneous emergence of a spiritual leader, claiming either to be the new Messiah or to know of his or her coming, who then proceeds to gather a devoted following who wish to share in the promised salvation. It is the leader or prophet who lures the popular imagination away from the incrementalism of reform and earthly revolution and into a divine world where transformation will be ecstatic and eternal. The price such leaders exact for this transcendental vision is invariably one of total control over the group. Charisma is an important feature of the English messianic communities described later in the chapter.

It is not always the case that such groups will see the need to establish their own separate community but often the sense of immediacy, the idea of a collective salvation on earth for the chosen ones, and their high level of cohesion will induce them to do so. When they do (though the life of the community may be limited by the date that has been set for the miracle, their legitimacy passing with the date of the promised event), they can present some of the most complete and challenging examples of community organisation. The total control which sects characteristically exert over their members amounts, in a community setting, to an unparalleled level of cohesion. Compared with many secular counterparts they exhibit a level of commitment and obedience which enables them (particularly where they believe the millennium has already started) to survive over long periods. At issue between the two types, secular and sectarian, is whether survival is worth the apparent loss of individual freedom and self-will, or whether these ideals are only realisable through collective submission.

The attraction of forming a community is increased when the biblical account of the millennium is transposed into a historical framework of world history, where communities are identified with the purity and brotherhood of the Early Church. Again, there are various interpretations, but commonly along the lines of a view of world history in three stages – the Golden Age of the Early Church in Jerusalem, the Fall of the Church (as a result of both struggles with the Turks and the emergence of an ecclesiastical structure vested in political privilege and material prosperity), and the restitution of the True Church and recovery of the original Christian principles. This third stage would see the restoration of true fellowship and equality, and for certain sects would best be realised through the establishment of separate communities.

Part of the model of the Early Church was an image of living the common life as brethren, and of sharing all things. In the words of the Bible: 'And all that believed were together, and had all things common; and sold their possessions and goods and parted them to all men, as every man had need' [6]. It was believed that private property was a sign of the drift from the principles of true brotherhood. With the established Church and secular society committed to the retention of private property, the formation of communities could be seen to offer an attractive alternative where a new system based on cooperation and communality could be created.

In spite of this loose allusion to history it is understandable that some of the more extreme manifestations of sectarian activity have encouraged the view that sectarianism in general, and messianism in particular, is the result of isolated and spontaneous outbursts that have little rational basis. Contrasts are drawn between sectarian communities, with no apparent pattern to them, and the secular communities, with their overt political aims. There is, however, the alternative view that sectarian activity is far from being random and apolitical. Instead, this type of community can be explained as a reasoned and comprehensible response of particular groups of people to specific historical circumstances and, although there are some differences with secular communities, there are also important points in common. In looking at the communities of utopian socialism and agrarian socialism in the late 1830s and 1840s, reference has already been made to the millennial tendencies that were in evidence. Moreover, the reverse is no less true, in that messianist communities are not without their own political origins or aspirations. The fact that their ideal is framed in religious terms is not to deny them a significant material basis.

Historically, messianism has flourished in the midst of crisis and wider social ferment: 'again and again, in situations of mass disorientation and anxiety traditional beliefs about a future golden age or messianic kingdom come to serve as vehicles for social aspirations and animosities' [7]. In English history this was true, for instance, in the case of John Ball and his followers in the peasants' revolt of 1381, in the aftermath of the Black Death; in the wave of messianism in the seventeenth century, amidst a wider background of religious persecution and political revolution; and in the Jacobin unrest towards the end of the eighteenth century, and the ensuing disorientation associated with early industrialisation. Although drawing on the same core of material discontent as the secular revolutionaries, in many cases the messianists, with their distinctive rhetoric and philosophical basis, were able to gather their own following. Consistently, this following has been drawn from the disprivileged – from those whom Hobsbawm refers to as 'primitive rebels' – and messianic movements have been cults of the poor [8]. In the Middle Ages Messianism appealed, especially, to those living on the 'margin of society' – peasants without land or with too little land, journeymen and unskilled workers living under the continuous threat of unemployment, beggars and vagabonds – all those who were not simply poor, but who could find no assured and recognised place in society [9].

The leaders themselves were also, characteristically, drawn from these classes, common folk with a direct and simple appeal to those of their own kind. Their rhetoric was directed with a forceful simplicity at the searing spiritual and emotional gaps in the lives of an alienated population. They replaced the material and rational impossibility of improvement, with the excitement and promise of immediate salvation. In effect, they provided a sense of purpose which neither established religion nor many of the political movements were able to do. It is this that Weber recognises when he contends that:

the sense of honour of disprivileged classes rests on some concealed promise for the future which implies the assignment of some function, mission, or vocation to them. What they cannot claim to *be*, they replace by the worth of that which they will one day *become*, to which they will be called in some future life here or hereafter. ... [10].

And it is this that D. H. Lawrence likewise recognises in 'Apocalypse', where he sees 'popular religion' meeting basic needs and impulses left untouched by 'thoughtful religion' – a powerful source of dissent barely beneath the surface of Victorian life. 'Strange marvellous black nights of the North Midlands, with the gas light hissing in the Chapel, and the roaring of the strong-voiced colliers. Popular religion: a religion of self-glorification and power, for ever! and of darkness ... the self-glorification of the humble' [11].

Messianism opens up the possibility of earthly salvation for those who have no other basis for hope, and in this lies both its revolutionary impulse and its inevitable limitations. It rests on a theory of change which is sudden, cataclysmic and total – where, with the future drawn into the realm of the present, the prospect of a world totally transformed and redeemed is at once within reach:

For the real Chiliast the present becomes the breach through which what was previously inward bursts out suddenly, takes hold of the outer world and transforms it. ... The Chiliast expects a union with the immediate present. Hence he is not preoccupied in his daily life with optimistic hopes for the future or romantic reminiscences. His attitude is characterised by a tense expectation. He is always on his toes awaiting the propitious moment and thus there is no inner articulation of time for him [12].

Their unstable, explosive potential presents an obvious threat to authority and has, at various times, led to the most extreme forms of repression and persecution. In certain ways – in their appeal to the subconscious, irrational forces in society – they present an even greater threat than so-called 'rational' revolutionary strategy, being both harder to foresee and afterwards to control.

4.2 The spread of sectarian communities

The sectarian communities in England were the product, not only of their immediate cultural environment, but also of a wider pattern of Christian dissent. The communities were themselves part of a network that originated in central and northern Europe at the time of the Reformation, and which later extended westwards to North America. There is much about the English communities that is distinctive, but also much that is common to this European and American experience. Sectarian eruptions on the Continent were invariably felt on this side of the Channel, and increasingly across the Atlantic too. The spread of Anabaptism is an early case in point [13].

Anabaptism (so called because of a belief in adult baptism) was a movement that rapidly gained a large following in the 1530s in the German states, Holland, Switzerland and Austria. Its most volatile achievement was to identify Münster in Westphalia as the New Jerusalem, and to take control of the city to await the destruction of the rest of the world. The fall of the city to the Protestant and Catholic authorities failed to quell the movement, which spread to other parts of Europe and to England in 1612 where it was met with repressive measures. What offended the governments of Europe was not only their religious heresy but the challenge they posed to material codes. For the sectarian there was no separation between religious belief and social practice. Together with a related group, the Familists (or Family of Love), they espoused a form of primitive communism, and spread the unsettling notion that perfection was possible on earth. It was an idea that rapidly gained support among the ranks of the disprivileged and, equally, was the subject of the most extreme persecution by an intolerant State.

Sectarianism was well-entrenched in England in the early decades of the seventeenth century, but reached a new climax with the struggle against the monarchy. For the sectarians this was seen not simply as a struggle for greater freedom, but as a millennial battle against the Antichrist in the form of the monarchy (just as in the nineteenth century the Antichrist took the form of capitalism). In the popular imagination the overthrow of the monarchy was perceived not merely as a political change but as the advent of the millennium, when Christ would appear at any time to put the seal of approval on the work of the revolutionaries. Understandably, the New Model Army, at the fore of the struggle, was an important source of these ideas, but the sense of expectation and claims to divine prophecy spread far beyond the military ranks. Anabaptists, Millenarians or Fifth Monarchy Men, Antinomians, Seekers, Ranters, Diggers, Levellers and Quakers all stem from or flourished during this period, though few of them were successful in establishing their own communities [14].

One example of a sect formed at this time, with an influence on later communities in England (and, indirectly, on the Shaker communities in America) is that of the Quakers. The movement dates from 1646 when George Fox experienced a spiritual unrest, and developed the belief that the Holy Spirit, the 'inner light' could be found within everyone. The immanence of the Holy Spirit was neither the prerogative of an elite, nor dependent upon bestowal by a Church hierarchy; salvation was available to all, and it could be achieved through the communication of spiritual experiences in meetings. With converts from the Anabaptists, Familists and Diggers, Fox set about organising small Quaker societies as the basis for further enlightenment. Less in Fox than among some of his followers, there was a distinct messianist leaning within the early movement.

From the outset there was an attachment to community projects. One of the more radical schemes was that of the Quaker, John Bellers, who in 1696 proposed a national network of 'colleges of industry of all useful trades and husbandry'. Each of these would operate with some 300 producers, and he likened the basis of community to that of primitive Christianity. There was little enthusiasm at the time for the scheme, although over a century later Robert Owen acknowledged the 'colleges of industry' as a model for his own 'villages of cooperation'.

Instead, Quaker communities have assumed a less challenging role, reflecting a balance between the introversionism and fervour of the early movement, looking inwards for salvation, and a growing concern for the problems of the outer world. As a result of individual conscience and a high standard of ethics in their everyday life, many Quakers achieved considerable success as businessmen and (in part to avoid prejudicing those very qualities which enabled it) an associated reputation as generous philanthropists. Quaker communities, introducing higher standards of living and working conditions without threatening existing patterns of ownership, are renowned. They include, for instance, the corporate industrial ventures of the iron-masters at Ebbw Vale and Coalbrookdale, the settlements associated with the chocolate manufacturers at Bournville and New Earswick, and land colonies like William Allen's experiment at Lindfield [15].

In the eighteenth century, a different type of sectarian community in England was that which was associated with the Moravians. The movement originated in Central Europe, around the revival of the Moravian Church, a model of Christianity that was seen to be close to that of the idealised Primitive Church. From 1738 disciples of the faith arrived in England to spread the message. Not unlike the Shakers in America in the following century, membership of the Moravians imposed a strict commitment to their particular notion of community. It was through participation in community that their socio-religious rules could be most fully observed, and converts were encouraged to live in a Moravian community.

In addition to a wider distribution of chapels, five Moravian communities were established in England in the middle of the eighteenth century. There were settlements in Bedford and Bristol, and at Ockbrook (near Nottingham), Fulneck (near Pudsey) and Dukinfield (near Manchester); the last-named was established in 1743 but was later relocated and known as Fairfield [16]. The settlements were, generally, very successful, earning a reputation for the industriousness of their members and the quality of their varied products. The Moravian schools gained particular recognition.

Each of the trades within a community was known as a 'diacony' and all profits were returned to the community as a whole, members receiving only a nominal salary. Behaviour within the community was controlled by a strict moral code – administered by a representative body of 'elders' at monthly meetings. Subdivisions within the community were known as 'choirs', each choir reflecting a different age and status group (married members, widowers, widows, single brethren, single sisters, youths, great girls, little boys, little girls, and infants). There was an extensive building programme in each community, the buildings and finances being managed by a third category, the 'elective congregation committee'.

Charles Kingsley, a century after their establishment, reflected that the 'Moravian Socialist Establishments' had succeeded because 'they were undertaken in the fear of God, and with humility and caution; because the Moravians have believed, and acted up to their own creed, that they were brothers and sisters, members of one body, bound to care not for themselves but for the Commonwealth' [17]. It is probably true that the severe demands imposed on new members served both as a source of success in the communities and as a constraint on the spread of Moravian principles among a wider following. But the Moravian example was the exception rather than the rule. Where they sought to establish their own communities it was more common for sectarians to leave the repressive atmosphere of Europe. The route westwards across the Atlantic was a long-established option for those in search of religious freedom – for instance, between 1620 and 1640 some 20,000 left

England for a new life in the new American colonies [18]. The resultant Puritan settlements in New England are part of a varied religious tradition in America that existed before the nineteenth century. But it is not until after the War of Independence, with the way open for a vast new influx of emigrants from Europe to settle the new lands, that one finds extensive evidence of extreme sectarian activity. It was in the turmoil of charting new ethical as well as physical boundaries in nineteenth-century America that messianism flourished. Messianist sects found rich ground in the mixture of despair over existing conditions and the hope for something better that motivated the emigrants. In their strict codes of behaviour and order, they also provided an alternative to the moral and legal uncertainties of frontier life.

The sectarians were not slow to exploit the popular vision of America as the land of salvation. Persistently, the virgin territories are epitomised as the Plains of Heaven, of Paradise itself, and the long journey across the sea was likened to the sufferings endured by the Israelites in their flight from the Egyptians. At the limits of the wilderness lay the Promised Land, and all who had been chosen for the journey would be saved. Messianists claimed that, of all the nations of the world, America had been chosen for the Second Coming, and the millennium of the saints (while essentially spiritual in nature) would be symbolised by a paradisaic transformation of the earth. The idea of emigration was raised from a purely social and physical level to supernatural heights, and for the believers new settlements in the backwoods shone with the aura of the Holy City [19].

The sectarians in America absorbed a long and varied European tradition, and many of their communities lasted for very much longer periods than they had been able to do in the Old World. It was not only the social milieu that was favourable to their growth, but also the simple issue of cheap and available land in which they could take root. In the major phase of community formation, between 1800 and 1860, it is likely that well over half of all those that were established were sectarian communities [20].

The point of their relative success was not lost to English observers who, while not necessarily agreeing with their religious basis, found much to admire in these early experiments. A significant example was that of Harmony in Indiana – the community of a sect known as the Rappites. Under their prophetic leader, George Rapp, the original group had come from Wurtemberg in Germany, first to Pennsylvania and then on to Harmony in 1814. It gained particular interest in English communitarian circles when Robert Owen bought the total settlement from the Rappites in 1825, as the location for his own experiment, New Harmony [21]. Letters and reports crossed the Atlantic with encouraging news for the English cooperators.

Owen's son, Robert Dale Owen voiced the humanist viewpoint in condemning the social organisation of an 'ecclesiastical aristocracy' while recognising its economic viability:

Harmony was a marvellous experiment from a pecuniary point of view, for at the time of their emigration from Germany, their property did not exceed twenty-five dollars a head, while in twenty-one years (i.e. in 1825) a fair estimate gave them two thousand dollars for each man, woman and child, probably ten times the average wealth throughout the United States [22].

Another admirer of Harmony – 'the name of the place being characteristic of the society that is settled there' – was William Hebert, who visited the Rappite community and subsequently reported back to prospective English communitarians:

These good people have literally made the 'barren wilderness to smile' with corn fields, meadows, and gardens upon a most extensive scale. Their little town, seen from the neighbouring hills, which are covered with their vineyards and orchards, has an exceedingly pleasing appearance. . . . Harmony is truly the abode of peace and industry [23].

At a time when nothing comparable existed in England, the likes of Harmony were important demonstrations that, given the right conditions, communities could indeed work. The English communitarians, with their faith in science and reason, were prone to look on such experiments as scientific evidence of the viability of an alternative social system.

There are other links between England and the American communities, in particular, where English sectarians emigrated in order to allow the freer development of their own faith, or as converts to indigenous American sects. Many who might otherwise have tried to form communities in England, chose, instead the more promising conditions of America. Probably the best example of sectarian communities whose beliefs stem from a group in England is that of the Shakers.

The sect originated in Lancashire, where two former Quakers, John and Jane Wardley encouraged the belief that Christ was about to return, and would do so in the form of a woman. Their following, known as the 'Shaking Quakers', were convinced that she had indeed arrived, in the person of Mother Ann Lee and, excited by her vision of an earthly paradise far from the world they knew, a small group followed her to America in 1774. They established their first community at Niskayuna, near Albany, in 1776, based on the principles of chastity, community of goods, confession of sins and separation from the rest of the world so that they could achieve their own measure of perfection. By 1800 the number of Shaker communities had grown to eleven and, at their peak in the nineteenth century, there were as many as fifty-eight [24].

The American observer, Charles Nordhoff, wrote in 1875 that:

the Shakers have the oldest existing communistic societies on this continent. They are also the most thoroughly organised, and in some respects the most successful and flourishing. . . . They assert that the second appearance of Christ upon Earth has been; and that they are the only true Church in which revelation, spiritualism, celibacy, oral confession, community, non-resistance, peace, the gift of healing, miracles, physical health and separation from the world are the foundations of the new heavens. In practical life they are industrious, peaceful, honest, highly ingenious, patient of toil, and extraordinarily cleanly [25].

The Shaker communities were of contemporary significance, not simply because of their numbers and their survival qualities, but also because of their experimentation with new communal (as opposed to individual or family) networks. They were also remarkably successful in material terms, managing their communities effectively and combining work on the land with a variety of crafts of the highest quality. Political communitarians in England (from the early socialists in the 1820s to the anarchists in the 1890s) viewed the Shaker communities with mixed emotions – aware that the reasons for their success were in contradiction to their own ideals. The strict social system, which reduced many of the tensions that occurred in secular communities, was unacceptable to those who sought a humanist basis for freedom. The Shakers were driven by the depth of their millennial beliefs, convinced that the millennium had already begun, and thus freed from the insecurity of waiting for something that is always imminent but always beyond reach. The chiliasm of the Shakers set them apart from the rest of society and though undoubtedly successful in one sense, their communities were models which could not easily be adopted by secularists.

Apart from the Shakers there were other sects with strong English links – the Swedenborgians, the Plymouth Brethren, the Oneida Perfectionists, the Millerites (later the Seventh Day Adventists), and the Disciples of Christ. But in terms of numbers who left England to build new settlements in answer to the message of God, there is nothing to compare with the attraction of the Mormons (The Church of Jesus Christ or Latter-day Saints). In the tide of Owenism and Chartism the prophet Joseph Smith held out new hope in the form of his ecstatic vision of the City of Zion. It was ordained that God's city be built in the United States and Smith knew where and how this should be done [26].

The call of Zion was eagerly answered. A Mormon publication in England, the *Millennial Star*, sold 25,000 copies weekly, access was gained to chapels and public halls throughout the country, and the exhortations to emigrate were strong – 'Every Saint who does not come *home* will be afflicted by the Devil'. The numbers who were converted ran into tens of thousands, and special ships were commissioned to convey the saved ones from Liverpool and Bristol to the Promised Land – twenty-one ships carried more than 4,500 converts between 1842 and 1846 and in the aftermath of Chartism in the 1850s the tempo increased to a still higher level. Mormon settlements were established in Ohio, Illinois, Missouri and, finally, in Utah as the sect moved westwards in search of earthly tolerance and divine authority.

For the English communitarians there were lessons to be learnt. In the first place, as with other sects the Mormons enjoyed a high level of commitment among their members, but in this case with the interesting difference of a wide involvement in the management of their own affairs. One in five formally participated in government, and that was a sound practical lesson which the secularists might well have pursued. In the second place, the ease with which the Mormons recruited members in England demonstrated, yet again, that beneath a thin surface of apparent submission and despair, there still existed a forceful potential for creative cooperation. In the next section we can look more closely at domestic attempts to release this impulse.

4.3 Nineteenth-century sectarianism in England

Compared with the century of the English Revolution and with the example of the United States, the intensity of sectarianism in nineteenth-century England was of a lower order and gave rise to few communities. There are a number of reasons for this.

For a start, some of its original revolutionary impulse was now diffused into the various non-conformist denominations which grew rapidly during this period. In 1851 the Religious Census showed that denominations derived from the dissenting Protestant sects had a majority following in the new industrial centres and, nationally, enjoyed nearly as much support as the Church of England. Their growth (like that of the sects in earlier periods) was still associated with a core of underlying material discontent, and with situations where a rational basis for improvement had receded. They attracted many who had lost all other hope with the collapse of political movements and for these the new denominations could only relocate hope within the abstract realm of life after death. They absorbed the frustrations of political failure and, in abandoning the idea of immediate change, developed what E. P. Thompson refers to as 'the chiliasm of the defeated and the hopeless' [27]. In turn, without a sense of immediacy, a major stimulus for community formation receded. In place of community and collective salvation, the individual and the family became the basic social units in the new non-conformist order.

Additionally, sectarianism lost many potential members to the more vigorous religious groups in the United States, and to a variety of new political movements in England. Not only did these latter organisations provide the disprivileged with an alternative means of material improvement but also, in some cases, their methods and rhetoric were barely distinguishable from full-blooded messianism itself. Reference has already been made to the messianic pretensions among the Owenites and the Chartists in the late 1830s and early 1840s, in their certainty that the millennium was about to dawn.

But although the heat of sectarianism had cooled it is equally apparent that, from time to time, often unexpectedly, it was still capable of flaring up. At the end of the eighteenth century the imagery of the millennium is captured in the works of William Blake, and lived on in the radical circles of Jacobins and Dissenters in London, in the mining and weaving villages of the Midlands and the North, and in the country districts of the South West. With the turn of the century, in the new industrial towns and among the labouring population in the countryside, there were always those who preferred the excitement of immediate salvation to the more indirect methods of political campaigns or emigration, or to more established forms of religion. Neither the Free Churches nor the new political organisations were able to satisfy for all, the full depths of spiritual and emotional need that were experienced in this period.

The pattern of nineteenth-century sectarianism is erratic, but there are some themes which can help to explain the setting for community formation. One such theme is that which originates with the self-proclaimed prophet, Richard Brothers. In 1794 Brothers announced his prophecies in the form of a publication, *A Revealed Knowledge of the Prophecies and Times, Wrote under the Direction of the Lord God.* It foretold of imminent doom and disaster when the rich would perish, and the poor, the honest, the virtuous, the patriotic would live to rejoice. The threat posed by Brothers was sufficient to induce the Privy Council to secure his arrest in 1795, and subsequent confinement to a lunatic asylum. But his influence continued through his followers for several years more, and through the response of rival prophetic groups. What is more, it was Brothers who revived the idea that England was the true Israel where the new Jerusalem would be built, an idea that was central to a line of prophets who followed him. It was also an idea which lent itself to community formation, and there are at least two cases where plans for housing the chosen ones went ahead – the Christian Israelite Institution at Wrenthorpe, and the New and Latter House of Israel at Gillingham.

Attracting a larger following than Brothers was 'the Exeter Prophetess', Joanna Southcott. From the time of her first booklet, *The Strange Effects of Faith*, in 1801, her following widened into a national movement that persisted almost throughout the period of the French Wars (themselves likened to Armageddon). It was always, essentially, a cult of the poor, appealing most strongly to those for whom superstition and the supernatural remained as important elements in their lives. Her support was strongest in the west and north of England – in Bristol, south Lancashire, the West Riding and Stockton-on-Tees [28].

The first peak of her popularity came between 1801 and 1804 with the widespread belief that Southcott was the female Messiah that had been promised, and that she could offer salvation. Those who she could save from the furies of the Hell to come received a seal, and as many as 100,000, the 'sealed People', may have done so. Excitement rose again some ten years later when she claimed she was about to give birth to the new Messiah but, instead, in 1814 she died and the peak of messianism passed. The tradition was far from dead, though, and two who claimed to be her successors, John Wroe and James 'Jezreel', were later involved in the communities at Wrenthorpe and Gillingham. She was also not the last to adopt the role of a female Saviour, one of a number who did so being Mary Ann Girling, the founder of a messianic community in the New Forest [29].

A renewed wave of messianism occurred in the 1830s, one of the more colourful characters being 'Sir William Courtenay, King of Jerusalem'. Posing as the Messiah, his promise of free land to his followers encouraged a sizeable and loyal support among farm labourers in the Canterbury area in Kent. He also condemned the Poor Law Amendment Act as a breach of Divine Law. Courtenay's promises came to nothing (he was shot in a clash with troops in 1838) but behind the rhetoric of allegory he was close to the undercurrent of grievance and yearning upon which messianists have always thrived [30].

Of greater significance, in overtly attempting to forge this link between spiritual need and materialist principles, was the Christian Socialist, James Elishama 'Shepherd' Smith. For Smith the millennium was due to start in 1840, and the way forward lay in blending Owenite and St Simonian principles with religious salvation – claiming that the establishment of the new social system was nothing but the Christian millennium.

Smith had met John Wroe and joined the Southcottians in 1830, but the 'destructive criticisms of church and society which he had learned . . . were transformed into a more comprehensive and theoretical critique of industrial capitalism, and his millennium became, in its practical aspects, socialist communitarianism' [31]. He looked towards a society equal in rank and privileges as well as in property, benefitting from the inevitable progress of technology, and exploring new frontiers of artistic and literary pleasures. To achieve this the idea of small communities was central to his plans – 'If priests and legislators knew their own interests they would establish the social system of communities at once' [32]. The Owenites, themselves veering closer to millennialism at this time, found much with which they could agree.

After the 1830s, messianism surfaced again from time to time but never attracted the volume of support that had been enjoyed by Joanna Southcott. Sectarianism in Victorian England generally persisted in less dramatic forms. Reference has already been made to the Quakers and the Salvation Army as national organisations, but sometimes new sects took the form of small and localised groups, pursuing their distinctive beliefs in a world of makeshift chapels and travelling preachers. One such group was that which was known as the 'Peculiar People', a sect whose activities were almost wholly confined to the farming districts and small towns of South Essex [33]. Founded in 1834 by John Banyard at Rochford, the name attributed to the sect has a biblical source for what they regarded as their privileged separation as true believers from the rest of the world [34]. Without establishing their own settlement, they distinguished themselves from the surrounding population through their particular beliefs and customs (which included a faith in spiritual healing). It was from a kindred group in London that John Sirgood left to establish his own sect in Sussex, the 'Cokelers', which, in contrast with the 'Peculiar People', did establish its own communities. The communities of the Cokelers, along with the various messianist communities, will be considered in the next section.

4.4 Community profiles

Of the five sectarian communities to be considered, four are of a messianist character. These are the Agapemone near Spaxton in Somerset (1846), the Christian Israelite Institution at Wrenthorpe in Yorkshire (1857), the New Forest Shakers in the vicinity of Hordle in Hampshire (1872), and the New and Latter House of Israel at Gillingham in Kent (1875). The fifth community – that of the Cokelers, centred on Loxwood in Sussex (1850) – is of a different order. In contrast with the fervour of the messianists (for whom cataclysmic change was always imminent), the Cokelers set about the quiet re-organisation of their own lives on earth in preparation for the privileged place they believed was awaiting them in heaven.

The Agapemone,
Four Forks, Spaxton, Somerset
The first of the sectarian communities is the 'Community of the Son of Man' or as it was more generally known, 'The Agapemone' (meaning 'abode of love') [35]. Set in the Somerset countryside, a few miles from Bridgwater, it consisted of some sixty believers who had gathered to save themselves. They were called together in 1846 by Henry Prince, who claimed that the Day of Judgement had already arrived, and that only those who joined his community would enjoy salvation. Prince was regarded by his followers as a prophet, and there were some who even addressed their letters to 'God, Somerset, England'.

As an example of messianism the community was unusual. For one thing, it was certainly not a community of the poor. Prince, himself, had been a Church of England minister, as had others in the community who had trained together for the Church and who, as students, had formed a select group known as the 'Lampeter Brethren'. It is true that, as minister of the parish church of Charlinch, Prince (and, later, one of his Lampeter friends, George Thomas) had aroused great excitement among the local population with his prophetic pronouncements, and was soon dismissed. Thomas managed to get an independent chapel built at nearby Spaxton, but local supporters were not, in the main, the people who joined the Agapemone. Instead, Prince looked first to wealthy spinsters and, through a series of arranged marriages ('commanded by God'), involving himself and three of his friends, sufficient capital was amassed for the experiment.

It was a community, not of tense expectation or doom, but one of

✻ THE AGAPEMONE

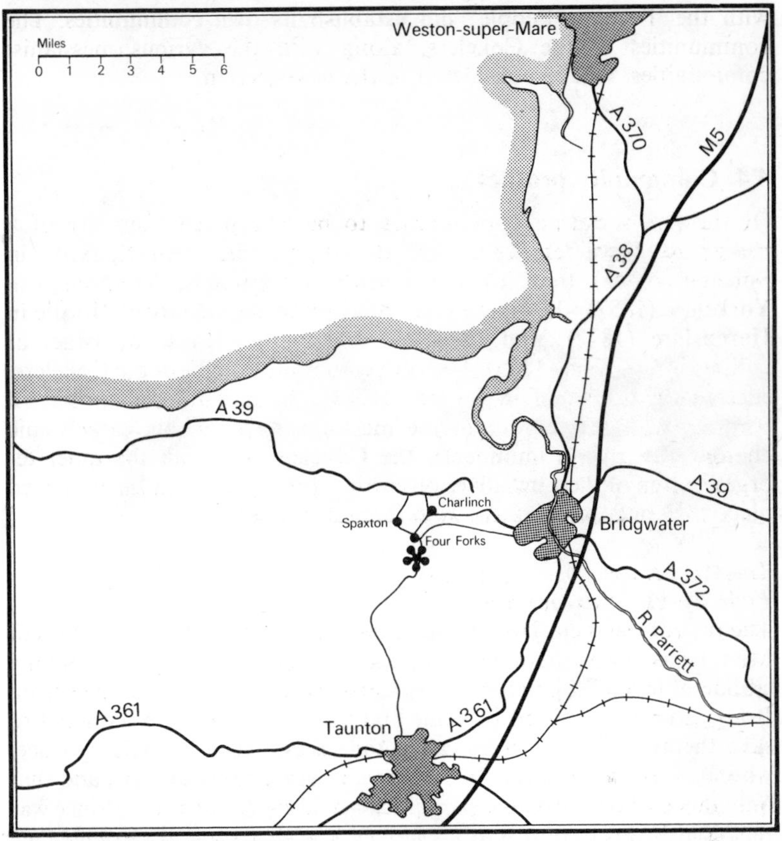

Fig. 4.1 Location of the Agapemone.

extravagant and leisurely enjoyment. Those who joined were assured they could sin no more and, with this to safeguard them, the protected ones soon earned a reputation for free-living, which even extended to hockey on Sundays. Capital from its rich sponsors was used to build an impressive complex of community buildings – a large house for Henry Prince and more modest dwellings for the lesser brethren, a banqueting hall (the gable surmounted by a lion rampant, flag and staff, and a scroll bearing the words 'Hail, Holy Love'), together with an aviary, stables and coach-houses for a distinguished set of carriages and horses, conservatories and a lawn known as the pleasure-ground. The community was secure in its knowledge of salvation, and what they produced was an unusual blend of sectarianism and mid-Victorian indulgence. A closer view of this apparent dichotomy is provided in a contemporary account of the community that appeared in the *Illustrated London News* in 1851:

Fig. 4.2 Impression of the Agapemone, included in a report in the *Illustrated London News*, 29 Mar. 1851.

The number of persons who composed the Family, in the summer of 1849, was about sixty, some married and others unmarried – the two classes being about equal in numbers. There were children in the establishment; but, in the phraseology of the brethren, this term seems to mean the unmarried, for the youngest of them was described as being about twenty-four years of age, and the eldest of them about forty! They do not call themselves a sect, but a private family. The brethren comprise several clergymen – four, at least – who have belonged to the Church of England, who have either left it or been deprived of their preferment on account of their peculiar opinions; a medical man, who attends the Family professionally; an attorney, who manages the legal business for the Family; a civil engineer, a farmer, etc. All the members of the Family appear to be persons of substance, though some of them have acquired their property by marriage. They live at their ease in much enjoyment and rather mock at solemn professional men for their seriousness and their care. They profess merriment. They ride out for pleasure, they hunt, they play at various games, and delight in hockey, especially on Sunday. They have money in the bank, the interest of which must, of course, be paid by the labour of some portion of that serious, care-taking community, which does not enter the Abode of Love, nor ride in carriage, nor play at hockey on Sunday. They have purchased a farm, but it does not appear that they cultivate the land themselves. Their property is managed in common by their chiefs, they take their meals in common, and have their pursuits in common. Their creed is typified by their practices. They have converted the chapel into a banqueting-house, and substitute feasting and enjoyment for privation and prayer. 'If God be not life, happiness, and love,' said one of the Family, 'then we do not know what God is'. Every family, the same jolly fellow declared, should be an Agapemone.

Latterly, it is said a stricter kind of discipline has been introduced into the Family, and its chief thinks it right to enforce some kind of sumptuary regulation on the Children. The ladies have been obliged, it is said, to lay aside caps, and cut off their hair, which is to be kept close shorn. The men, too, are treated like the Russians, and contrary to most other sects, which encourage the growth of hair, they are ordered to shave close, annihilating whiskers and all, and keeping their heads like those of charity-boys. It is said, too, that one of the children of the Family having taken lessons in love beyond the walls, was seized by force and carried back to the Agapemone. Not liking his treatment he made his escape, and has since carried pistols, according to report, to protect himself from the love of his friends. These stories may be only scandal, for it is always the fate of such societies to have much said of them that is not true.

Though Mr Prince and some of his chief disciples have gone about the country making converts; have visited Brighton, Suffolk, and other places to spread abroad the doctrines of love; and though the brethren have especially given their lessons to ladies of a certain age, who possess property, and have no objections to some wives, transferring their property to some of the brethren, yet

Figs. 4.3, 4.4 and **4.5** Current views of the Agapemone.

Fig. 4.3 The former residence of Henry Prince, now divided into flats.

Fig. 4.4 One of the summer-houses, carefully preserved by the owners of a new bungalow on the site.

Fig. 4.5 The former Banqueting Hall, now used as a puppet workshop.

the sect appears to have no very well defined dogmas. They act as God tells them to act, and do everything for his glory. They renounce prayer; they sing the praise of the Lord sometimes in the open air, and sometimes in unintelligible gibberish. They act as their feelings prompt them. They say the day of grace is past, and the day of judgement is come [36].

Sustained by fresh inputs of capital from new followers, the Agapemone endured over a very long period. When Prince died in 1899, at the age of eighty-eight, his place as spiritual leader of the community was assumed by the Rev. J. H. Smyth-Piggott. Three years later, Symth-Piggott stood before a crowded congregation and publicly proclaimed himself as the Messiah – he later rejected the condemnation of the Church of England on the grounds that he was no less than God. After a brief period in London he took up residence in the Agapemone, where he gained some notoriety for the continuing practice of encouraging 'spiritual wives' to join the community. He died in 1927, but the estate at Spaxton remained in the hands of Agapemonites until 1962, when the various buildings were finally sold. Prince's house has since been converted into flats, with new housing in the grounds, and the chapel (once described as a mighty temple which to the world is not known) has assumed a new use as a puppet workshop. But the layout and elevations remain not radically different to the way they were portrayed in *The Illustrated London News* in 1851 – probably the most complete physical survival of any of the communities.

The Cokelers,
Loxwood, Sussex

Compared with the Agapemone there was nothing so extravagant about John Sirgood's Cokelers, a sect that believed in salvation through separation from the corrupt ways of the rest of the world [37]. Their ascetic life included a rejection of alcohol and tobacco, of secular books and music, and of flowers in the home; marriage was tolerated but discouraged as an earthly obstacle to the relationship between the individual and God. They attended three religious services every Sunday and two during the week, the men wearing dark suits, the women in a black costume of straw and velvet bonnets, shawls, coats and long skirts.

On divine authority, Sirgood left London for Loxwood in Sussex in 1850, and started to preach from his own cottage. His beliefs were similar to those of the Peculiar People (with which he had previously been associated), but faith-healing was never central to the new sect. Formally known as 'The Society of Dependents', the group acquiesced to the locally-derived name of 'Cokelers' [38]. They developed an Antinomian doctrine where true members of the sect could do no wrong. Having chosen Christ instead of the pleasures of the world, the brethren were considered each to possess a part of his divine body, and to be as without sin as Christ himself. They were his favoured people – peculiar to Christ and a law unto themselves, assured of a privileged place in heaven:

Though in this world we take our place,
As other mortals do,
We're all imbued by Him with grace
And he will see us through.
He will know his sparkling jewels
Those in whom His image shines,

�֍ THE COKELERS

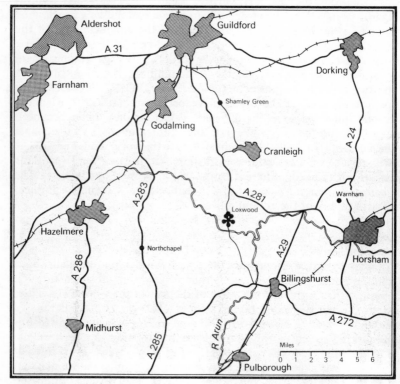

Fig. 4.6 Location of the Cokelers.

He will spare us and preserve us,
He will say, Yes these are mine (from a Cokeler hymn).

The sect grew rapidly from its small beginnings at Loxwood in 1850 to a membership of about 2,000 at the time of Sirgood's death in 1885. Chapels were built in a number of neighbouring villages, and in some the proportion of the population who were Cokelers rose to nearly a half. Characteristically, the sect drew most of its members from poorly-paid occupations – small farmers, labourers and women in domestic service; and, no less characteristically, local clergy, landlords and employers combined to quell what they saw as an unwarranted act of insurgency. Cokelers were evicted from their homes, and servant girls and labourers lost their jobs. At one stage the parish authorities served notice on Sirgood, warning him that unless he desisted from holding 'unlawful' meetings he would be legally prosecuted – 'it is a very general opinion that your illegal proceedings have been allowed to go far enough, and that it is quite time they should be controlled' [39].

This wave of opposition, in about 1860, came to nothing. Changes in

Figs. 4.7 and **4.8** Current views of Loxwood.

Fig. 4.7 The 'Dependents chapel' in Spy Lane, which is still used for services.

the law (through the repeal of the Conventicle Act) removed any legal threat to their existence, and the prejudice of local employers and traders only spurred them to greater independence. It was partly to overcome the restrictions imposed on servants who wanted to attend weekly services that led to the Cokelers establishing their own shops (with living quarters above and nearby) as an alternative source of employment and accommodation. The shops were run on strictly cooperative lines, financed and owned wholly by members of the sect.

Fig. 4.8 The former Cokeler stores, with associated living accommodation for its members, now used for a variety of purposes.

They were central to the economic system of the sect – a means of communalising wealth, as well as meeting more practical needs such as providing their members with a wide range of goods and services at a fair price, a market for their farm produce, and a source of help in times of hardship. Their activities were extended over the years and, in addition to the supply of goods, they included bakeries and workshops and, at the turn of the century, even bought and maintained cars in each locality to transport their members to chapel. Shops were established at Loxwood, Northchapel, Warnham and Shamley Green (and further afield at Norwood in South London). As an example of their scale, the one at Northchapel consisted of three departments and employed thirteen saleswomen and assistants, besides delivery carts and their drivers, and a cycle workshop – and this was a pattern that was repeated in each of the other enterprises.

In spite of the strength of their economic base, the membership declined after the death of Sirgood – to about a thousand at the turn of the century, and only a few score today. It is inevitable, though, that their presence should have left an interesting legacy to the Sussex landscape. A number of the chapels remain, including that in Spy Lane at Loxwood, where all the members of the sect used to congregate on Bank Holidays. The chapel is well-maintained, and adjoins the burial ground where Sirgood and his fellow Cokelers lie in unmarked graves. All the shops have changed hands, and the simplicity of the associated cottages and apartments have generally been obscured by modern conversions. But it is not many years since the Cokelers were numbered in hundreds rather than in tens, and there are still many in the district with memories of the group that, for all their integration into the economic life of the area, never lost the measure of detachment that was essential to their beliefs.

Christian Israelite Institution,
Melbourne House, Wrenthorpe, Yorkshire

Unlike the Cokelers, John Wroe's Christian Israelite Institution at Wrenthorpe in Yorkshire was firmly based in a messianist tradition [40]. Wroe – 'a man of peculiar appearance who inspired uneducated and wonder-loving people with a strange fascination' [41] – claimed his lineage from the prophet Richard Brothers and the prophetess Joanna Southcott, declaring himself as the Fifth Messenger. For more than forty years, following Southcott's death in 1814, Wroe fanned the flames of messianism in the West Riding, building on the support that Southcott had left behind. He also travelled extensively overseas, and attracted a sizeable following to which he later looked for funds.

The beliefs of the Christian Israelites were compounded from both the law of Moses and the gospel of Christ. They included the specific claim that full and complete salvation (of 'body, soul and spirit') would be enjoyed by a chosen few of the world's population, restricted to 144,000. These, the descendants of Abraham, would be immortal, and would be joint rulers with God of the eternal kingdom shortly to be established. Their separation from the rest of society was emphasised by peculiarities of dress and diet; especially noticeable was the fact that they never

�֍ CHRISTIAN ISRAELITE INSTITUTION

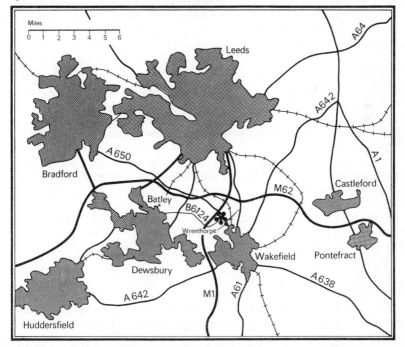

Fig. 4.9 Location of the Christian Israelite Institution.

shaved or cut their hair, a characteristic which earnt them the name of 'beardies'.

Wroe's credibility as a prophet had been tested on a variety of occasions. In 1824, before a reported crowd of 30,000 he was publicly baptised at Idle Thorpe in Yorkshire, and to demonstrate his Divine authority he announced that he would divide the waters of the Aire and walk across dry-shod. The continuing flow of the river failed to extinguish his fervour (or, in the long term, his credibility) and when, some thirty years later, he declared that the time had come for the elect to gather together there was no shortage of financial support from all over the world. He was also able to attract £2,000 from funds that had been collected with the original intention of publishing the *Eternal Gospel*, symbolically, forty years after Joanna Southcott's death. In a dream in 1853 he claimed that the Lord had told him to build a mansion where the Messiah could dwell, along with some of his following.

The Lord also gave him specifications as to how the mansion should be built but, in the event, his divine construction was based more on what Wroe had remembered of Melbourne Town Hall [42]. The original site was 100 acres in extent, and the construction of 'Prophet Wroe's Temple' (or 'Melbourne House') was seen by Wroe as a spiritual struggle of good over evil. 'It is a fiery trial over this House that is building, and hitherto those in Satan's spirit have overcome and swelled, yet it will be built because he who builds it, his name is Israel' [43].

At a cost of some £9,000 the mansion was completed two years later. Its opening was attended by:

... about 250 of the body assembled in Wakefield, from the principal towns in this country, America, Germany and Australia, for the purpose of attending the annual conference, and on Sunday morning the ceremony of formally opening the temple was commenced by the entire number, attired in white robes, marching in procession around the grounds in which the edifice is built. They then entered the temple, followed by the prophet; but as no persons were permitted to be present except members of the sect, we are unable to describe the ceremonial observed [44].

As a lavish and well-designed project it attracted unqualified praise from visitors.

Prophet Wroe's Mansion. . . . It stands on a fine commanding eminence which slopes gently to the south from which a view of the whole country for many miles round can be obtained. The grounds, consisting of several acres, are well ordered, and abundantly stocked with beautiful trees, and at each of the four corners there is a porter's lodge, and a carriage drive sweeping round to the south front of the hall. The forcing-houses are extensive and full of vines and various fruits from many lands. The stables furnish abundant accommodation for a numerous stud. The house itself is a fine mansion-like structure with south, east and west fronts; and the principal rooms are said to be panelled with cedar [45].

In other respects the community was less than successful. John Wroe

Fig. 4.10 Current view of Melbourne House. The stone notice ('Stick no bills on these premises') to the left of the gatepost, dates from Daniel Milton's claim to occupancy of Melbourne House after Wroe's death. His campaign included pasting bills on the wall of the property.

was by then 75 years old, and was to discredit his claim to immortality by dying six years later. The property was built for all members of the House of Israel, but on Wroe's death was transferred to his grandson, and the community disbanded. The estate remained in the hands of the Wroe family until the 1930s and it is reported that for some years after his death, a room was set aside with his slippers and a suit of clothes ready for his return.

Today the house is used as an old people's home, the Melbourne House Pentecostal Eventide Home. On the entrance wall is a stone notice – 'Stick no bills on these premises'. It is a reminder of the dispute which continued over a number of years before and after John Wroe's death. Leadership of the sect was assumed by an American, Daniel Milton, who contested that the Christian Israelites had the right to occupation of Melbourne House. His campaign for rightful occupation included pasting bills on the walls of the property, which provoked the notice in question. Milton's refusal to take heed of the notice led subsequently to legal proceedings, and a fine of 6*d.* damages with 14*s.*6*d.* costs.

The New Forest Shakers,
Hordle, Hampshire

Perhaps even more than the other examples of its type, the community known as the New Forest Shakers exhibits the full intensity of messianism – the suddenness with which it can flare up around a local leader, the extreme cohesion among its immediate following, and the persecution compounded of fear and uncertainty that is never far beneath the surface of established society [46]. The location for these events, a few square miles within the New Forest, gives little indication of the fervour that the community excited at the time; and the same point is made by a writer fifty years ago who was able to speak to surviving members of the community:

It is difficult for present day residents in Hordle to realise that, in the words of an old inhabitant, 'they were exciting times in those days some fifty years ago, to be sure they were', but I am assured by several of the old folk still living in the district, that on Sunday afternoons Vaggs Lane and Silver Street, right along past the Three Bells almost as far as the corner of Woodcock Road, were packed with vehicles of all sorts from donkey carts to large brakes drawn by 3 or 4 horses, which had brought day trippers and sight-seers from places as far away as 20 miles to see and hear 'the Shakers', as the community at Forest Lodge had been dubbed by those who saw nothing but cause for ridicule in the peculiar manner in which Mrs Girling's followers showed their joy when 'moved by the Holy Spirit' in their worship of God [47].

The leader or 'Mother' of the community, the female reincarnation of Christ, was Mary Ann Girling. It was said that one sign of her divinity was the stigmata which appeared on her hands, feet and side. She was afterwards able to describe in minute detail the extraordinary emotion which overwhelmed her at the moment when she experienced the Divine

�֍ THE NEW FOREST SHAKERS

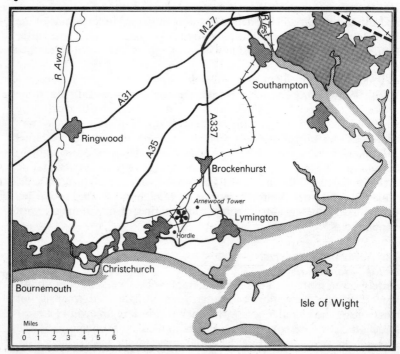

Fig. 4.11 Location of the New Forest Shakers.

call. From that time she travelled through the country districts of East Anglia, preaching the brotherhood of mankind and the imminence of the second coming of the Messiah. At first she had access to the Methodist chapels, but soon this was barred to her and she took to preaching in the streets and market squares. The echoes of radical dissent in her teachings attracted a following among the farm labourers for whom Methodism was too moderate. With some of her followers she came to London in 1870 to continue her work, and in time the group formed themselves into a community at 107, Bridge Road, Battersea. There they lived together and shared all things in common, modelling their lives on the original disciples of Christ.

In the face of local antagonism the group turned to a wealthy sponsor, Miss Julia Wood, who secured alternative property for them in the countryside – at New Forest Lodge, Vaggs Lane, Hordle in Hampshire.

Fig. 4.12 The former 'New Forest Lodge' in Vaggs Lane, Hordle, where Mary Ann Girling and her followers first settled.

The building into which Mary Ann Girling and her twelve disciples (three families from Suffolk, three girls and three elderly men) moved in January 1872 is still intact, though now extended and used as a nursing home.

The community stayed at New Forest Lodge for three years during which time their numbers grew to some 160 of whom between forty and fifty were children, about forty men, and about seventy women of all ages, 'principally drawn from the agricultural classes'. They called themselves the 'Children of God', and it was outsiders who gave them the name of 'Shakers' on account of their habit (comparable to their American namesakes) of dancing when moved by the Spirit of God.

Their life was modelled on the most rigorous principles of

community. The group practiced celibacy as necessary to the true worship of God, the children in the community being brought in by newcomers. Again like the American Shakers, the men and women sat at separate tables at meal times and occupied separate apartments, meeting only in connection with the routine of their daily duties and at the religious services. Clothing was made in the community, and the style was strictly regulated. The women wore what is described as a bloomer costume for their work on the land, and white dresses on Sundays. The girls wore their hair in curly ringlets down their back, which apparently gave them an unusual appearance when dancing, and encouraged rumours that Mrs Girling mesmerised them to keep them under her control.

The men were responsible for the farmwork, made boots and shoes, and maintained the property and farm-buildings. There were no wages paid within the community, and work done for neighbouring farmers at harvest-time was seen as a labour of love (though small contributions to the general fund of the community were always welcome). All who came to join the community gave up their material possessions for the good of the whole family. In the words of Mary Ann Girling: 'We bought, but we did not sell – Christ did not sell. We have no marriages or giving in marriage. We never close our doors at the service, or wish to keep people out. We have no secrets and defy the world to say we have not lived in purity' [48].

In its three years at Hordle Grange there were apparently few who left the community; the rules were strict but commitment was high. Inevitably, though, local residents saw fit to remove the community. Rumours of immorality abounded, and an unsuccessful attempt was made to have Mrs Girling certified as being insane. In the end, though, it was on the issue of property that the community foundered. Increasing difficulty in paying interest on their mortgage, worsened by the unlawful seizure of some of their stock by the authorities, led eventually to their eviction. The circumstances surrounding their eviction were cruelly reminiscent of the severe treatment accorded to sectarians 200 years previously. According to a contemporary report in the *Hampshire Independent*:

The mortgagee gave notice to foreclose, and the Sheriff's Officer ejected them. The household goods were placed upon the high road with 2 or 3 pianos and harmoniums, 77 beds and bedding, farm produce, &c., supposed to be worth about £1,000. Then the inmates numbering upwards of 140, including 40 children, were ejected, Mrs Girling the 'Mother' being the first to be moved. . . . The others grouped themselves round her and commenced singing, appearing to regard their hard lot as only a portion of the persecution which those who are the Lord's must expect to undergo in this world. Hundreds of visitors were on the spot to witness the ejectment. There was a fierce east wind blowing with heavy rain and sleet and snow. The keen icy blast penetrated the thin dresses of the women and little ones. The furniture was soaked and spoiled. Hay, straw and beans were strewn about the road and the scene was one of terrible privation and desolation. After some hours of misery, the children were removed to a

Fig. 4.13 Arnewood Tower, built by Mr A. T. T. Peterson, who had been convinced that Mary Ann Girling possessed mesmeric powers, and who subsequently built the tower under instruction from the soul of Sir Christopher Wren.

neighbouring cottage. A woman who was ill at the time, was removed by her husband to a place of shelter. The Rev. E. Clissold offered the others the shelter of a barn but they declined it. They said they would not leave their 'Dear Mother' and through all the terrible night they remained in the rain and snow, the sound of their hymns and prayers mingled with that of the storm, and the morning found them half-perished with the bitter cold, but defiant of all consequences and sturdily refusing to leave the spot, saying they were in the Lord's hands and

He would do with them as seemed to Him best. Bread and cheese and milk were kindly bestowed upon them, otherwise they had scarcely anything to eat. In the evening a heavy snowstorm came on and there was every prospect of another terrible night, but about 9 o'clock they were persuaded by Sergeant Simpkin (partly with the threat of removal to the Workhouse) to accept the shelter of a barn about half a mile distant [49].

In spite of their hardships, the nucleus of the community remained in the district, leasing barns and subsequently a small farm at Tiptoe, until the death of Mary Ann Girling in 1886. Her body, with eleven of her followers, is buried in a line of graves in Hordle Parish Churchyard. Instead of headstones, a macrocarpus tree was planted above each grave. In the belief that the second coming of the Messiah was imminent, Mrs Girling had not arranged for anyone to carry on her work.

But a more dramatic reminder of the community's involvement in the district is not in the line of twelve graves, but in Arnewood Tower, the extraordinary 218 feet high concrete tower built by a local resident, Mr A. T. T. Peterson. Peterson had travelled extensively and spent most of his career as a barrister in India. His retirement to Hampshire coincided with the arrival of Mary Ann Girling, whom Peterson was convinced possessed mesmeric powers. An interest in mesmerism led, in turn, to spiritualism and it was in communication with the soul of Sir Christopher Wren that Peterson received his instructions to build the tower. He had already experimented with concrete in some of his farm and garden buildings, and the building of the tower represented a strange mixture of spiritual energy, a fascination for concrete, and a desire to provide help for the unemployed. It remains as a distinctive, and somewhat macabre, feature of the local landscape – its dominance in sharp contrast to the more tenuous hold of Girling and her followers in the same countryside.

The New and Latter House of Israel, Chatham Hill, Gillingham, Kent

During the last quarter of the nineteenth century James Jersham Jezreel (originally known as James White) gathered around him in Gillingham a following of the elect people of Israel, 'who are never to see death, and when the ingathering is complete they are to live for a thousand years with Christ upon Earth, which is to be converted into Heaven'. It was a community in the tradition of John Wroe's at Wrenthorpe [50].

Jezreel had, in fact, joined the Kent following of the Christian Israelites in 1875, and was soon to send a 'divine message' to the inheritors of the Wroe estate, declaring himself as the Sixth Messenger. His letter was promptly burnt and White (as he was then known), unsure of his own destiny, took up a military post in India. It was while he was abroad that God revealed his 'last message to Mankind', which White wrote up as *The Flying Roll*. It transpired to be a mixture of John Wroe's writings combined with his own beliefs, and served as the scripture of the sect that formed around him on his return to Kent in 1880.

❈ THE NEW AND LATTER HOUSE OF ISRAEL

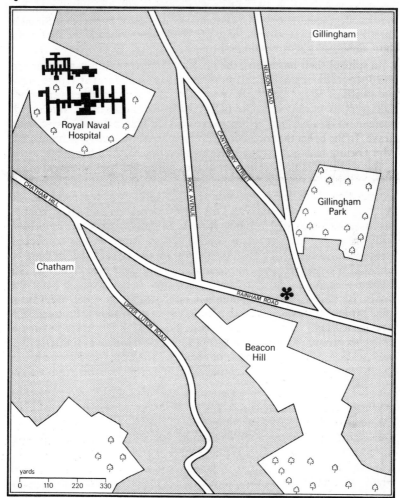

Fig. 4.14 Location of the New and Latter House of Israel.

While waiting for the 'ingathering' of the chosen 144,000 [51] the group prayed together, and made their presence known locally. On Sundays both secret and open services were held, at the latter of which young children recited portions of the *Flying Roll*, and sang to the accompaniment of harps. Like the Christian Israelites in Yorkshire the men's hair was long and looped up at the back, but their dress was not distinctive. They opened shops and involved themselves in local industries, but the focus of their efforts was consistently that of building a great temple to serve as the sectarian centre for their faith. Jezreel exhorted the elect to come from all countries of the world to undertake this task, converting all their property and belongings into gold for the purpose. In July 1884 he wrote a letter to some of the brethren in the United States, saying that the Immortal Spirit had revealed to him that it was the Lord's will that the brethren should settle up their affairs, and then come with their wives and children to Gillingham. 'The time has now come for each one to be put to the test, to see whether they love gold, silver, or land, or house, more than the bones of my body, my bride, my church, saith the Lord. . . . All help me by every means in their power to get up the building' [52]. Many apparently answered the call.

The choice of a site for the building on Chatham Hill came to Jezreel through a divine message (though practical difficulties forced him to take another site nearby), and the specifications he adopted from Revelation (21:16), where 'the city lieth foursquare, and . . . the length and the breadth and the height of it are equal'.

The following description of the plans for the building is based on information given by the architects in a local newspaper report at the time:

The structure was to be built of steel and concrete with yellow brick walls, and eight castellated towers of the same material. On each side of the outer walls emblems and symbols of the 'New and Latter House of Israel' were to be portrayed in stone, standing out in bold relief. Chief of these were the Trumpet and the Flying Roll, the Crossed Swords of the Spirit, and the Prince of Wales Feathers, signifying the Trinity. A large basement was to be constructed for storage purposes, machinery for working lifts, heating apparatus etc. Above the basement the entire ground floor was to be used for twelve large printing presses, designed to turn out thousands of copies of the Flying Roll and other literature of the sect.

Above the ground floor was to be the Assembly Room, which was undoubtedly Jezreel's finest and most original conception. It was to be circular in shape like an amphitheatre, was to reach almost to the top of the building, and was to accommodate 5,000 people. In the roof of this great room or hall there was to be a glass dome, 94 feet in diameter, and invisible from outside the building. The dome, supported by twelve massive steel ribs, was to rise 100 feet above the floor, and in the dome a revolving electric lantern 45 feet in diameter was to be the source of light, since the Assembly Room was not to have any windows. Under the dome three circular galleries or balconies were to supplement the seating accommodation on the main floor. The curved space between the dome and the outer walls was to be used, on three floors, to provide offices, reading rooms, and other requirements of a headquarters building.

The tower was to embody a number of remarkable features. Chief of these, perhaps, was the circular platform in the centre of the floor of the Assembly Room. It was to be 24 feet in diameter, and capable of being raised by hydraulic pressure to a height of 30 feet. It was to accommodate the choir and the preachers, and was to be made to rotate slowly so that each part of the congregation in the vast circular hall could be faced in turn.

All doors in the building were to be made to open outwards, to ensure swift and orderly evacuation of the premises in case of fire. Jezreel tried to guard against such a calamity, however, by insisting that the tower should be made as fireproof as possible by extensive use of non-combustible materials such as steel, concrete, and brick.

From the outside, the first floor of the building (the floor of the Assembly Room) was to be approached by eight flights of steps, each pair leading to a main door in the centre of each front. The offices and other apartments in the upper floors of the building, between the dome and the outer walls, were to be reached by means of staircases in three of the four castellated corner towers, and by a lift in the other. Gas and electric light were both to be used for lighting, and – a remarkable innovation for the time – Jezreel made plans for the towers at the corners to be illuminated with electric lights on special occasions.

The roof of the building surmounting the dome was to be flat, and asphalted, and was to be used as a promenade, from which because of the commanding position on rising ground at the top of Chatham Hill magnificent views extending for miles on every side would be enjoyed.

Jezreel planned to lay out the land immediately surrounding the building as gardens, and to construct stately avenues from the tower to Nelson Road and the junction of Canterbury Street with Watling Street, making it thus something of a focal point. Lastly, around the perimeter of the grounds he aimed at building a number of Jezreel shops, new accommodation for 'Israel's International College', and a small meeting hall [53].

But the building, though partially completed, never served the purpose for which it was intended. The faith of the sect was seriously challenged by the death of Jezreel himself in 1884, and although his wife

Fig. 4.15 'Jezreel's Tower' as it looked when work on it was stopped.

assumed the leadership of the sect as Queen Esther, the Mother of Israel, and laid the foundation stone for the building in September 1885, her immortality was also disproved in 1888. With funds still arriving from America, construction continued for a few more years, until the sect finally dispersed in 1905.

Jezreel's Tower, as it came to be known, remained as a local landmark until 1961. Built of iron and stone, the sect had claimed that it would withstand all powers of earth and hell. Though the claim was discounted by events, demolition took thirteen months and claimed the life of a worker. The site was then set aside for industry, and is now partly occupied by a new factory. Though not immortal, the name of the Prophet of the Flying Roll is enshrined in 'Jezreel's Tower Works' and nearby 'Jezreel's Road'. Of more lasting significance, his major written work, *The Flying Roll* was reprinted nearly a century after its original publication in 1879, and the doctrine of the 'New and Latter House of Israel' still attracts its own following.

Chapter 5

The communities of anarchism

In the last decade of the nineteenth century there was an upsurge in community activity, the majority of the communities identifying with the various anarchist ideas that were current at that time. While there are several ideologies and strategies within anarchism, the essence of anarchism – of society without compulsion – is a natural ally to the idea of community.

In the first section of this chapter the basis for this affinity between anarchism and community will be explained, and attention will be drawn to the background of ideas and experiments in Europe and America to which the English communitarians later referred. The second and third sections will show how much of this experience was drawn into 'anarchist communism' and 'religious anarchism', which provided an ideological and organisational framework for the English communities in the 1890s. The details of these communities will be examined in the final section.

5.1 Anarchism and community

Anarchism embodies the idea of a new form of social organisation, where there is no authority and, in particular, no government [1]. Far from upholding order the State is seen as the source of dissent and the enemy of natural cooperation. The State, in promoting specific property interests and resultant economic inequalities, is responsible both for wars between States and for internal crime and punishment. While the very nature of the State is abhorrent, the capitalist system, in maximising competition and inequality, is the specific manifestation of authority that is the object of revolutionary struggle. The conjuncture of anarchist activity in general and of community formation in particular in the period 1890 to 1900 is historically significant in this respect.

The period was one of intensifying revolutionary activity, induced by economic recessions and the increasing consciousness of labour to their real situation. Within this growing ferment, the split between Marxism, anarchism and parliamentary socialism as alternative political strategies became more sharply defined. And for the anarchists in particular, the increasing scale of capitalist State activity in the form of bureaucratic government, industrial monopolies, and the advent of conurbations provided both a material basis and incentive for the development of a theory that was opposed to the State.

It was a period when revolution was widely regarded to be possible and, as a revolutionary theory, anarchism flourished. Although there are differences amongst anarchists as to the use of violence to achieve revolution, there is agreement both in the need for social preparation and in the revolutionary nature of the process itself:

If your object is to secure liberty, you must learn to do without authority and compulsion. If you intend to live in peace and harmony with your fellow-men, you and they should cultivate brotherhood and respect for each other. If you want to work together with them for your mutual benefit, you must practice co-operation. The social revolution means much more than the re-organisation of conditions only: it means the establishment of new human values and social relationships, a changed attitude of man to man, as of one free and independent to his equal; it means a different spirit in individual and collective life, and that spirit cannot be born overnight [2].

For the majority of anarchist communitarians revolution was construed as a non-violent process, where the formation of community could be seen both as a form of social preparation for a new order that would spread through the rest of society, and as a revolutionary action in itself.

Either way, by violence or by peaceful evolution, the dissolution of the State would usher in a new era of cooperation. It is a belief that rests on a naturalistic philosophy where human beings are inherently social (though not necessarily inherently good) and will associate together for their mutual benefit. It is cooperation rather than competition that is seen to be natural, the latter having been foisted upon society by the artificial intervention of the State.

Of particular importance to the communities is the identification of anarchism with a questioning of established norms of material progress and the establishment of a decentralised and possibly simpler form of society. The anarchist notion of progress has been described as a retreat along lines of simplification, a desire to get back to the roots of existence, and to base what little organisation is necessary on the point of production [3]. By the end of the nineteenth century it was clear that capitalism had already created a type of society where the scale of operations would increase with the size of the world market, and where production was dictated by the profit motive at the expense of unequal distribution and an alienated labour force. A simpler, decentralised society was advanced on economic grounds, in that labour would be directly involved in essential production and distribution, and that the wasteful services and distorted pattern of consumption under capitalism would be eliminated; on social grounds, in that it would enable free individuals to participate without the repressive mediation of a higher authority; and morally, in that the replacement of competition and authority by cooperation would have the purifying effect of a return to one's natural state.

In seeking their ideal of a simpler society many anarchists have looked to the ideas of spiritual unity and community in the early Christian church, to an adapted model of the mediaeval commune, and to a variety of idealised portrayals of peasant society. As an illustration of this tendency the following argument for the 'free commune' was put forward in a periodical which was circulated amongst communitarians in England at the end of the last century:

Most anarchists usually base their ideas of future social organisation on the absolute independence of individuals, and guilds of producing groups. But it seems to me that these are sectional associations, apt to look at things from a sectional point of view, and not that of the whole community. Therefore I think that there should be, in addition to these special groups which embody the idea of individuality, another association, consisting of the same people, which embodies that of the community; and that I consider would be the 'commune'. Why the commune it may be asked, why not the State? Because the latter concentrates collective power in the hands of a central body whilst we, who believe in Freedom, would diffuse it amongst all. The special business of the commune or collective society, as distinct from the guilds or the more private groups, would be to deal with those things, that more specially and immediately concern the life of all, such as the distribution and exchange of wealth, and the public works and utilities (as halls, parks, roads, etc.) so as to prevent undue waste of wealth and labour, and ensure to all a full share of the results of social effort.

As for production, that is another matter. It would probably be best to leave that under the control of the workers themselves, as men work best when working as they will. The communes would doubtless be managed by mass meetings of all the people – the folk mote – with such delegates and agents as necessary ... If I am asked what would prevent the commune or unit of collective society from encroaching too much upon individual liberty, I should say: first of all, the free spirit of men who were able to express themselves as they would; the claim of each to secede or withdraw without losing the means of living by so doing; and probably the claim which reasonable people would recognise of free arbitration in all cases of dispute.

If I am asked would communes recognise majority voting, I should say that if they occasionally adopted it as a temporary expedient they would reject it as a general rule, but common sense would generally decide each matter upon its own merits without any set form of action.

My ideas can be put into three phrases: communal possession of wealth or social equality, communal autonomy, or in other words, the folk-mote as the basis of social organisation; and individual liberty, or the right of persons and groups to the most complete self-activity, limited only by the rights of all [4].

Beyond broad areas of agreement on the essence of anarchism, there are also ideological differences which are significant in relation to the communities, some preferring a collectivist and others a more individualist form of organisation. These differences were worked through in a variety of ideas and experiments both in Europe and America during the nineteenth century. When anarchism is accepted in England as a rationale for communities it is as two distinctive ideologies, 'anarchist communism' and 'religious anarchism', a division which reflects the persisting tension between collectivism and individualism.

5.2 Society without the State

In order to understand the origins and relative importance of anarchist communism and religious anarchism (the latter being more directly associated with community schemes than the former), some of the earlier developments can be traced. In particular, one can look to the ideas of the English anarchist, William Godwin, in raising the possibility of 'a simple form of society without government'; to the rich current of revolutionary anarchism on the Continent, especially to Proudhon's theory of 'mutualism' as the economic and political basis for cooperation; and, finally, to the theory and practice of American 'individualist anarchism'. Practical anarchism came late to England and both Kropotkin and Tolstoy, as central figures for the communitarians between 1890 and 1900, acknowledge their debt to these earlier developments.

'A simple form of society'
Nearly 100 years before the anarchist communities, William Godwin implanted the idea of a decentralised society without government, founded on voluntary federation [5]. Godwin's theory of society was couched in unmistakably eighteenth-century terms, preoccupied with the nature of political right and justice and confident in the power of reason. Yet it forms an important bond with earlier strands of anarchist thought and experiment (notably that of Winstanley and the Diggers). And, in turn, it provoked both a critical response and an immediate following. While Thomas Malthus voiced the misgivings of the liberal theorists [6], the Romantic poets, Shelley, Southey, Coleridge and Wordsworth warmed to the prospect and imagery of the annihilation of that 'brute engine' political government [7]. There is also a relationship between Godwin's ideal and the utopias of the later English Romantics, William Morris and Oscar Wilde [8].

From Godwin's extensive critique of existing society and his utopian alternative it is, particularly, his views on decentralisation which have the most direct bearing on the later formation of communities. His views on an alternative form of government stem from his notion of ethics. Like his contemporary liberals he started from a strictly utilitarian standpoint, judging actions and relationships in terms of the greatest benefit to the community. But, unlike the liberals, he believed that the unequal amounts of happiness that individuals experienced was neither natural nor desirable; indeed, a full measure of happiness would accrue only when individuals defined their own rights with benevolent regard to the rights of others. He argued that, as the inequalities that he observed were the result of external circumstances, rather than of inherent human weaknesses, it was possible to change these circumstances and to improve society. With the spread of reason, progress towards a happier society was inevitable, though the process would be accelerated when all knew the 'truth' of their condition. A knowledge of this truth would reveal that the real obstacle to improvement, and the very cause of inequality and suffering, was no less than the institution of government. Society was a natural condition for mankind, but government was an artificial and corrupting force.

Without government, humans would be free to determine their own lives in free association with others:

It is earnestly to be desired that each man should be wise enough to govern himself, without the intervention of any compulsory restraint; and, since government, even in its best state, is an evil, the object principally to be aimed at is that we should have as little of it as the general peace of human society will permit [9].

Godwin then outlined the nature of what he termed 'a simple form of society without government' – reducing the scale of organisation to that of the parish, and removing the distinction between rulers and ruled. As far as possible the parishes would be autonomous, and formal relations between each other would be limited. In a decentralised society the tyranny associated with centralised control would disappear and, where one's actions would be known by all, there would be greater sincerity between individuals:

The ideas of a great empire and legislative unity are plainly the barbarous remains of the days of military heroism. In proportion as political power is brought home to the citizens and simplified into something of the nature of parish regulation; the danger of misunderstanding and rivalship will be nearly annihilated. In proportion as the science of government is divested of its present mysterious appearances, social truth will become obvious and the districts pliant and flexible to the dictates of reason [10].

Simplicity and sincerity were carried through into the economic arrangements, where Godwin envisaged a primarily agrarian economy based on necessity rather than luxury, and directed towards economic equality – 'a state of the most rigid simplicity'. But it was also a state with utopian lure where, though everyone would perform some manual labour, no one would be required to work in this way for more than half an hour a day:

In such a community, scarcely anyone can be expected, in consequence of his situation or avocations, to consider himself as exempted from the obligation to manual industry. There will be no rich man to recline in indolence, and fatten upon the labour of his fellows. The mathematician, the poet and the philosopher will derive a new stock of cheerfulness and energy from the recurring labour that makes them feel they are men. There will be no persons devoted to the manufacture of trinkets and luxuries; and none whose office it should be to keep in motion the complicated machine of government – tax-gatherers, beadles, excise-men, tide-waiters, clerks and secretaries. There will be neither fleets nor armies, neither courtiers nor lacqueys. It is the unnecessary employments that, at present, occupy the great mass of every civilised nation, while the peasant labours incessantly to maintain them in a state more pernicious than idleness [11].

With this prospect, Godwin could confidently ask who there was that would shrink from this degree of industry. And is it possible 'to contemplate this fair and generous picture of independence and virtue, where every man would have ample leisure for the noblest energies of mind, without feeling our very souls refreshed with admiration and hope' [12].

Godwin presented the idea of decentralisation as a novel and inseparable part of a revolutionary philosophy, and the prospect of a simplified form of society is one that is later to be explored in various community settings. But the acknowledged debt to Godwin in community history is far from clear [13]. What seems likely is that, in the first instance, it was the utopian socialists (William Thompson in particular) who forged a link between some of Godwin's ideas and practical attempts at community formation. There is also evidence that Emerson introduced some of Godwin's ideas to the American individualist anarchists who, in turn, had some influence on the later English schemes.

'Property is a decentralising force'

In spite of the foundations that were laid by Godwin, and the embellishments of the English Romantic poets, it was on the Continent and in the United States that anarchist ideas were developed as a significant revolutionary theory. In the history of anarchist thought Michael Bakunin is a major figure, extending anarchism into a collectivist realm with possession by voluntary institutions rather than by individuals. But he was not of direct interest to the communitarians. His assessment of revolution was that change would be violent and sudden, and that efforts to change society by means of the example of peaceful associations were naive [14].

Of greater bearing on the later communities were the ideas of Pierre-Joseph Proudhon. Avoiding an extreme adherence either to individualism or to revolutionary violence, Proudhon's idea of 'mutualism' provided what seemed to be a plausible middle route towards a new society. It was an idea which rested on a belief in the advantages of economic and political cooperation in small groups, in opposition to the State, in modified property rights, and in ultimate equality within society. In essence, mutualism was seen to be a natural form of economic cooperation between groups of labour, which would form the basis for new social and political relationships:

... a theory of 'mutuality', a system of guarantees that resolves the old forms of our civil and commercially based societies and satisfies all the conditions of efficiency, progress and justice pointed out by the critics. It will be a society that is based not on convention, but on reality; a society that converts the division of labour into a scientific instrument; a society that stops men from being slaves of machines and foresees the crises that these will cause. It will make competition profitable and transform monopoly into a guarantee of security for all. Through the energy of its principle, instead of asking the capitalist for credit and the State for protection, it will make both capital and the State subordinate to labour.

Through the genuine nature of exchange it will create true solidarity between people. It will, without prohibiting individual initiative or domestic thrift always restore to the community the wealth that has been privately appropriated. It will be a society that will, through the movement of the outlay and the return of capital, insure the political and industrial equality of its citizens, and through a vast system of public education bring about equality in functions and aptitudes through constantly raising their level. Through justice, prosperity and virtue it will bring a renewal of human consciousness and insure harmony and equilibrium between the generations. . .This synthesis is as old as its constituent parts since it merely means that society is returning through a maze of inventions and systems, to its primitive practices as a result of a six-thousand-year-long meditation [15].

A number of general points can be illustrated from this. Firstly, Proudhon was motivated by a notion of equilibrium, where the contradictions of existing society, with its conflicts between socialism and capitalism, could be resolved through mutualism. He believed that Man is naturally equal, and agreed with socialist contemporaries that it was the capitalist system which had created inequalities. He did not see the need for sudden political revolution, but contended that the political principles of the French Revolution could be extended into the economic sector. He advocated political action through mutualist associations rather than political parties.

Although Proudhon advocated fundamental changes in the organisation of society there were, at the same time, elements of conservatism. In particular, in spite of his early and widely misinterpreted contention that 'property is theft', Proudhon retained a fundamental belief in Man's natural rights to own land and to trade one with another. He criticised the capitalist system in which land and the labour applied to it was exploited in the same way as other sources of production. In its place he envisaged a new system of small-scale ownership with a direct link between those owning the land and those who worked it, and where the only area of State intervention would be to restrict excessive ownership. Private property in this sense was seen as an important source of power decentralisation:

There is a corollary to this principle that property is the only power that can act as a counterweight to the State, because it shows no reverence to princes, rebels against society and is, in short, anarchist. The corollary is that property, an absolutism within an absolutism, is also an element of division within the State. State power is the kind of power that absorbs everything else into it. If it is allowed to take its own way, all individuality will quickly disappear, swallowed up by the collectivity, and society will sink into communism. Property, on the contrary, is a decentralizing force. Being itself absolute, it is anti-despotic and anti-unitary. Property is the basis of any system of federation. This is why property, which is by nature autocratic, automatically becomes democratic when it forms part of an ordered political society [16].

His preference for individual ownership and mutual trading was of more direct appeal to the peasants and petty bourgeoisie than to the new industrial proletariat. In his later writings Proudhon even exempted agriculture from the need to organise in mutualist associations, believing instead that the family could serve as the basic unit for society.

The underlying theme in Proudhon's proposed form of organisation is one of decentralisation from the control of large capital units and State bureaucracy. Although he could not conceive the total abolition of all forms of central control he argued that this could be countered through mutualist associations. The very need for State intervention, with its vast apparatus of laws and regulations, is removed by substituting a new order of contractual relationships for the old order of coercion. If society is based on equality and cooperation there would be no longer a need for the institutions of a police force, repression and restrictions. Instead, power would be diffused through a series of autonomous units, developing from the base 'upwards', rather than in the pattern of the traditional hierarchy. Mutualist associations of producers would be linked into communes, to make up a federation. To Proudhon, 'federalism' was the political arm of mutualism – together they could provide the basis for full political and economic revolution.

Apart from his influence on later anarchists, notably Kropotkin, the contribution of Proudhon to the anarchist communities is, perhaps, twofold. Firstly, his theory provides a strategy for revolutionary change which, in line with the communities, rests on direct action without recourse to violence. At the same time (as Kropotkin was later to demonstrate) the incentive for revolution rests not simply on abstract reason but on economic good sense and the underlying belief that a decentralised society is natural. Secondly, Proudhon offers an attractive balance between individualism and uniformity. He is concerned to break down the monolithic structure of the State yet, at the same time, to avoid the total fragmentation of a society composed simply of individuals. More than the individualist anarchists he sees history in terms of social formations, and his desire to protect individual freedom rests on a commitment to association. His belief that individualism is best preserved in a relationship with a social group – which sees individual freedom as inseparable from the natural processes out of which society itself evolves – is one that appears in various forms among the later communitarians. It is a fundamental belief in all anarchist thought that diversity and individual freedom is the basis not of competition but of cooperation – that, in the words of Proudhon, 'Liberty is the mother not the daughter of order'.

'Infinite diversity is the universal law'

Proudhon's ideas proved to be particularly attractive to the American anarchists, developing their own form of individualist anarchism in the more open conditions of the new society. It was a form of anarchism that was characterised by a consistent emphasis on individualism (with similarities to Proudhon's advocacy of limited property rights), and a close association with Nature and the virtues of a simpler mode of existence [17]. The American experience was of considerable interest to the later English communitarians, with Thoreau referred to among the Tolstoyans almost as essential reading.

It is Joseph Warren, though, rather than Henry Thoreau who was responsible for a new wave of anarchist community experiments. As early as 1834 Warren, 'the American Proudhon' [18], founded the Village of Equity in Ohio – claimed to be the first anarchist community in any country since Winstanley's venture on St George's Hill almost two centuries before [19]. Further anarchist communities founded by Warren were Utopia in 1846 and Modern Times in 1850.

Warren had previously observed both Owenite and Fourierite communities and rejected their hierarchical structure in favour of one based on mutual agreements [20]. He believed that earlier experiments had failed because they had been unable to deal with the tensions between the united interests as opposed to the individualities of persons and circumstances. Instead he contended that society must be converted so as to preserve the sovereignty of every individual inviolate – 'infinite diversity is the universal law' [21]. In his community experiments Warren was constantly searching for ways of enabling universal individuality:

I do not mean to be understood that all are of one mind. On the contrary, in a progressive state there is no demand for conformity. We build on Individuality. Any differences between us confirms our position. Differences, therefore, like the admissible discords in music, are a valuable part of our harmony. It is only when the rights of persons or property are actually invaded that collisions arise. These rights being clearly defined and sanctioned by public opinion, and temptations to encroachments being withdrawn, we may then consider our great problem practically solved. With regard to mere difference of opinion in taste, convenience, economy, equality, or even right and wrong, good and bad, sanity and insanity – all must be left to the supreme decision of each 'individual', whenever he can take on himself the cost of his decisions; which he cannot do while his interests or movements are united or combined with others. It is in combination or close connection only that compromise or conformity is required. Peace, harmony, ease, security, happiness, will be found only in 'individuality' [22].

But at the same time there is an awareness of the fundamental difference between this notion of 'individuality' and the liberal meaning of 'individualism' especially as it was expressed in the 'free-for-all' situation of American land colonisation. While the anarchist under-standing of individuality is one of universal application, where no individual takes more than he needs and where no harm is done to others, for the *laissez faire* liberal it is a question of 'every man for himself'. With the one system, freedom would be universal in its distribution, with the other it is inherently unequal. For the anarchist there are natural limits to what an individual would want, and it is exploitation that is unnatural.

A further source of individualist anarchism is to be found in the writings and actions of Ralph Emerson and Henry Thoreau. In their own way, both conveyed the spirit of the frontier, with its prospects for freedom and affinity with Nature, to a European society more industrialised and under far more rigid State control. It was a romantic message for the communitarians in England, in the language of the backwoods: 'The life in us is like the water in the river. It may rise this year higher than man has ever known it, and flood the parched uplands; even this may be the eventful year, which will drown out all our muskrats. It was not always dry land where we dwell, I see far inland the banks which the stream anciently washed . . .' [23].

For two years Thoreau worked for Emerson, where he learnt of the philosopher's resistance to the State. Emerson (seemingly influenced by Godwin) opposed the State as a corrupt force, numbing human conscience and stemming liberty. He taught that 'good men must not obey the laws too well', a lesson taken to heart by Thoreau who was later arrested for refusing to pay his poll tax and subsequently wrote *On the Duty of Civil Disobedience* [1848]. In this work Thoreau used his unlawful action to explain his attitude to government generally, concluding with the view that 'there will never be a really free and enlightened State, until the State comes to recognise the individual as a higher and independent power, from which all its own power and authority are derived, and treats him accordingly' [24].

Understandably, though, for the communitarians who were themselves confronting Nature, it was Thoreau's account of the period he spent alone in a wooden hut on the edge of Walden Pond (near Concord, Massachusetts) which provided more direct inspiration. Thoreau's simple way of life lasted between March 1845 and September 1847, and is recounted in his book *Walden or, Life in the Woods* [1854]. It was widely interpreted as a utopia of Man finding purity in his natural surroundings.

Thoreau's experience was solitary rather than communal but the Tolstoyans, especially, were to find his search for essential truth and the reduction of life to its simplest elements both instructive and inspirational. 'I went to the woods because I wished to live deliberately, to confront only the essential facts of life and see if I could not learn what it had to teach, and not, when I came to die, discover that I had not lived' [25]. He provided both a critique of modern civilisation, with its elaborate veneer of useless activities and goods, and an object lesson that it was possible to live at a very much more basic level and, in the process of so doing, experience a purification. The only cure for civilisation's ills was seen to be 'a rigid economy, a stern and more than Spartan simplicity of life and elevation of purpose' [26].

Walden is an account, not simply of detailed observations of Nature but of the ideal of fusion between body, soul and surroundings. As with many of the communitarians it is diet which frequently figures as a focal point in this analysis. For two years Thoreau lived on 'rye and Indian meal without yeast, potatoes, rice, a very little salt pork, molasses, and salt; and my drink, water' [27]. A simple diet was one means of liberating mind and body and it is understandable that vegetarianism is a recurrent subject of interest within communities. Thoreau, himself, was not a vegetarian, and, living alongside a lake, fishing presented a particular ethical problem: 'I found in myself, and still find, an instinct towards a higher, or, as it is named, spiritual life, as do most men, and another toward a primitive rank and savage one, and I reverence them both. I love the wild not less than the good' [28].

But above all *Walden* was about transcending rather than suc-cumbing to problems, and Nature provided a mediation. The pure, natural surroundings are a means by which Thoreau searched for the meaning of soul and the essence of life. In the simplicity and perfection of Nature he found constant inspiration. The season of Spring itself is likened to the illusory Golden Age of distant past and future:

The Golden Age was first created which without any avenger
Spontaneously without law cherished fidelity and rectitude.
Punishment and fear were not; nor were threatening words read
On suspended brass; nor did the suppliant crowd fear
The words of their judge; but were safe without an avenger.
Not yet the pine felled on its mountains had descended
To the liquid waves that it might see a foreign world,
And mortals knew no shores but their own.
There was eternal spring, and placid zephyrs with warm
Blasts soothed the flowers born without seed [29]

Thoreau was by no means the most important of the anarchist theorists, but in his practical example, in his rejection of standardised society, in his exploration of Nature, and in confronting such topics as diet, dress and craftsmanship, his appeal to the communitarians is understandable. The image, if not the reality, of log cabins in a natural setting where life took place at a simple level, was not far from the minds of the Tolstoyan anarchists in England half a century later.

5.3 Anarchist communism

The anarchist ideas that had been developed by the middle of the century reflected their own historical and geographical origins – Godwin's in the manner of an eighteenth-century philosopher, Proudhon's with his sympathy for French agrarian life, and Warren and Thoreau in the unique conditions of the American frontier. Many of these ideas were carried forward, but the English anarchists towards the end of the century looked to more immediate sources of reference, to what is termed 'anarchist communism' and 'religious anarchism'.

Anarchist communism is a revolutionary doctrine, envisaging the local commune as the unit of production and distribution, with each giving according to their means and taking according to their needs. It developed in England more as the result of ideas brought from the Continent by political refugees and foreign workers, than from a continuing tradition of native anarchism. The international clubs in

London were early anarchist strongholds, the scene of both meetings and the publication of newspapers. *Die Freiheit* (1879), the first anarchist paper to be published in England, was associated with the exiled German, Johann Most, and his followers at the Rose Street Club in Soho. Later publications which advocated anarchist communism were *Freedom*, founded in 1886 by a group centred around Peter Kropotkin, and *Commonweal* which from 1889 expressed the views of the anarchist-controlled 'Socialist League'. The two papers existed side by side for eight years, *Freedom* with an intellectual readership, and *Commonweal*, more directly involved in day-to-day issues, with an activist following. In 1895 the two groups combined, and *Freedom* continued as the main exponent of anarchist communism [30].

Most influential of the theorists of anarchist communism in this period was Peter Kropotkin. Apart from his own works and contacts with the communities, there is an affinity with his contemporaries, William Morris, Edward Carpenter and Oscar Wilde, who each make their own contribution to the ideal of the community in a decentralised society.

'The free commune'

Peter Kropotkin's anarchist theory of the 'free commune' offered one of the strongest theoretical foundations for the English communities in the late nineteenth century. In essence, Kropotkin sought to demonstrate that 'mutual aid' is a natural basis for social relationships, and that a natural outcome of its application would be to replace the oppressive authority of the State with a system of decentralised, cooperative communities – the free commune. As a figure of international standing Kropotkin was able to argue for communities, not simply on their own merits, but also as part of a theoretical perspective which explicitly rejected both the alternative revolutionary theory of scientific socialism, and the counter-revolutionary liberal support for Darwin's 'jungle law' of evolution.

Kropotkin's influence in England was enhanced by his personal presence in this country (in 1876, 1881 to 1882, and 1886 to 1917). For Kropotkin, England was not simply a base for his writings and lectures but, in itself, a society of imminent revolutionary potential. He enjoyed contact with the various anarchist groups in London, he was a close friend of William Morris, and he appears to have met most of the leading English socialists of that time [31].

Kropotkin was aware of the interest in the immediate establishment of communities yet, while in many ways they were modelled on his ideal of the free commune, there never appears to have been any question that he would become directly involved himself. In his association with Edward Carpenter and in lecturing at Sheffield on the prospects of individual freedom through mutual aid, he may well have contributed to the establishment of the Norton Colony [32]. He was also a visitor to the Clousden Hill Free Communist and Cooperative Colony, and is acknowledged as the inspiration behind the venture [33].

But, undoubtedly, Kropotkin saw himself increasingly as a strategist of revolution rather than as a tactician. The growing severity of industrial crises led Kropotkin to believe that the whole edifice of capitalism was about to be brought down. 'All is linked, all holds together under the present economic system, and all tends to make the fall of the industrial and mercantile system under which we live inevitable. Its duration is but a question of time that may already be counted by years and no longer by centuries' [34]. Capitalism was crumbling and Kropotkin saw a greater need for his intellect in London, rather than in Norton or Clousden Hill – the free commune would inevitably follow the collapse of the old system.

In spite of his lack of direct involvement, for the anarchist communitarians Kropotkin's theory of evolution and social organisation provided a means of dealing with two basic tasks which confronted them. The first was to justify the assumption underlying the communities that 'cooperation' rather than 'competition' represented the natural pattern of social relationships; and the second was to demonstrate that small communities without State control were not only morally preferable to the existing order but also that they could be economically viable. In tackling these issues Kropotkin added the weight of his own international reputation to the communitarians in their struggle against orthodoxy.

The idea that cooperation was the natural basis for society was not, in itself, particularly novel – but its reformulation after a century where economic, philosophical, and biological arguments had been advanced to reinforce the hegemony of competition is, in historical terms, significant. The classical economists, the utilitarians and, more topically for Kropotkin, extreme advocates of Charles Darwin's theory of evolution, had jointly provided a rationale for competition and social inequality, both in domestic and overseas colonial policy. Kropotkin sought to demonstrate that competition was not, in fact, the natural order of things and, as such, was morally unacceptable. Instead, Kropotkin pointed to 'mutual aid' as being the predominant fact of nature, fundamental both to preservation and to progressive evolution. He used examples of animal species and earlier forms of human development to argue that, far from existing in isolation, there had always been a natural tendency to cooperate. He argued that society had been conditioned to believe that without the intervention of the State, disorder would prevail. But if society could exist before the State, then there was no inherent reason why it should not exist again on that basis.

Whereas the State could be seen to intervene in order to promote the interests of some over those of others, mutual aid would ensure justice and equity and that, in turn, would enable morality:

Mutual Aid – Justice – Morality are thus the consecutive steps of an ascending series, revealed to us by the study of the animal world and man. They constitute an 'organic necessity' which carries in itself its own justification, confirmed by the whole of the evolution of the animal kingdom, beginning with its early stages (in the form of colonies of the most primitive organisms), and gradually rising to our civilised human communities. Figuratively speaking it is a 'universal law of organic evolution', and this is why the sense of Mutual Aid, Justice and Morality are rooted in man's mind with all the force of an inborn instinct – the first instinct, that of Mutual Aid, being evidently the strongest ... [35].

Kropotkin's moral vision of a new society is therefore rooted in what he saw to be a 'scientific' analysis of history. His thesis was that it was the State which represented an aberration in the history of cooperative forms of organisation (free confederations of tribes, village communes, parishes, guilds, cooperative forms of production) rather than the reverse, and that revolutionary struggle would be directed towards reasserting mutual aid as the true principle for social organisation. As revolution was seen to be imminent so, too, was the recovery of a society based on mutual aid. Yet that would not be the end of it. Kropotkin's view is not that conflict is absent as a social characteristic, but that it is checked by the existence of a stronger tendency towards unity and mutual sympathy. But the balance would never be absolute, and rather than portray a profile of a static future he introduced the important notion of a social structure that is never finally constituted. The society of the future:

will be composed of a number of societies banded together for everything that demands a common effort: federations of producers for all kinds of production, of societies for consumption; federations of such societies alone and federations of societies and production groups; finally, more extensive groups embracing a whole country or even several countries and composed of persons who will work in common for the satisfaction of those economic, spiritual and artistic needs which are not limited to a definite territory. All these groups will unite their efforts through mutual agreement.... Personal initiative will be encouraged and every tendency to uniformity and centralisation combated. Moreover this society will not ossify into fixed and immovable forms, it will transform itself incessantly, for it will be a living organism continually in development [36].

On the second issue, that of giving specific support to the notion of small free communities, Kropotkin turned both to historical evidence and to his own statistical assessment of the viability of reorganisation along these lines. His historical ideal was that of the free commune of mediaeval Europe:

It is a natural development, belonging, just as did the tribe and the village community, to a certain phase in human evolution, and not to any particular nation or region. The commune of the Middle Ages, the free city, owes its origin on the one hand to the village community, and on the other, to those thousands of brotherhoods and guilds which were coming to life in that period independently of the territorial union [37].

Far from being a historical dream, Kropotkin saw the realisation of this ideal as the inevitable outcome for society. The modern development of technology itself was seen, not as a threat to an earlier model of decentralisation but as a means for its achievement.

For the communitarian Kropotkin provided both political idealism and practical guidance. At the theoretical level he argued that:

Political economy has hitherto insisted chiefly upon 'division'. We proclaim 'integration'; and we maintain that the ideal of society – that is, the state towards which society is already marching – is a society of integrated, combined labour. A society where each individual is a producer of both manual and intellectual work; where each individual is a worker, and where each worker works both in the field and the industrial workshop; where every aggregation of individuals, large enough to dispose of a certain variety of natural resources – it may be a nation, or rather a region – produces and itself consumes most of its own agricultural and manufactured produce [38].

And for the communitarians, developing theory through practice, there was also some sound practical advice on the viability of localised production in small workshops coupled with intensive cultivation. He illustrated his point with a utopian profile of some 200 families 'making the best use' of 1,000 acres of shared land [39]. About 340 acres is given over to growing cereals, another 400 acres for grass and fodder for the herds of dairy and beef cattle, and some 20 acres for intensive fruit and vegetable production. Each household would enjoy half an acre for its own use, leaving another 140 acres for workshops, public gardens and squares. His comments on labour are of interest [40]:

The labour that would be required for such an intensive culture would not be the hard labour of the serf or slave. It would be accessible to everyone, strong or weak, town bred or country born; it would also have many charms besides. And its total amount would be far smaller than the amount of labour which every thousand persons, taken from this or from any other nation, have now to spend in getting their present food, much smaller in quantity and of worse quality. I mean, of course, the technically necessary labour without even considering the labour which we now have to give in order to maintain all our middlemen, armies and the like. The amount of labour required to grow food under a rational culture is so small, indeed, that our hypothetical inhabitants would be led necessarily to employ their leisure in manufacturing, artistic, scientific, and other pursuits [41].

Kropotkin saw no technical reason why this model of cooperation would not work. He recognised that the obstacles that prevented its realisation were not in the imperfections of agriculture, in the infertility of the soil, or in a hostile climate, but rather in the conservatism of existing institutions, and that it was necessary to clear these away before the free commune could flourish. The utopia of the free commune was, therefore, both within reach and yet not – the anarchist communities of that period were necessarily, in these terms, both real and yet illusory, practical attempts to create dreams. They represented a variation of Kropotkin's ideal, but in advance of the political revolution that he saw to be necessary to ensure their full development.

'To the land of freedom'

Apart from Kropotkin there were others at that time who wrote on the vision of a free society, in which work would be fulfilling and the products of labour shared. It was in no sense a doctrinaire 'anarchist communist' movement but the general direction in which they moved, direct associations with the Norton Colony, and personal friendship with Peter Kropotkin lent support to the idea of a reorganised society along the lines that he proposed. They shared Kropotkin's belief in the imminence of revolutionary change and in the urgency of addressing themselves to the nature of future society. 'Of the possibility of a free communal society there can really, I take it, be no doubt. The question that more definitely presses on us now is one of transition – by what steps shall we, or can we pass to that land of freedom' [42].

The question of transition and of what might follow was precisely that which interested William Morris. He differed from Kropotkin in his adherence to the Marxist notion that a strong, central State, in the hands of the proletariat, would be necessary to secure the revolution. But he shared with Kropotkin many of the features of an eventual stateless society, the conditions that Morris termed 'pure communism'. Amongst his varied works, the utopian romance *News from Nowhere* is of significance in inviting the imagination to envisage how a cooperative form of society might look and work in practice [43]. It provided an idealisation of communitarianism – though, for Morris (and, in practice, for the communitarians) an idealisation impossible to achieve in a short period and with the corrupting influence of the State.

Morris portrayed an image of England transformed into a society where relationships were cooperative rather than competitive. The iniquities of the old system – private property, centralised government, money – were abolished and replaced by a system of free and equal exchange. The products of competitive society – crime, punishment and rivalries – disappeared with the abolition of the institutions which gave rise to them. Large-scale technology is replaced by crafts and manual work, to produce a pattern of labour that is fulfilling and creative. The focus of production and distribution is the locality, in place of international trade. And the physical environment is transformed into one of 'sweet cottages' and proximity to nature. The society of the future is decentralised and simplified to resemble a model not dissimilar from an idealisation of the fourteenth-century commune. It is one of perfect harmony, of individual fulfilment, between society and nature. It is the ultimate romantic dream – an impossible model for the communitarians to attain yet, at the same time, with roots firmly entrenched in a realistic theory of historical change.

A friend of both Kropotkin and Morris, with an interest in communities, was the writer Edward Carpenter. Although he did not himself participate in a community, it was partly as a result of his exhortations that the Norton Colony in Sheffield took root. Carpenter had some years previously acquired a smallholding, 'Millthorpe', only a few miles from the city where, as his visitors put it '. . . you carry on your simplification of Life'. He had read and was impressed with Thoreau though, in his own words, 'was not intoxicated'. But his philosophical mind and the lure of simplification, attracted to the smallholding a wide range of visitors – 'vegetarians, dress reformers, temperance orators, spiritualists, secularists, anti-vivisectionists, socialists, anarchists'. His own commitment was to socialism, with a leaning towards anarchism – but he generally displayed a certain detachment from direct involvement in political activities, a role of prophet and philosopher more than that of an activist.

His contribution to anarchism and to the growing interest in the communities at that time took the form of writings and lectures on the corruption of existing society, and on the benefits of returning to a more natural way of life on the land. Carpenter was often acknowledged by the communitarians and wrote widely in their publications, but more often his language was far-removed from the practicalities they faced. He wrote in a style that was both prophetic and impassioned:

I see a great land poised as in a dream – waiting for the word by which it may live again.
I see the stretched sleeping figure – waiting for the kiss and the re-awakening.
I hear the bells pealing, and the crash of hammers, and see beautiful parks spread – as in a toy show.
I see a great land waiting for its own people to come and take possession of it [44].

For Carpenter, freedom, democracy and the land are passionately intertwined:

Between a great people and the earth springs a passionate attachment, lifelong – and the earth loves indeed her children, broad-breasted, broad-bowed, and talks with them night and day, storm and sunshine, summer and winter alike. . . . Owners and occupiers then fall into their places; the trees wave proud and free upon the headlands; the little brooks run with a wonderful new music under the brambles and the grass. . . . Government and law and police then fall into their places – the earth gives her own laws; Democracy just begins to open her eyes and peep! and the rabble of unfaithful bishops, priests, generals, landlords, capitalists, lawyers, Kings, Queens, patronisers and polite idlers goes scuttling down into general oblivion, faithfulness emerges, self-reliance, self-help, passionate comradeship.
Freedom emerges, the love of the land – the broad waters, the air, the undulating fields, the flow of cities and the people therein, their faces and the looks of them no less than the rush of the tides and the slow hardy growth of the oak and the tender herbage of spring and stiff clay and storms and transparent air [45].

Another romantic contribution to the debate was that provided by Oscar Wilde. He also acknowledged his debt to Kropotkin and believed, no less, in the imminence and desirability of socialism – though questioning whether this would necessarily bring individual freedom:

Socialism, Communism, or whatever one chooses to call it, by converting private property into public wealth, and substituting cooperation for competition, will restore society to its proper condition of a thoroughly healthy organism, and ensure the material well-being of each member of the community. It will, in fact, give life its proper basis and its proper environment. But, for the full development of life to its highest mode of perfection, something more is needed. What is needed is individualism [46].

The way to achieve individualism was to prevent a new form of centralised, authoritarian government replacing the tyranny of 'political power' with its own 'economic power'. Relationships in the new society should be voluntary in all spheres – 'it is only in voluntary associations that man is fine' [47]. Unlike Morris, Wilde saw no virtue in manual labour, and looked to the widespread application of technology – to 'mechanical slavery' – to replace 'human slavery'. It was, on Wilde's own admission, utopian, but for someone who believed that 'progress is the realisation of utopias' [48] hardly regressive.

5.4 Religious anarchism

The parallel influence of religious anarchism in this period can be explained, in part, as a reaction to the association of mainstream anarchism with violence. It is probable that only one death resulted in England from an anarchist bomb (and even that took the form of a home-made device exploding in the possession of a Frenchman who had intended to use it abroad), yet anarchism suffered from what, at times, amounted to hysterical condemnation. There were many who, while sharing their rejection of the State, could not see the way to its destruction by means of bombs or even by mass industrial action. Their strategy, instead, was to 'confront capitalist organisation by fraternal organisation' [49], to achieve a social revolution first to ensure that a meaningful political change could follow. It is understandable that this strain of anarchism was a powerful source of inspiration for the communities. The route to salvation was not, in the first place, through mass action, but through gentle cooperation. At the heart of this philosophy are the ideas of Leo Tolstoy.

'A new life-conception'
Although Tolstoy remained in Russia throughout the 1890s and was not involved directly in the practical aspects of any of the schemes, through his writings and through personal contact with a number of the communitarians his influence on the English community movement was profound. In contradiction to his own teachings on humility, the relationship that developed was charismatic – to the point where visits by his followers to his estate of Yasnaya Polyana were described as 'pilgrimages', and the communities that were shaped according to his ideas were known as 'Tolystoyan'. Such communities were attempts to put into practice the philosophy of Tolstoy as it was then emerging through various translations of books, pamphlets and letters. The Purleigh Colony (1896), the Ashingdon Colony (1897), the Brotherhood Workshop in Leeds (1897), the Wickford Colony (1898), the Whiteway Colony (1898) and the Blackburn Brotherhood (1899) were all attempts to reorganise life on Tolstoyan lines.

A number of Tolstoy's ideas were already well-developed and

available to English readers before this late nineteenth-century phase of community formation. From as early as 1852 in *The Cossacks*, Tolstoy was articulating a preference for 'Nature's simplicity' in contrast to the artificial sophistication and, as he saw it, futility of city life. It is a theme which was explored in his better-known novels, *War and Peace* and *Anna Karenina* – a theme where '...Happiness is being with Nature, seeing Nature, and discoursing with her' [50]. It led him to an idealisation, not only of Nature but of the simple life generally, and of the life of the peasant in particular.

There was also, well before the English community phase, a relationship between Tolstoy's developing ideals and practice. In an attempt to reduce the contradictions of his own position as an aristocratic landowner, Tolstoy introduced, first, reformist measures on his estate and, in 1880, a denunciation of property (in effect, more symbolic than real) and a commitment to dress and work in the fields as a peasant.

However, it was from an intensive period of religious writings (between 1879 and 1882), in a series of works where he sought to prove that the State church no longer accorded with the Gospels, that Tolstoy was led into the political realm of questioning (in the words of one of his own works) 'What then must we do?' In examining his religious and political answers, two issues will be explored. The first is to question what there was in Tolstoy's ideas that made them so attractive to the community movement in England, and the second is to consider the relationship between his emerging ideas and the experience of practice.

It would seem that two main sets of ideas can be identified, the one relating to a revolution of moral consciousness, and the other relating to a rejection of the State and its associated institutions. It is as a reflection of this duality that Tolstoy is sometimes referred to as a 'religious anarchist'. In practice, the communities offered a way of resolving this division.

Tolstoy's notion of Christianity, a return to the principles of the Sermon on the Mount, is explained in his book *The Kingdom of God is Within You: or, Christianity not as a Mystical Doctrine, but as a New Life-Conception* (first published in Russia in 1893). In the book, Tolstoy develops three principal ideas, proceeding from an understanding of the essence of Christianity to a call for social action:

... the first, that Christianity is not only the worship of God and a doctrine of salvation, but is above all things a new conception of life which is changing the whole fabric of human society; the second, that from the first appearance of Christianity there entered into it two opposite currents – the one establishing the true and new conception of life, which it gave to humanity, and the other perverting the true Christian doctrine and converting it into a Pagan religion, and that this contradiction has attained in our days the highest order of tension which now expresses itself in universal arguments, and on the Continent in general conscription; and the third, that this contradiction, which is masked by hypocrisy, can only be solved by an effort on the part of every individual endeavouring to conform the acts of his life – independent of what are regarded as the exigencies of family, society and the State – with those moral principles which he considers to be true [51].

Tolstoy advanced the belief that society had progressed from a state of individualism to one of 'social life-conception' and that a new phase of 'Christian life-conception' was imminent. He argued that society was already experiencing serious contradictions, and that these were manifested along class lines. As such, he provided a spiritual rejection of capitalism:

One needs but to compare the practice of life with its theory to be horrified at the extraordinary contradictions between the conditions of life and our inner consciousness. Man's whole life is a continual contradiction of what he knows to be his duty. This contradiction prevails in every department of life, in the economical, the political, and the international . . . every man in these days knows that in the matter of life and wordly goods all men have equal rights; that no man is either better or worse than his fellow-men, but that all men are born free and equal. Every man has an instinctive assurance of this fact, and yet he sees his fellow-beings divided into two classes, the one in poverty and distress, which labours and is oppressed, the other idle, tyrannical, luxurious; and not only does he see all this, but, whether voluntarily or otherwise, he falls in line with one or the other of these divisions – a course repugnant to his reason. Hence he must suffer both from his sense of the incongruity and his own share in it [52].

It was a revolutionary challenge, where the Christian foundations of life – equality, brotherly love, community of goods, non-resistance of evil by violence – would replace the principles that supported the family and the State as basic institutions of capitalist society. The challenge was sharpened by the messianic prophesy that the time for change was at hand, that 'each man has but to begin to do his duty, each one has but to live according to the light within him, to bring about the immediate advent of the promised Kingdom of God, for which the heart of every man yearns' [53]. The rationale for immediate revolution, of social change in advance of the abandonment of the State, was of obvious attraction to those who were already predisposed towards community formation.

In some of his later works Tolstoy went on to develop his ideas of society without the State, without property and without a need for money, where there would be no exploitation, and where non-resistance would replace violence. Individually, the communities experimented with these ideas which, taken together, provided an overall rationale for their localised efforts. The revolution would occur, not with the sudden overthrow of the State, but through the growth of 'rational conscious-ness'. Tolstoy argued this on the following basis.

He started by noting that exploitation and 'slavery', was an inevitable product of capitalism. It had resulted from the dominance of the landowner over those who owned insufficient land, from the imposition of taxes by governments, and from the competition of capitalists who controlled both labour and markets. 'So that, in one way or another, the labourer is always in slavery to those who control the taxes, the land, and the articles necessary to satisfy his requirements' [54].

Tolstoy then argued that this slavery was legitimised and perpetuated by legislation which, in turn, rested on the organised violence of the State. It was laws which perpetuated inequalities in property (both land and acquired goods) and which, in legalising taxation, ensured the dominance of State institutions:

It is said that the law defends equally the property of the mill-owner, of the capitalist, of the landowner, and of the factory or country labourer. The equality of the capitalist and of the worker is like the equality of two fighters, of whom one has his arms tied and the other has weapons, but to both of whom certain rules are applied with strict impartiality while they fight [55].

It followed, then, that to remove slavery one had first to remove the State. But the change must not be by means of violence, as this would only sow the seeds for a new form of exploitation. Instead, power must be abolished by the rational consciousness of men, which would expose this power (and its manifestation in the State) as being both useless and harmful. Rational consciousness would itself be shaped, not by materialistic theories, but by a:

spiritual weapon ... a devout understanding of life, according to which man regards his earthly existence as only a fragmentary manifestation of the complete life, and connecting his life with infinite life, and recognising his highest welfare in the fulfilment of the laws of this infinite life, regards the fulfilment of these laws as more binding upon himself than the fulfilment of any human laws whatsoever. Only such a religious conception, uniting all men in the same understanding of life, incompatible with subordination to power and participation in it, can truly destroy power [56].

There were immediate, practical steps that could be taken to challenge the State. Individuals should desist from holding any Government post, they should refuse to pay taxes or to receive government pensions, and they should refuse to call on State laws for the protection of their property. He went on to advocate a return to the land for the majority of the population, which he argued would be possible with the cessation of overproduction and without the manufacture of 'useless' goods, and with the perfection of cultivation that was possible (acknowledging the arguments developed earlier by Kropotkin). For the communitarians these guidelines for immediate change almost took on the nature of a charter – Nellie Shaw, for instance, describes the solemn burning of the land deeds of the Whiteway Colony, and their collective refusal to pay rates [57].

'Fraternity spells revolt'

The second question that was posed in the preceding section was to examine the relationship between the ideas as they were still emerging in the 1890s and the experience of practice in the communities at that time. What is interesting to speculate is the extent to which ideas and practice were in a dialectical relationship, with the communities exploring and evaluating the worth of Tolstoy's ideas and, in turn, Tolstoy's later writings benefitting from his knowledge of their experience. It is a difficult proposition to pursue, but possible, at least, to establish the existence of a rich flow of contacts between Yasnaya Polyana and the English communities.

These contacts took one of a number of forms – the circulation of journals to spread the ideas of Tolstoy to an English public, the translation of Tolstoy's works by participants in the community movement, and the 'pilgrimages' to the Russian estate by community supporters who would then return with fresh insights and inspiration to disseminate to their comrades. The communities (Purleigh Colony, in particular) also received a number of Russian refugees from Tsarist oppression, including Tolstoy's close friend, Vladimir Tchertkoff.

To explain these various but related contacts it will be helpful to look first at the conjuncture of events that took place in Croydon from about 1890. For it was there, through the Croydon Brotherhood, that an attempt was made to synthesise Tolstoyan philosophy with a growing English sympathy for a notion of brotherhood and peaceful revolution. It was also the base from which the significant Purleigh community venture was launched [58].

The origins of the Croydon movement are twofold. One source is to be found in the movement known as the 'New Fellowship' (originating as the 'Fellowship of the New Life' in 1883). The Fellowship was convened by Thomas Davidson, a former teacher and educational theorist who had travelled widely in Europe and North America and who had, at one time lectured with Henry Thoreau's mentor, Ralph Emerson. Davidson dreamt of a new form of communistic society composed of people spiritually purer and maintaining a 'higher life' than in present society. The Fellowship emphasised the subordination of material things to spiritual, and aimed at the cultivation of a perfect character in everyone. As a reaction to Davidson's commitment to communitarianism a group of the Fellowship hived off to form the 'Fabian Society' [59].

From 1889 the New Fellowship spread their ideas to a wider audience through the medium of a new publication *Seed Time* (originally named *The Sower*). It was in *Seed Time* that the links with Tolstoy were demonstrated, and the role of conscience in social revolution was stressed:

We are agreed concerning the diseases and miseries of this present order of society; we are agreed that these are established in the monopolies of property, by which the means of production are put into the control of a limited class, who use them to enslave and exploit the mass of the people. And we see that the remedy can only be found in a reorganisation of society which shall give to all free access to the means of production, which shall secure to each one a brotherly participation in all wealth; which shall destroy the servitude of all menial forms of labour, and establish that honesty and simplicity of life which must distinguish every society of equals.

... We recognise in the evolutionary processes, more than the mere outward progression of social forms. We know that 'conscience' has a part to play in the evolution of the new order [60].

The journal was concerned more with philosophising about a simpler, purer life than with the practicalities of achieving it. It was prepared for an intellectual, middle-class readership and, as well as publishing abstract papers, carried reports of lectures and other activities of the Fellowship. 'Rustic gatherings' were popular events, where members were invited to gather at a suitably rural venue to hear a paper, and then to proceed through the countryside to an appropriate tearoom. At one such event the paper was on the subject of 'the return to Nature'[61], and amidst 'the winds, the woods and water' the author spoke of a new unity between Nature (all that we recognise as not ourselves) and Soul. The rediscovery of this unity would reveal a new understanding of truth, of beauty and of simplicity. The members then returned by railway to the metropolis, but the message of the afternoon was not lost on the later communitarians.

Seed Time was printed at Croydon, and it was there that some of its contributors met. The second arm of the Croydon movement stemmed from the influence of the social mystic, J. Bruce Wallace and, from 1894 the avowed Tolstoyan, John Kenworthy. Wallace had already started a 'Brotherhood Church' in North London, with a publication *Brotherhood* which reported on social issues and on community experiments in various parts of the world. He was described as 'a man of intensely devoted and spiritual nature, who was convinced that it was possible to establish some kind of cooperative system in place of the present capitalistic system and commercialism generally' [62].

At the same time, a group known as 'The Croydon Socialist Society' decided to emulate Wallace's example, and establish a comparable 'Brotherhood Church' in Croydon. The word 'church' was used to refer to a number of people inspired by a common aim, but with no established religious or theological imputation. Something of the eclectic origins of the community experiments that followed is captured in Nellie Shaw's memories of their early gatherings:

It may be doubted if ever a more mixed and diverse crowd gathered within four walls than used to assemble weekly at the old Salvation Army tin tabernacle in Tamworth Road. Every kind of 'crank' came and aired his views on the open platform, which was provided every Sunday afternoon. Atheists, Spiritualists, Individualists, Communists, Anarchists, ordinary politicians, Vegetarians, Anti-vivisectionists and Anti-vaccinationists – in fact, every kind of 'anti' had a welcome and a hearing, and had to stand a lively criticism in the discussion which followed. As many came from a distance, tea was provided at a moderate charge in the adjoining room ... [63].

John Kenworthy brought with him a familiarity with the American anarchist movement and a firm commitment to Tolstoy's ideas, which he 'preached' from the pulpit of the Brotherhood Church. He combined with Wallace in 1894 to establish the Brotherhood Trust, as a means to create a voluntary cooperative system in England. It was a scheme of cooperative trading and industrial ventures, from which the profits were to be used for the purchase of land for communities. Wallace and Kenworthy had hoped to enlist a million participants within four years as the first step towards the dismantlement of capitalism. Kenworthy wrote frequently in *Seed Time*, urging the establishment of communities as a means of transforming society.

Another important development at Croydon was the new publication *The New Order*, which from 1895 reported the meetings and ideas of the Brotherhood, and later reported progress in the Tolstoyan communities. The printing activities formed the basis of the 'Croydon Brotherhood Publishing Society', which was subsequently relocated in the Purleigh Colony and became the means of printing the Tolstoy translations that were made by Aylmer Maude (who also lived at Purleigh). Tolstoy had granted full printing rights to the press, following a visit by Kenworthy to Tolstoy's estate in 1896.

The New Order was a more evangelical and practical publication than *Seed Time*, and played a more direct part in the process of community formation. Kenworthy again figured both as editor and regular contributor, constantly reminding readers of the principles of the new life:

equality (the socialist idea), fraternity (the communist idea), freedom (the anarchist idea), honest labour (the way of salvation), spreading the truth (the way of Jesus) . . . their fulfilment in practice means revolution to the lives of all who have their places in this unjust and unhappy state of society, the Mammon System. But in time the principles they express will revolutionise society altogether, and overthrow Babylon to bring in the New Jerusalem [64].

The journal also carried regular notices and advertisements, exhorting their members to take immediate and practical steps to revolutionise their lives – coal from the cooperative colliery at Swadlincote, the new vegetable butter at 6s. for a 14 pound tin, and dresses cut and fitted on scientific principles by the Croydon Brotherhood Dressmakers (Fig. 5.1).

In addition to the publications, while it does not seem that new points of substance were gleaned from 'pilgrimages' to Tolstoy, the process itself certainly contributed an interesting dimension to the relationship. Nellie Shaw claimed that 'the connection with Tolstoy became personally intimate' through contact with someone who had visited the master. Aylmer Maude (for long a resident in Russia), John Kenworthy, Tom Ferris (of the northern communities) and Francis Sedlak (who later settled at Whiteway) all made the journey to the Russian interior, the latter two in accord with Tolstoy's 'no money' doctrine. Kenworthy wrote a series of letters in 1896, in the first of which he described the purpose of the journey as being to see Leo Tolstoy and friends of his, and to arrange with them ways and means of carrying forward in England

72   THE NEW ORDER   Sept. 1897.

CROYDON INDUSTRIES.

CROYDON BROTHERHOOD STORE supplies groceries, fruit, vegetables, flour and semolina (which the manufacturers claim to make from pure English wheat). A speciality is made of pulse, grain and other vegetarian foods. Books and stationery ; labour, socialist, vegetarian and other advanced periodicals and literature. Goods delivered by cart every Friday. Arrangements have been made with a local tailor for clothes to be made with co-operatively produced materials. Also for natural undyed wool clothing. Please address all orders, remittances, advice, complaints or other communication on store business, to ARTHUR St. JOHN, Brotherhood House, Waddon, Croydon.

CROYDON BROTHERHOOD DRESSMAKERS carry on business at Brotherhood House. Dresses cut and fitted on scientific principles (artistic and rational costumes specially designed by Chas. E. Dawson). Women's and children's millinery. Knitted hose and underwear to order. Particulars from the Secretary, NELLIE SHAW, at the above address, or at 146, Beckenham Road, Penge, S.E.

JUST OUT.

72 pp., Large Post 8vo., 1s. Paper, 2s. Cloth.

The Fallacy of Marx's Theory of Surplus Value.

BY HENRY SEYMOUR.

This important treatise is a logical analysis of the theory of Surplus-Value as set forth by Karl Marx.

MURDOCH & CO., 26, PATERNOSTER SQUARE.

SCHOOL FOR BOYS AND GIRLS.
SUTTON, SURREY (NEAR CROYDON)

PUPILS BOARDED IF DESIRED.

NO PUNISHMENTS, NO MARKS, NO PRIZES.

For particulars and terms apply to MISS FRASER,
1, Carshalton Road, Sutton, Surrey.

BROTHERHOOD CHURCHES.

Southgate Road, N. (Nearest Stations—Haggerston and Mildmay Park, N.L.R.)
Pastor : J. BRUCE WALLACE, M.A.
Sunday, 11 a.m., and 7 p.m.
During the week—Classes, Guilds, Recreation Evenings.

Post Office, Chestnut Walk, Walthamstow. (St. James's St., G.E.R.)
Pastor, J. TAVENER.
Sunday, 7 p.m.

Queen's Park Hall, Harrow Road, W. (Westbourne Park Metr. Ry.)
Pastor, W. G. PIGOTT.
Sunday, 11 a.m., 3 and 7 p.m.

A MEETING
of friends in North London, who are studying and trying to follow the teaching of Jesus, is held every Sunday evening. All are welcome. For particulars apply to SIDNEY R. GOODE, 10 Torriano Cottages, Leighton Road, London, N.W., from whom THE NEW ORDER and other literature may be obtained.

THE BROTHERHOOD COLONIES' AGENCY,
26, PATERNOSTER SQUARE, E.C.

SUMMER HOLIDAYS AT REASONABLE RATES.

The B.C. Agency is now taking up the catering of holiday facilities on the Purleigh Colony. Sympathisers are invited to get some fresh air into their lungs free of charge by working on the land. Implements provided free, and they can work as hard as they like. All they have to pay for is food and lodging.

DAILY SUPPLIES OF NEW LAID EGGS

from Purleigh Colony and kindred sources, will be sold to friends who can take a weekly supply ; also

HONEY IN COMB (per section)	1/-
BRAZIL NUTS (14lb.)	4/2
DATES (56lb.)	8/2
NUCOLINE, the New Vegetable Butter, can be used either for cooking or table (14lb. tin)	6/-
WHEATMEAL, Finest (14lb.)	2/2
Do. Do. (28lb.)	4/-
Do. Do. (56lb.)	7/6
HOMINY & GROUND RICE, same price as wheatmeal.	
OATMEAL, Finest Scotch (14lb.)	2/9
LENTILS, HARICOTS, PEAS, SPLIT PEAS, RICE, &c., &c., at usual rates.	
FRESH RIPE BLACKBERRIES (20lb.)	5/-

PLEASE NOTE.—The B.C. Agency are now supplying the New Oil Soap (extracted from Cocoa Nut), free from colouring matter or other impurities (12lb.) 3/-.

BROTHERHOOD PUBLISHING CO.,
LONDON OFFICE
26, PATERNOSTER SQUARE, E.C.

BY LEO TOLSTOY.
The Four Gospels, Harmonised and Translated. 2 Vols. now published. Crown 8vo., art linen, gilt top, price   each 6s. 0d.
(Vol. III in preparation)

Work while ye have the Light	2s. 6d.
Christ's Christianity	3s. 6d.
What to Do	3s. 6d.
The Kingdom of God is Within You	3s. 6d.
The Gospel in Brief	3s. 6d.

BOOKLETS. In Box, price 2s. each.
Vol. I. Where Love is, there God is also.
Vol. II. What Men Live By.
Vol. III. The Two Pilgrims.
Vol. IV. Master and Man.
Vol. V. The Parables. (cloth only.)
May also be had separately, in paper cover, price 1s. each.

BY JOHN C. KENWORTHY.
Each, crown 8vo. paper, 1s. ; Cloth, 2s.
The Anatomy of Misery : Plain Lectures on Economics.
The Christian Revolt : Signs of the Coming Commonwealth.
From Bondage to Brotherhood : A Message to the Workers.
The World's Last Passage. A New Story. (Cloth only.)

"NEW MORAL WORLD" SERIES,
By ARTHUR BAKER, M.A.
Threepence each.
1. A PLEA FOR COMMUNISM.
2. SHAKERS AND SHAKERISM.
3. THE BROOK FARM EXPERIMENT. (Nearly ready.)
Other issues to follow.

Just out—A DREAM OF AN IDEAL CITY. By Albert Kimsey Owen. Price One Penny.

Pamphlets and books on all subjects procured to order.

Printed for the Brotherhood Publishing Company, Croydon, at the "Brotherhood Press," 28, Clerkenwell Road, London, E.C.
Published at 26, Paternoster Square, London, E.C.

Fig. 5.1 From *The New Order*, September 1897. Each month, *The New Order* included a page of advertisements for a variety of publications and activities with which the Tolstoyans at Croydon were sympathetic.

the work to which they in Russia gave themselves [65]. Again, it was Nellie Shaw who described something of the excitement occasioned by these visits and by the arrival of others who knew Tolstoy:

I well remember the Sunday following Kenworthy's return from Russia . . . how excited we all were to hear first-hand about the great Russian, Count Tolstoy, and to learn that he was a vegetarian, dressed like a peasant and lived so simply and frugally. He had been greatly interested to hear all about our little venture, and particularly about the Sermon on the Mount class. We heard, too, about the poor persecuted Doukhobortsi, interest in whom was shortly afterwards greatly stimulated by the arrival in Croydon of a number of Russians, friends of Tolstoy's – Vladimir Tchertkoff, with his wife and son, Dr Skarvan from Austria, where he had suffered imprisonment for his Tolstoyan principles, Helena Petrovna, a Caucasian princess, with quite a retinue of dependants and two servants ... (and) Mr Aylmer Maude, having left Moscow, arrived in Croydon with his wife and family, settling temporarily at Brotherhood House ... [66].

But the focus of activity was already shifting from Croydon. In the winter of 1896 a number of the more active members of the group decided that enough preparations had been made and that the time had come to set up a community. In the first place it was in the Purleigh Colony and the neighbouring Essex communities that this new wave of activity was centred. Later, with the demise of Purleigh, the Tolstoyan trail extended to Whiteway in Gloucestershire. Croydon, Essex and Whiteway were important landmarks of Tolstoyan community activity in the late 1890s, but they were not alone. From April 1898 anarchist groups in the north of England, sharing a similar ideology, circulated a new publication, *The Free Commune:* 'a quarterly magazine of libertarian thought', which carried news of their various activities. In one edition there was news of anarchist groups in Leeds (Brotherhood Workshop at 6, Victoria Road), Manchester (where an anarchist group met every Tuesday in the City Coffee Rooms in Swan Street), Liverpool (at the Wellington Monument every Sunday), Derby (at Comrade McGinnis's in Sitwell Street) and Sheffield (the Norton Colony, advertised as the Sheffield Free Communist Group). The establishment of more communities was urged as a revolutionary deed:

We urge all comrades, that wherever possible, they should group themselves together and acquire land; establishing small colonies adjacent to the towns. They could after the manner of the Clousden Hill Colonists, go in for intensive and glass culture, producing quantities of glasshouse fruits etc. In this manner a large part of their own food could be produced, and the surplus disposed of – preferably to the Co-operative Societies – in exchange for labour notes, or drafts upon the stores, which would be a mutual advantage, relieving as it would the necessity of legal tender so often the great difficulty in such enterprises. This would provide for those necessities or luxuries which owing to the exigencies of climate or other circumstances they could not otherwise acquire. If attempts of this character were dotted up and down the country they would prove powerful examples of our principles, and would, no doubt, be largely imitated.

They would help to form the nucleus of a better society, and what is more to the point, find a haven of refuge for those who were victimised in the fight against authority and exploitation.

Agricultural co-operation would produce these results ... It would remove men from the contaminating influence of commercialism, and by bringing them in contact with Mother Earth, purify and broaden their characters.

Everything that purifies life helps the Revolution; the mere change of social forms does not necessarily bring Socialism but Fraternity spells Revolt [67].

5.5 Community profiles

Of the two anarchist ideologies, anarchist communism and religious anarchism, the latter provided a clearer rationale for the communities. While both accepted the need for revolution, the latter saw this process as one of immediate moral and social regeneration which would undermine the very foundations of capitalism. The establishment of communities could, therefore, be seen to be a first step in that direction. In contrast, the anarchist communists, while adhering to communities as a long-term ideal, were less enthusiastic about their prospects within capitalist society.

It is understandable that less communities identified with Kropotkin than with Tolstoy, though it would be a mistake to draw too fine a distinction between the two types – they were both agreed that a society of communities would be infinitely preferable to one based on the State. There were two communities which looked more to Kropotkin's writings – the Clousden Hill Communist and Cooperative Colony near Newcastle (1895) and the Norton Colony in Sheffield (1896), and six that were essentially Tolstoyan – the Purleigh Colony in Essex (1896), the Brotherhood Workshop in Leeds (1897), the Ashingdon Colony (1897) and the Wickford Colony (1898) in Essex, the Whiteway Colony in Gloucestershire (1898) and the Blackburn Brotherhood in Lancashire (1899).

Clousden Hill Free Communist and Cooperative Colony,
Clousden Hill, Forest Hall, Newcastle
Of all the communities in this period the one most closely associated with Kropotkin's ideas was that known as the Free Communist and Cooperative Colony, a few miles north of Newcastle. It appears to have been seen, primarily, as a scientific experiment to prove that this type of system could work; and an advertisement in *The Labour Annual* announced it as 'a free communist and cooperative colony to demonstrate the superiority of free communist association, over the competitive production of today'[68]. The same point is made in a brief report which appeared in *The Clarion* in 1897:

The history of the experiment may be told in very few words. Two years ago several Newcastle Communists resolved to test, experimentally, the theories propounded by Prince Kropotkin in his work *'La Conquete du Pain'*. With that object they took a farm at Clousden Hill, consisting of twenty acres of inferior land ... There is, we believe, nothing else like it throughout the length and breadth of the British Isles. It is an experiment in Communism, as applied to farm life. In other words, a number of people who have chosen the business of agriculture are putting to the test of practice the principle of having their goods in common [69].

The 'Newcastle Communists' referred to in the report were brought together in 1895 by Frank Kapper, a Czech tailor, who was responsible for establishing the community. Others came from Denmark, Switzer-

�'ve CLOUSDEN HILL FREE COMMUNIST AND COOPERATIVE COLONY

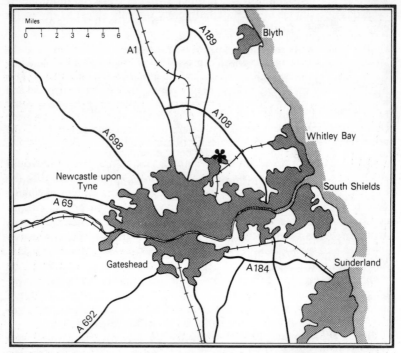

Fig. 5.2 Location of the Clousden Hill Free Communist and Cooperative Colony.

land and Belgium to number amongst the twenty or so who lived in the community during its few years of existence. They farmed about 20 acres, and Kapper provided some details of how this was done:

In taking over the above place on a twenty years lease, at an annual rental of £60, we took over from the last tenant stock consisting of hay, oats, potatoes, fruit bushes, vegetables, sixty two fowls, and various agricultural implements, at the agreed price of £100. Of this sum we have up to the present paid £75, leaving a balance of £25 yet to be paid. We have increased our livestock by one cow, one goat, two pigs, twenty two hens and chickens, six ducks, sixty four geese, eight turkeys and two pairs of rabbits, at a total cost of £38. 7s. 1d. The hay and oats we intend, if possible, to reserve for the feeding of the stock, which ought to be still more considerably increased. The sale of milk which during two months alone amounts to £7.15s.3½d. convinces us that an increase in dairy stock would mean a valuable addition to our income. We fattened the geese and turkeys and disposed of them at Christmas time at a fairly good price, a considerable portion of our outstanding accounts being part of this transaction. For intensive cultivation we have built a glass house 100 feet long by 15 feet wide, which is ready for glazing and inside fittings; and for forcing purposes we have constructed four frames, besides which many other improvements have been made [70].

And then, with the familiar dialectic between theory and practice that distinguishes the communities, Kapper switches from the minutiae of everyday life (down to the last halfpenny on milk sales) to the wider context of their efforts:

On the whole we are more than satisfied with the results of our efforts, and the same general satisfaction has been expressed by numerous visitors, including Kropotkin, Kampffmeyer, Tom Mann, and other well-known reformers . . . Our membership for the present consists of four men, two of whom are married and have small families; but with better resources at our disposal the number could be considerably increased. The number of applications which we have received clearly shows the desire of workers to return to the land, and demonstrates the necessity of agricultural colonies similar to our own [71].

On establishing the community, Kapper had vowed that there would never be any formal authority, and that if ever there was, he would be the first to leave. It appears that his intention was met and that, even when a vote was taken, it was done so only for consultative purposes, with no compulsion for the minority to accept the decision. The work was arranged, from time to time, by the members themselves, and it was found unnecessary to fix any stated number of hours for a working day. Kropotkin's contention that in a non-competitive situation the management of one's affairs could be settled without compulsion, was borne out. But so, too, were his doubts that this type of voluntary association could survive in capitalist society and, like other communities, Clousden Hill was not without its contradictions.

One of the colonists, Ben Glover, was later to recall that all those who started the colony 'were true Labour men'. He recounts how they pooled what money they came with into a common fund. There were no wages, and each got pocket money according to how the fund stood. Eating was a communal event. Yet, on the other hand, they were forced to make compromises with the outside world. As well as the support of the local Sunderland and Newcastle Cooperatives which took much of their produce, they traded with a firm in Newcastle Green market. And, in the words of Ben Glover, '. . . I had all the dances to supply them with their button-holes which brought good prices, 1s. 6d. for ladies and 1s. for gentlemen' [72].

But for all its problems and compromises the colony stayed in existence until the turn of the century, providing a valuable mainstay of experience for the northern anarchist groups. The *Free Commune* carried reports on the community, and exhorted others to follow their example. The April 1898 edition referred to a conference of northern cooperatives held at Sunderland, and an associated visit to Clousden Hill, where some of the colonists spoke of their experiences. The community finally broke up as a result of disagreements within the group, and the site has long been engulfed within the northward limits of the Newcastle conurbation.

Norton Colony,
Norton Hall, Sheffield

A year after the start of the Clousden Hill community another group of
anarchists leased a cottage and some land in the grounds of Norton Hall,
on the outskirts of Sheffield, and lived and worked communally for
about four years. It was less of a scientific experiment than Clousden
Hill, and more of an immediate commitment to lead a new way of life in
close association with the land. Edward Carpenter, who lived nearby,
was a familiar figure in the Sheffield district, urging others to leave the
city and return to the land. And the anarchist communist publication
Freedom (echoing the theme of Kropotkin's *Fields, Factories and
Workshops*) also carried articles deploring the urban way of life. 'To the
Anarchist, who places the happiness of men, women and children,
above all other aims, the freedom of the human race not merely from
authority, but also from bad surroundings, bad conditions, and hard
and uncongenial work, there can be no cry more fascinating and so full
of hope as "Back to the Land"!' [73]

Hugh Mapleton, a founder member of what was known as the Norton

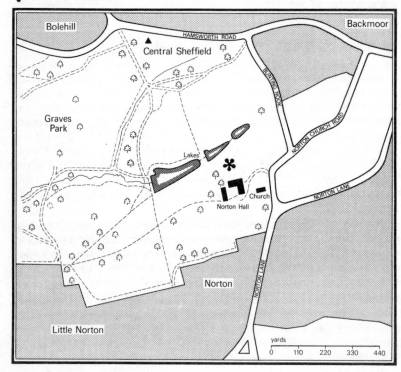

�֍ NORTON COLONY

Fig. 5.3 Location of Norton Colony.

Colony (or sometimes the Norton Community Colony) wrote of their aims and organisation:

Our little beginning here is strictly on communistic lines; we have no rules, all business is discussed and work arranged over the communal breakfast table. We commenced business about two years ago with two members; others have joined from time to time, bringing our number to seven at the present time. Our holding consists of a large garden, five greenhouses and a cottage. Our drawbacks were heavy rent, small capital and inexperience in practical horticulture.

We grow our own vegetables and fruits in fair variety. But we wisely determined to confine ourselves to very few varieties of produce for market; thus our attention was concentrated the first season on tomatoes and cucumbers and the result was a splendid crop, our tomatoes being especially praised and the flavour commended. This year our tomato crop is even larger, and we have also cucumbers, mushrooms, grapes, and many varieties of plants in pots; and our large cos lettuce has commanded the highest price in the Sheffield wholesale market.

We created a market for our tomatoes, cucumbers and mushrooms by selling them from door to door in the neighbouring villages, and although we all disliked the idea at first, yet it has been entirely successful, everything having been sold week by week, the people preferring to buy our fresh produce instead of the often stale market goods. Early last spring we commenced the sale of seeds, buying them in bulk, and this department proved very helpful just then when there was very little other income.

We also made the most of our capital by buying our food stuffs wholesale and by keeping careful accounts of all income and expenditure. With a weekly balancing we have been able to pay our way from the first, and distribute a small amount as pocket money weekly. This summer we have added sandal making to our activities; and as this form of footwear is rapidly becoming popular we hope to find this department helpful. We wear sandals ourselves, much to the astonishment of the villagers many of whom supposed we were 'Egyptians' in consequence. We hope our indoor sandals at 3/- per pair will be a means of introducing them to people who otherwise would not venture to try them.

Included in our 'Return to Nature' principles is vegetarianism, teetotalism, non-smoking, and abstention from salt, chemicals, drugs, and minerals and all fermenting and decomposing foods [74].

He also warned potential newcomers that the work was very hard, and that:

only those determined to face the monotony of hard and poorly paid labour, to sacrifice nearly all studies and recreation and to live under continuous discouragements, disadvantages and difficulties are suited to pioneer this work; men and women without backbone, grit and energy are only a drag and had better stay where they are till things are made smoother for them [75].

Another member of the community, Frank Johnson, recalled that Edward Carpenter had been the impetus behind the scheme. Carpenter never joined the community, but engaged in similar activities to the Norton anarchists. He made sandals and grew vegetables and 'to show his solidarity with the working class', stood behind his vegetable stall in Sheffield Market [76].

There were plans to make Norton a larger and more self-contained

Fig. 5.4 A group taken at Norton Hall at the time of the colony.

Fig. 5.5 Current view of Norton Hall and grounds.

community, and hopes were expressed that other groups would follow their example. Capital was always short, though, and when, in addition, the landowner refused to renew the lease the community broke up (in the spring of 1900). Some thought was given to joining the Starnthwaite Home Colony in the Lake District, but after two of the Norton colonists had visited it the idea was rejected. Among the reasons given was the belief that several small groups gradually increasing in strength would be more effective than a single large community. 'So we decided to disband and carry our ideals with us in the outside world. We were happy: we never had a quarrel. If the land had been freehold we might have been able to keep the colony going' [77].

Norton Hall still stands, its current use a private clinic. But with its grounds – once farmed in free association, in uneasy juxtaposition to the great house – now open to the people of Sheffield as a public park, something of the old contrast remains.

Purleigh Colony,
Purleigh, Essex

Of different origins to those of the Sheffield community, the Purleigh Colony was an important link between the Tolstoyan ideas that were developed at Croydon, and their subsequent application at the neighbouring Essex communities of Ashingdon and Wickford and the more important experiment at Whiteway in Gloucestershire.

After several years of discussion and more limited cooperative ventures at Croydon, it was felt that the time had come to extend what had been learnt into a fuller community setting. 'As agriculture seemed to be the basis of all constructive work . . .' [78], a land colony was preferred to a continued urban setting. Not for the first time, though, the Surrey

❈ ANARCHIST COMMUNITIES IN SOUTH ESSEX

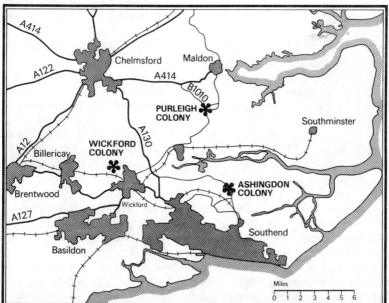

Fig. 5.6 Location of anarchist communities in South Essex in the 1890s.

countryside proved to be infertile ground for this type of venture [79]. In contrast, not for the last time, it was the less prosperous Essex countryside that yielded ground for community experiments – in this case, initially an area of 10 acres at Cocks Clark near the village of Purleigh. The first three colonists arrived in the autumn of 1896, to prepare the way for the main settlement the following spring.

The links, not simply with Tolstoyan thought, but directly with Tolstoy himself were always strong. The Croydon Brotherhood Church was the source of a number of those who went to Purleigh. Indeed, Purleigh's gain was Croydon's loss, and as a result of losing key members in this way the church soon had to close – though this was interpreted as a sign 'not of defeat, for the interest had been transferred elsewhere, and Tolstoyism was not merely talked about, but those who had gone away were now attempting to put the ideas into practice' [80]. There were also those in the community – John Kenworthy, Aylmer Maude and Vladimir Tchertkoff – who had visited or lived in Russia and were personally acquainted with Tolstoy. These links were retained throughout the period of the community's existence, and Tolstoy lent his support to the scheme in various ways. And, finally, for a time the community attracted some of the Russian Doukhobors, members of the sect that was forced to leave Russia to avoid political persecution. Together, these mixed origins created an unusual blend of Russian and English culture, in the unlikely setting of an Essex hamlet [81].

In a local newspaper report the community was described as being '. . . composed chiefly of men who have spent a city life, and a few Russians who find life in England more desirable than in their own country. One of the colonists is a Russian princess. One of the men held a good position in a London bank, and another was connected with a business firm' [82]. Understandably, it was the Russian contingent that attracted the persistent interest of visitors although, in some ways, it was the refugees from banks and businesses that offered a sharper lesson in social transformation. The sight of a princess 'hewing wood and drawing water in true Tolstoy fashion' was not an everyday encounter for an *Essex County Chronicle* reporter. Tolstoy's friend, the exiled noble, Vladimir Tchertkoff, who settled at Purleigh with his wife and son, was also an obvious source of interest. His romantic background of an aristocratic upbringing in St Petersburg, and subsequent transformation and exile on account of anarchist activity, contrasted sharply with his simple existence at Purleigh. There he and his wife entertained visitors with simple vegetarian cooking while he proclaimed that 'as long as there are starving men in the world we hold that luxury is wrong. We try to have only what is necessary for us' [83].

The spirit of Purleigh was one of tolerance – of encouraging others to '. . . wake up to the real meaning of life and follow 'their' best perceptions of right in whatever direction these may lead. None of us are likely to reach perfection in one jump' [84]. Or, as another colonist interpreted their position, 'without any intention of forming a monastic brotherhood, we each desire to develop our lives along the lines which appeal to our inner consciences. While endeavouring to cultivate a spirit that esteems others better than ourselves, we still see that if we wait till everybody toes the same line no progress will be made' [85].

Victorian summers are always recalled as being hot and sunny, and idealistic profiles were drawn of hard but cheerful labour on the land by day, followed by lengthy discussions and reading in the evening – the elusive goal of manual and intellectual labour long sought by utopians. A more restrained but informative account of how the colony took shape is provided by one of the colonists, Hubert Hammond:

Most of us have come here with the wish to live simpler and more useful lives than we found possible in our former positions. We put what money we had into one common fund, and bought with a portion ten acres of land. Four acres are now in cultivation, and the rest in pasture. In addition we have the use of six acres for a time, and vegetables are grown in the gardens of the hired cottages in which some of the colonists live. The rest of the money has been used to carry on the work necessary to the development of a colony, and to buy food.

Owing to many years of misuse and many more of disuse, the land here is rather poor, but we hope to work it up to good condition in a few years. During the first winter about three acres were dug over by the three colonists then on the land, with occasional outside help. Rather more than half-an-acre of this was deeply dug, and last autumn fruit trees were planted in it. The rest of the dug ground was treated last year in a more or less experimental manner. Potatoes helped to clean the land and supplied food, various vegetables were grown, and some patches of oats and wheat were planted. From the results we expect to be able to raise corn here in future. We also grew a very successful crop of tomatoes under glass. Some planted out-doors were not so successful.

Various buildings have been put up – a tool shed, a 100-foot green house (thirty feet fitted with heating apparatus), a workshop with carpenter's bench, a stable to accommodate a horse and pony, some fowl houses, a cow shed large enough to hold six cows, a coal shed and a six-roomed brick cottage. The cottage is occupied by the family and one of the single men, and most of the colonists come in to dinner every day.

During last year we made about 7,000 bricks, at first with the help of a practical brick maker, and afterwards by ourselves. These bricks turned out moderately successfully. Many were spoiled through lack of a kiln for burning, but there were enough good ones to build the cottage, and there are a good many left which will do for a part brick-built barn when we can afford to build it.

We have a horse which has been very useful in carting building materials, manure, etc., and a pony and cart used to carry produce and provisions to and from the railway station (about three miles off), and the nearest town – Maldon – about five miles from here.

There are two cows which are shortly to calve, two goats, and about forty hens. The majority of the colonists are vegetarians, some because they dislike the killing of animals, others because they believe a vegetarian diet is cheaper and healthier, while others occasionally eat meat.

The necessary business affairs of the colony, and details of work, are discussed and arranged at a weekly committee meeting at which all the colonists who care to, attend. Nothing is undertaken unless all the colonists are unanimous in desiring it. This arrangement has been found very satisfactory in actual working.

At the end of the business meeting all have tea together, and the evening is spent in music and other amusements, or some reading and discussion. Latterly a drill class has been held on Tuesday evenings for the younger members and anyone else who cares to come. This generally winds up with some dancing.

We most of us (the colonists and those connected with the colony) meet together on Sunday afternoons in the hope of getting spiritual help from one another. By this I mean bringing an open mind to the consideration of any subject that may be read or talked about and stating one's best thoughts on the matter. There is no fixed form of proceeding and anyone who cares to come is welcomed to these meetings. Very often Labour Church songs are sung, and the evening is spent in a more or less serious discussion, or music, or both.

We have no rules. Each one is left to do as he or she likes, held in check only by one's good sense and the general opinion of comrades. Neither have we fixed rules about the admission of new members [86]. Some have brought money with them, others have not. Usually we try to give people wishing to join a clear statement of our position, and leave it to them to decide whether they will cast in their lot with us to work towards the same ideal or not.

That ideal is to live lives worthy of men; to endeavour more and more to develop tolerance and unselfishness, and to work earnestly for a time when we can welcome all who care to come [87].

Early reports on the community were generally favourable. Outsiders were especially enthusiastic about the colonists' rapid success with intensive farming methods – such as the *Essex County Chronicle* reporter, clearly impressed at the sight of a 'forest of sunflowers', at the 'goodly store of potatoes', and the 'gay array of ripening tomatoes'. In addition to its farming the colony acquired a printing press, and took over from Croydon the work of the Brotherhood Publishing Society. As well as producing *The New Order*, it also enjoyed printing rights for the publication of Aylmer Maude's translations of Tolstoy's works [88]. The numbers who settled at Purleigh increased steadily – one estimate of the colony at its peak being sixty-five, with a further twenty-three Russian exiles. Altogether '. . . a very promising beginning with real grit among the workers' [89].

But in spite of the hopeful start, within a year or two there were reports of dissent. Apart from insanities and eccentricities within the colony, more divisive issues developed. There was, firstly, the question of whether the colony should be open to all or whether it should be selective in admitting new members. Something of a 'vanguard' approach seems to have prevailed in which those who looked as if they would fail to play a full part in the work of the community were excluded. Others thought this was not only wrong in principle but was also an example of class prejudice, discriminating against working-class entrants who lacked capital. In the event, this issue was responsible for a small group eventually leaving Purleigh to set up the new colony at Whiteway. Another issue arose over how they should market the Tolstoy translations without succumbing to commercial pressures. Formally, they held the view that all forms of business were dishonest and selfish, yet faced a dilemma which could not be resolved in such a

Figs. 5.7 and **5.8** Purleigh was a centre for Tolstoyan publishing.

Fig. 5.7 At Hill Farm a printing press produced copies of the English versions of Tolstoy's works.

Fig. 5.8 For a time, *The New Order* was also published at Purleigh.

Fig. 5.9 'Colony House' marks the site of the former community.

clear-cut way. They were also taken to task for advertising their products in *The New Order* – seen by one reader as pure competition: 'Why not wait till orders come by recommendation, which God will surely see to?' [90]. A third problem was posed by the close relationship that developed with the Doukhobors. As well as accommodating some of the refugees at Purleigh, most of the colonists were actively concerned to secure the safe resettlement of the main group. In the event, land was obtained in Canada, and some of the more experienced colonists left Purleigh to join the Doukhobors in their new settlement. Taken together, the stresses proved too much for the colony's survival, and by 1899 letters were written to Tolstoy to tell him of the collapse of the experiment.

Today there is little in the outward appearance of the village and countryside to recall the occurrence of this brief but colourful period in its history. There is the occasional physical reminder in the form of 'Colony House' at Cocks Clark, some early greenhouses on the site, and the building that once housed the Brotherhood printing press. In the main, though, what remains is an intangible spirit and vague local recollections of 'Russian anarchists who once lived on the hill'.

The Brotherhood Workshop,
Victoria Road, Leeds
In spite of the earlier examples of anarchist communities in rural settings, the establishment of the Brotherhood Workshop in 1897 in the

❈ THE BROTHERHOOD WORKSHOP

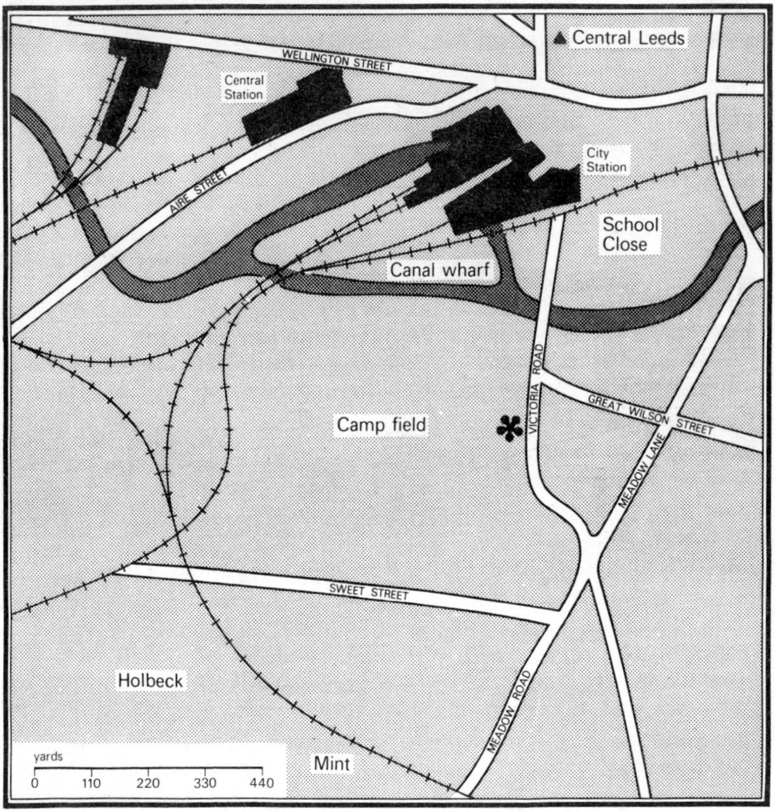

Fig. 5.10 Location of the Brotherhood Workshop in Leeds.

very centre of Leeds (and, in little more than a year later a similar enterprise in Blackburn) showed that an urban location was not incompatible with anarchist principles. Nor did it matter that the urban-based groups were making bicycles and mending electrical apparatus rather than growing lettuces and making sandals. The northern anarchists were steeped in Tolstoyan philosophy, but found the possibilities of spreading outwards in an industrial centre 'almost overwhelming in their extent' [91].

The initial group was formed largely of engineering workers who had been victimised in an industrial dispute, and who were provided with capital by a small manufacturer who was attracted to the ideas of Tolstoy:

A little while ago, one G. Gibson owned an Electrical and Cycle Engineering business and was . . . in the 'Samuel Smiles' sense, a promising young man. But alas! for our good thrift-mongers, the 'promise' is not fulfilled, for our comrade has come to the conclusion that he had been helping to perpetuate the property system and must alter his ways. In coming to this conclusion we are glad to say that he was greatly helped by the 'pernicious' teaching of J. C. Kenworthy. The upshot of it all is, that he has thrown his business into a communist workshop, and there to-day, with several other comrades, is busy making bicycles and other things, as merrily and as joyfully as one would picture men doing in the good time to come.

The organisation is entirely Anarchist and Communist in character. Each man receives according to his needs, on the basis of a common agreement, without the aid of any laws or rules. The profits from the business are to be devoted to its extension and ultimately to the establishing of a regular Communist Colony – an oasis in the desert of commercialism.

Needless to say we want to see every comrade, who needs anything in the shape of cycles, tyres, electric apparatus, etc. to patronise the place.

Good sound 'bikes' not made of gas pipes but equal to many sold at double the price can be had from £9-0-0. The address is 6, Victoria Road, Leeds [92].

As well as bicycles and electrical repairs the workshop diversified with woodwork, cobbling and tailoring. One room was put aside as a meeting room, and there were two more rooms where some of the comrades lived (with plans for further communal accommodation). With new activities and members, reports on the workshop's progress were encouraging. A year after its inception it was described as 'something like a beehive, there is plenty of work for all concerned, and gradually the thing is becoming systematised and more conducive to right relations. The spirit of the comrades is excellent and bids well for the future' [93].

Reports suggested that the anarchists were succeeding in organising a diversity of activities without curtailing individual freedom. At the same time, they were acutely conscious of the familiar contradiction between running a cooperative workshop and then having to sell their products in the open market. One of their members, Tom Ferris (who later joined the Blackburn Brotherhood) found it particularly hard to reconcile commercial practice with his firm belief in the abandonment of money. With a comrade he is reputed to have travelled without any money to Russia to visit Tolstoy. Certainly, in 1899 he visited the Whiteway colony, where he:

preached the gospel of no-money to us, asserting that it was incompatible with good Tolstoyism to use money. Money in itself had no intrinsic value, and was received as a means of exchange only because of the Government's superscription, which being based on force (soldiers, police, etc.) was morally wrong. Also, people should be content to produce to the best of their ability, share freely all they had with their fellows and trust to God for the rest. This was elaborated in an eloquent and forceful appeal. The idea caught on like the measles, and was accepted by nearly all the colonists. . . . [94]

Beyond their own circle the members gave public lectures and open-air meetings in Leeds to tell others of their work and beliefs. They claimed that socialists, anarchists and members of Christian churches were watching with curiosity and interest the success or otherwise of

Fig. 5.11 *The Free Commune* (produced at Leeds) was an important means of communication for the northern anarchists at the end of the century.

their experiment in 'industrial communism'. They numbered among their own members the experienced speaker, J. C. Kenworthy, who had been so influential at Croydon, and others who had spent some time at Purleigh and Whiteway. But although trying to convince others, they were more concerned to see 'new advances on the lines of action, than to draw a large congregation of people who, like so many around us, stop short of theory' [95].

Ashingdon Colony,
Ashingdon, Essex

The landscape along the unmade road known as The Chase in Ashingdon is evocative of anarchism in the 1890s, perched, as it was, on the very edge of established society. In spite of more recent housing, there is still in The Chase an atmosphere of untidy solitude within the semi-urban sprawl of Hockley and the South Essex conurbation. The road is narrow and deeply-rutted, the plots are large, with goats and orchards, the banks are thick with primroses and trees, and some of the cottages are weatherboarded. One such example of the latter is 'Brotherhood Cottage'; another house carries the name of 'Walden'.

The telling landscape is not matched by extensive records of the community, but it appears that the 4-acre plot in which 'Brotherhood Cottage' now stands was bought by James Evans in 1897. Evans had previously been in contact with Tolstoyan anarchism through the Brotherhood Church and was a member of the branch in Southgate Road in North London. From there he came to Ashingdon, keeping goats and growing vegetables. An advertisement in the 1897 edition of the *Labour Annual* spoke only of 'a small Anarchist Group' and invited interested parties to write to James Evans [96].

Fig. 5.12 Remains of an 'anarchist landscape' in The Chase, Ashingdon. Brotherhood Cottage (the former home of James Evans) is on the right.

There is little evidence to suggest how many responded to the invitation. One who did, Frederick M. von K. Browne (of Anarchae Keep, Ashingdon), gained some notoriety in the local press through his verbal attacks on society which the magistrates deemed to be indecent: 'The prisoner was an Anarchist and in his case anarchy expressed itself in most virulent attacks upon everyone with whom he came into contact. The indecent observations which he wrote referred not only to people to whom the remarks were addressed ... but to people generally' [97].

In 1940, 'Brotherhood Cottage' passed into the hands of Evans's son, and remained so until recently; it is now empty, the garden is overgrown and the cottage in a state of disrepair. But the links with anarchism lingered long after the collapse of the community itself, primarily through the arrival in 1941 of the Tolstoyan publisher, C. W. Daniel, who set up his press in The Chase itself. Daniel's early involvement in anarchist circles is illustrative of the world in which the Essex anarchist communities were formed – not only Ashingdon but also Purleigh (with its interest in publishing Tolstoy's works) and the Wickford Colony (with which Daniel was also associated):

In the late 1890's C. W. Daniel got his first job in publishing – in the London offices of Walter Scott, where the manager was F. R. Henderson. Henderson was an idealist, a philosophical anarchist: later on he ran the celebrated 'Bomb Shop' in Charing Cross Road, but in those days his main activity was publishing Tolstoy. Thus Daniel came under the spell of the thinker (Tolstoy) who was to be the major influence in his life. Soon he was organising a regular series of Sunday evening lectures on the great man's teaching which were given in a big first floor room in a house off the Edgware Road: the group ultimately became known as the 'London Tolstoyan Society'.

In 1902 he started his own small publishing business in Cursitor Street off Chancery Lane with the express purpose of propagating Tolstoy's ideas: he was given the agency of the Free Age Press publications of the master's works then being edited by Tchertkoff, and these books and pamphlets became his principal stock in trade. By 1908 master and disciple were in direct communication. Daniel had sent Tolstoy some copies of a monthly magazine ('The Open Road') that he published and to which he himself contributed under the pseudonym of 'The Odd Man.' Tolstoy wrote: 'I like all the pages signed by 'Odd Man'; I would be very glad to know your name and be in direct intercourse with you.' Soon, correspondence led to personal encounter. In December 1909 Daniel made the pilgrimage to Yasnaya Polyana, where by night he slept in the library and by day sat at the great man's feet ... [98].

More than forty years after James Evans had first invited others to join him, Daniels settled at Ashingdon – and until the 1950s he was still involved in spreading the Tolstoyan gospel. He returned to a part of the world where once he had contemplated his own community – a journey full-circle that mirrored a wider persistence of Tolstoyan ideas throughout this period.

Wickford Colony,
Downham, Wickford, Essex

In the same part of Essex as Purleigh and Ashingdon, and sharing the same belief in Tolstoyan ideals, another group set about establishing their own community [99]. 'Our aim is broadly to found a group of free neighbours animated by mutual goodwill, and to see what will come of it' [100].

The idea of a community grew out of the regular meetings of a group of friends ('all were in some sense socialists') at the Central Vegetarian Restaurant in London [101]. The writings of Tolstoy, especially what he had to say about non-resistance, dominated their discussions, and links were soon established with the Croydon Brotherhood and the Purleigh Colony. Arnold Eiloart, who was a member of the Purleigh Colony, brought to what might have been simply abstract discussions the benefit of his practical experience, and it was not long before the group looked for their own land.

In the event, they were not prepared to go as far as the Purleigh colonists – 'the members of this new group are not able to shake themselves so free from their commercial fetters, and to this extent fall far short of the example set by their fearless brothers' [102]. When it came to it, the attraction of Wickford was as much a question of easy access to a cheap and fast rail connection with London where the colonists could continue to earn a regular income, as one of proximity to their 'fearless brothers' at Purleigh. It was for this reason that it was first known as a 'Colony for City Men'.

In the longer term, though, they had hopes of encouraging wider social change, based on the familiar belief among communitarians that a working example of freedom and cooperation would serve to activate others. Henry Power (who was a member of the Croydon Brotherhood, and a founder member of the Wickford Colony) was far from underestimating the enormity of their task but believed that a start, however small, should be made:

The motives actuating this movement are those at the back of every such movement, and briefly stated consist in a desire to cultivate a more helpful and brotherly feeling towards each other, and to neutralise, according to our strength, the effect of generations of selfish competitive struggle, the evils of which are so manifest in the lives of all of us. Most of the members have reached their present state of mind by a slow process of evolution. They feel that it is useless waiting for the millennium, but hope to get a little nearer to it by endeavouring to act on the brotherly precepts. At least, they hope it will be found practicable to show their children the possibilities of a more social, helpful and truthful life than most of us have had the opportunity of realising, and perhaps this is as much as can be expected of the present generation.

Some people accuse us of building 'Castles in the air'. It is certainly not a mere affair of brick and mortar, or comfortable conditions that we are after. Our projected move amounts to a confession which comparatively few at present understand. The sympathy of that few strengthens us [103].

After discussing what would be the ideal arrangement, the group settled, in the summer of 1898, for the purchase of 29 acres of land and three cottages, at a total cost of £700. The site of the former community, nearly opposite Downham Hall, to the south of Downham Church, overlooks the Thames Valley. It is an attractive site, and understandable that the group of thirty-three who met there on the 23 July 1898 in order to assess its suitability were well pleased with what they found: 'The land was visited in the afternoon and general satisfaction was expressed as to its suitability to the purposes of the group. The beauty of the surrounding country was also generally appreciated' [104].

It was announced in *The New Order* that the intention was to divide the land into lots of 1 acre or more, and to allow members to subscribe for as many as they thought to be necessary. The plots could be paid for in one sum or by monthly subscription, and after the first round of claims, none had applied for more than 3 acres.

The move towards a more complete system of cooperation was to be taken slowly. For a start, the various plots were conveyed separately, and could be cultivated along the lines each of them thought best. There was a conscious attempt to avoid compelling anyone to adhere to a particular system – 'perfect freedom is the watchword of the colony' [105]. But there was also confidence that a more cooperative system would naturally evolve from a group of people who shared similar aims and ideals, and who would be drawn closer together in their common tasks. So, while the land was separately conveyed no fences were built to divide one plot from another and, from the outset, they were engaged in discussing ways of working the land in common. The same was true for building their own houses. There was talk of using building societies on an individual basis in the first place, with hopes for more cooperative methods as time went on.

The evolution of a fully-developed cooperative system at Downham was not to be, however, and it achieved nothing of the acclaim that was accorded to Purleigh. In any case, by that time, the interest of Tolstoyans was switching away from Essex to the Gloucestershire Cotswolds where, in the Whiteway Colony, the fullest expression of this type of anarchist ideal was already taking form.

Whiteway Colony, Whiteway, Gloucestershire

I do not remember that rain ever fell in that sweet Arcady; probably it did . . . If our feet were down in the potato trenches, our heads were up in the stars. We felt we were gods [106].

Whiteway occupies a special place in the history of the communities. For one thing, it survived (albeit with modifications) over a longer period than other English communities, and there are lessons to draw from that alone. Endurance is normally the product either of firm rules and adherence to a particular doctrine or, like Whiteway, of adaptation to new situations. From an initial commitment to Tolstoyan ideals the group shifted towards a Proudhonian form of individual possession, with a later injection of what they regarded as a more materialistic type of anarchism. There were lingering attempts in the 1920s and 1930s to retain a communal hold over its future, but gradually it assumed a more individualistic character.

For another thing, Whiteway is significant because it was such an open and wide-ranging experiment, embodying many areas of potential change. With the belief that 'true fellowship' was indeed possible on earth, and with a common abhorrence of the industrial system, the Whiteway communitarians tried to restructure all that they had found wrong in established society. They rejected the city in favour of the country, they opposed any form of private property (and some of them refused to use money at all times), they were pacifist and practised non-resistance in their own lives, they worked towards equality for women in the community, they favoured free union rather than State marriage, they looked for more liberating forms of clothing for both men and women, and (like so many of their predecessors) their pacifist philosophy was matched with a vegetarian diet.

The Whiteway Colony is in the tradition of the Croydon Brotherhood and the Purleigh Colony. Reference has already been made to the dissent at Purleigh over the question of selection, and further disagreements developed over the extent to which Tolstoyan orthodoxy should be enforced (particularly regarding insistence on hard work, and the question of sexual abstinence as a virtue). Those who felt that their freedom was being threatened at Purleigh decided to look for a new site, where all would be welcome and none excluded on account of their work output or views on sex. The outcome of their search was Whiteway in Gloucestershire:

forty-two acres of hilly ground with limestone rock underneath, quite shallow soil in parts, only really deep in the depressions and the valley, along which ran a small stream. In the middle of this unsheltered land, for there was not a single tree on it, stood a bare stone house, flat fronted, two storied, with two rooms on the ground floor, two on the second floor, and an attic running over both. The country in the immediate neighbourhood was most lovely and romantic, but our house and land were excessively plain [107].

At the outset, in August 1898, the small group (eight to start with, though others were already making arrangements to join) split into two factions – a 'village group', which saw its future in small industries and integration in the life of the nearby village of Sheepscombe, and a 'land group' at Whiteway itself, with farming as its main activity. It was intended that the two groups would support each other, but most joined Whiteway, and the few who were associated with Sheepscombe were never so committed to a communal way of life.

On the surface, many of the early descriptions of Whiteway exude a world of idyllic fantasy and political naivety. 'Perfect weather, agreeable companionship, raking, turning the sweet-smelling hay, then piling it in

❋ WHITEWAY COLONY

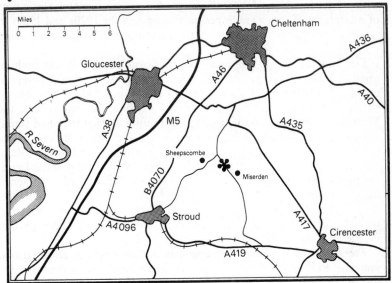

Fig. 5.13 Location of Whiteway Colony.

heaps, taking our refreshment and rest in the shade of the haycocks, working on even until the moon rose in the sky, going home at night tired and happy feeling that at last we had done some *real work*' [108]. The community survived its first year on 'the two living principles of freedom of action and goodwill towards everybody', and friendships and understanding were cemented in the hot summer of 1899. Tolstoyan brotherhood was possible, but readers of *The New Order* were warned that, like the Kingdom of God it could only be reached by hard climbing [109].

Yet it is important to extract from the world of fantasy the substance of a serious political challenge that was inherent in their new way of life. During the first years the land was worked communally on the basis of voluntary cooperation, meals were prepared and eaten together, and there was a common laundry. Their belief in common property was demonstrated symbolically through the burning of the deeds of property, and a proclamation that the land in question would never again be held privately. There was no formal organisation, and no leaders. Possessions in the community were freely available to all, including outsiders, on the principle that things should belong to those who need them most. Abuse of what many saw as their bountiful behaviour was met with non-resistance.

The women in the community enjoyed more freedom than they had previously experienced in Victorian society. Nellie Shaw (who came from Croydon to help start the community) told a young women's class that 'the women do exactly the same kind of work as the men, and do not find it too tiring' [110]. In her rightful exultation, what she failed to say was that the reverse was not true – it was a step towards equality, but limited by the failure of the men at Whiteway to abandon their own work in favour of domestic chores. Shaw was also an advocate of 'rational dress', which took the form of a freer, more practical style of clothing than convention normally permitted. There was freedom to choose whether to marry or not, but free union was generally favoured as an important branch of Tolstoyan teaching. 'Those of us who were attempting to go the full length of the Tolstoyan teaching welcomed the idea of free unions as a great improvement on legal marriage, in which, according to law, a woman became a chattel, being ringed and labelled as a man's property, losing even her name in marriage – almost her identity' [111]. Inevitably, this practice attracted no shortage of external criticism, an attack on free union being used as an effective way to undermine the moral standing of the community.

Their vegetarian diet, too, was a conscious attempt to practice a doctrine of non-aggression:

We live simply and economically. Bread and a little butter, porridge and tea or cocoa for breakfast; beans, lentils, or some other pulse, cooked with onions and potatoes are the chief dishes at dinner time, varied occasionally with rice, rhubarb, or wholemeal pudding, or bread and cheese. We never have jam or cake unless it is given to us, and then it is much appreciated [112].

The bread was baked in a brick oven by Sud Protheroe (who had learnt his art while at Purleigh Colony), and in time it became his full-time activity, with customers in Stroud and Cheltenham.

But for all its early achievements it was not without its problems. The hot summer was followed by a cold winter, with only a meagre supply of food and material comforts, while the policy of free-entry attracted those who clearly exploited the rest of the community. Like others before it, Whiteway might well have collapsed but, instead, at the end of the second year they jettisoned their principles of pure communism and took a new course. One of the pioneer colonists explained the reversal:

The communal system of working went on for a couple of years, and experience showed clearly enough that a change of methods was necessary. Free harmonious communism is possible only among people who have the utmost consideration for each other and who are ready at all times to be as exacting with themselves as any employer could possibly be. . . . It seems to be a law of human progress that pressure is inevitably put on from without until such time as people put it on from within themselves. Certain people had drifted into Whiteway with the idea that freedom consisted in throwing off all external restraint and giving the reins to every whim and desire that came across them [113].

Abandoning communism might well have been regarded as a setback, but it seems to have been treated more as a relief, exchanging one system for another which they felt would work better. Their intention had never been blindly doctrinaire, but always more pragmatic.

Figs. 5.14, 5.15 and **5.16** Housing at Whiteway.

Fig. 5.14 The bricks and hut were made in 1901 by William Sinclair (standing by the door) for his own use. It was a significant act in the move away from the original ideal of 'free harmonious communism'.

Fig. 5.15 and **Fig. 5.16** Later buildings have developed their own distinctive style.

We do not set ourselves up as reformers of society, but try to reform ourselves ... Wearing reformed dress, and educating public opinion in that way is better than making other people semi-reformed dress; and growing potatoes and cabbages, or building, is better than adding up people's banking accounts. To live as far as possible up to our idea is what we are striving for [114].

The original system was replaced with a form of individualism, though one based on possession rather than legal ownership. It was agreed that each of the colonists should take responsibility for as much land as they could reasonably work – in practice this generally amounted to 2 or 3 acres. The habit of communal eating also ceased; the communal washing of clothes continued for a while longer, until 'each man had to wash his own shirt, and so disappeared the last vestige of communism'[115]. The main thrust of innovation was over, though the arrival of a new group of anarchists from the Continent in the First World War provided a brief new lease of life. Thirty years after its inception, Nellie Shaw reflected on the various waves of newcomers to Whiteway:

Fig. 5.17, 5.18 and **5.19** Views of Whiteway.

Fig. 5.17 Colonists building the Hall in 1925.

Fig. 5.18 Current view of the Hall.

Fig. 5.19 'Protheroe's Bakery and Stores', which started when Sud Protheroe baked bread for the colonists, and developed into a full-time business with sales in the surrounding towns and villages.

The principle of 'dilution' has been steadily at work since the first days. There were giants in those days, says the Book of Genesis, and some of our first colonists were indeed spiritual 'giants', by whom we could measure ourselves and see how puny we were by comparison. The next settlers, the young married people, were sincere, earnest folk, with their ideas of 'back to the land' and simple productive work. Then came the continental anarchists, who brought in a totally different trend of thought, materialistic and psychoanalytical, but they had the courage of their convictions and were distinctly people of character. But now, of late years, we have been joined by some whom it is difficult to place or find reason for their presence here, for idealism seems to play no part, nor the desire to get 'back to the land'; also they evince very little community spirit [116].

In spite of Shaw's disappointment at what she saw as the dilution of the pioneer spirit, Whiteway has never completely reverted to the system of private property that is normally practised elsewhere. Plots were allocated according to what was needed until all the land was used up. A committee of residents currently has a say in how it should be allocated when people leave, and Whiteway is still known locally as 'the colony' [117]. There are also striking physical reminders of its early history – the community hall (built as a collective effort in 1925), Protheroe's bakery, some of the early wooden houses, and the spacious plots which were once their main source of livelihood. Contrasted with the neighbouring village of Miserden, trim and aristocratic, one can sense, too, something of the spirit of freedom for which Whiteway initially stood.

Whiteway had to make compromises to survive, but always in pursuit of freedom. It is interesting that Nellie Shaw herself regarded survival as something which should not be bought at any cost, and she compared the continuing free spirit of Whiteway with the restrictions of the enduring Shaker communities in America:

Whiteway was born of an idea; it was a 'love child'. Nothing was planned or arranged, hence much of its spontaneous charm and also many of its shortcomings. Undoubtedly, had we formulated a scheme, made rules as to work, thought out the means by which we could continue when our small amount of capital was exhausted; above all, restricted our numbers to those who actually thought on the same lines as we did, we might have had something like a cohesive community, but at the cost of our liberty and also our intellectual and spiritual growth and development.

The Shaker Community in America, by practising celibacy and working very industriously, has achieved great wealth, but at a terrible cost; for they are hidebound and prejudiced in their mental outlook, their natural feelings held in abeyance, living an unnatural life, their numbers only kept up by the fact of widows and widowers with families of children joining them. So with us, material success might have been gained at the price of spiritual sterility [118].

As a last word, another of the pioneer colonists, Joseph Burtt, wrote that 'materially, Whiteway failed, as it was bound to do, but it can only be rightly judged by the ideals which brought it into being' [119].

The Blackburn Brotherhood,
Blackburn, Lancashire

J. C. Kenworthy, who had been active at Croydon and instrumental in starting the Brotherhood Workshop in Leeds, was also responsible for carrying the message of Tolstoy across the Pennines to Blackburn. It seems that, as early as 1895, Kenworthy had been invited to speak at meetings that were sponsored by the Independent Labour Party. He paid two visits and implanted the idea of a Brotherhood Church in

❋ THE BLACKBURN BROTHERHOOD

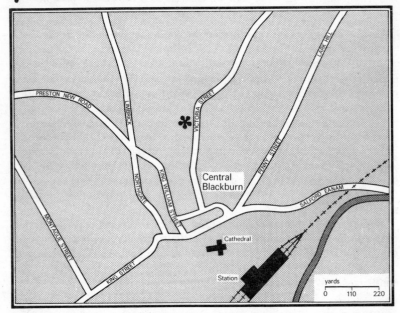

Fig. 5.20 Location of the Blackburn Brotherhood in central Blackburn.

Blackburn. The idea was eventually taken up and, in early 1899, the group involved acquired their own premises at 35, Victoria Street. There were about ten of them at the start, including Tom and Lilian Ferris who came from the Leeds community. Their message was a mixture of hope and humility: 'We in Blackburn are like a city set on a hill; and it is a source of wonder to us that our tendency towards a simpler, truer and, therefore, happier way of living should be deserving of so much notice. One realises at once both the strenuous need of a right example and inadequacy of one's fulfilment of it' [120].

Described as an offshoot of the Leeds group, it shared both its urban character and its Tolstoyan principles of organisation. The main activity of the Blackburn Brotherhood was the repair of electrical apparatus, and a sign in their window which announced that this was undertaken on 'non-commercial' lines aroused understandable local interest. Alongside examples of their work in the shop window were copies of Tolstoy's books and pamphlets.

Tom Ferris explained to a puzzled visitor that:

we call ourselves a church because we believe in Christ; we call ourselves the Brotherhood Church for want of a better name, and we read and circulate the writings of Tolstoy not because we are his followers, or recognise him as our head or teacher, but because we think his conception of the ideal life is the nearest to ours, and we think his literature among the best we can publish [121].

Fig. 5.21 35, Victoria Street. The shop window where a sign once advertised electrical work on 'non-commercial' lines, and which displayed copies of Tolstoy's works, now contains second-hand furniture.

In essence, what they were trying to do was to put into practice the principles of the Sermon on the Mount, and Ferris traced the previous efforts to do this – first at Croydon, and then to Purleigh, Leeds and Whiteway. They believed that love is the denial of force, even of resistance to evil by any form of compulsion; that truth involves perfect openness and sincerity in all dealings, that spiritual life is only coexistent with entire purity; and that these principles when carried out would bring peace and goodwill to all:

We believe in the kingdom of heaven upon earth, which embodies everything good that is in socialism without its attendant disadvantages. We believe in the socialist's principles, but insist on their being carried out by Christian methods. I don't see the slightest reason why a number of people, holding the convictions which I have expressed, should not form a society within society, which should be an example of communism such as was realised in the early Christian Church [122].

It was recognised that the fulfilment of their principles amounted to a total revolution, but that a start could be made through individual and communal acts of truth. One such act at Blackburn was to practice the no-money principle:

We say that where exchange comes in love is not. Now you see how it is that I cannot accept money payment for what I do as an electrical engineer. If anyone came to me and requested me to do some electrical work, I would do it cheerfully, only they would have to provide the materials. Not having them I cannot give them, and not using money I cannot buy them. If I had the materials I would give them also. But I could not accept payment for work [123].

In fact, only Tom and Lilian Ferris went to these lengths, and the rest of the community found the abandonment of money too drastic at that stage.

More difficult than getting agreement on single issues like the no-money principle was that of developing a true understanding of each other and of what was believed to be right, which was essential for their high ideals of spiritual community. Their reports on the availability of work, and the increasing numbers who attended their meetings were encouraging, compared with their recognition of the spiritual barriers that had to be crossed. Practical experience strengthened their belief that the only difficulties in living the right life were internal, not external [124].

The truth is that it was probably both internal and external difficulties which rendered their ideal of a 'society within a society' beyond reach. It appears that the community did not persist for very long, and that it did not diversify its activities, even to the extent of their comrades in Leeds [125].

Chapter 6

Appraisal

In the preceding chapters an explanation has been offered as to why the communities came into being. A consistent theme has been that their origins are located within a general process of historical change, and are the product of specific material conditions rather than of individual whim and eccentricity. The communities have variously taken on the dual role of a political method to achieve wider changes in society, and that of a social end in itself – the form of a new social order. It is in respect of both these roles that the communities can be evaluated.

The intention for the rest of this chapter is threefold. It is, in the first place, to evaluate the relative success of the nineteenth-century communities. In effect, did they achieve in any way what they set out to do? The second intention is to bring the history of the communities up to date, and to locate the nineteenth-century experience within a continuing historical process. It will be suggested that the renewed phases of community formation in the twentieth century can also be explained in relation to the conditions of industrial capitalism, together with a more universal resistance to State centralisation. A final section will draw together some general comments on the relative evidence of communities in different periods.

6.1 The communities and nineteenth-century change

There is a sharp division of views between those which assess alternative communities as being radical and innovatory, and those which see them as being conservative and even counter-productive to social change. This division is not simply one that has emerged with hindsight, but was a constant source of tension throughout the period of their existence. The extravagant claims and excitement within the communities themselves was constantly tempered by outright opposition or, more tellingly, by the effective indifference of most of society.

In itself, the empirical record of the communities is not impressive. Throughout the century, at a time of massive urbanisation and population increase, the alternative communities never amounted to more than a handful. The numbers living within any of these were few, and the duration of most of the settlements was short. There were periods (notably the 1840s and the 1890s) when there was something of a collective impact, but even at these times they remained very much a minority form of revolutionary activity. In the 1897 edition of the *Labour Annual* (a year book of 'industrial progress and social welfare'), only two pages are devoted to recording progress in the various communities at that time. There were also long periods, such as the third quarter of the century, when evidence of any new communities is sparse. Although alternative communities represented one way of countering capitalism, in terms of the numbers they attracted over the nineteenth century as a whole, it was a way that never had more than a minority appeal. The fact remains that the main thrust of protest took the form of mass working-class movements rather than a commitment to isolated communities. It was the cooperative movement, Chartism, the new trade unions, the growing struggle for parliamentary reform, and revolutionary socialist factions towards the end of the century, which attracted the greater share of working-class involvement. While the communitarians toiled in their few acres, and dreamt of a world transformed, the major battles for change were taking place elsewhere.

'Sitting among the dandelions'

Significantly, the capitalists, whose system the communitarians were committed to replace, generally took little notice of their efforts. Only in the few cases when the communities assumed national renown was there a serious response from political and religious leaders. There were also, at times, local attacks on the communities, on account of the threat it was claimed that they posed to the morals of 'respectable neighbours'. The villagers of Staunton in Gloucestershire, for instance, were doubly affronted to find not one, but two, rebel communities on their doorstep! [1].

But, for all the concern of indignant moralists and neighbours, capitalism was in no serious danger. What is more, the communities were, in most cases, heavily dependent on the rest of society for their early development. The Owenite communities, for instance, relied on private capital for their establishment, and were forced into a contradictory declaration as to their true intent. In launching his Devon community, Jasper Veysey gave the assurance that 'capitalists who are friendly to the system, have here we think an opportunity for the safe investment of their funds' [2]. And most of the communities were dependent on local markets for their produce. Established society was assured, in economic terms alone, that isolated examples of radical, if not revolutionary, behaviour could quite easily be contained.

As such, the communities were treated more as an item of social interest than as a threat. Their progress was regularly reported in established newspapers and journals and, particularly in the early communities, this interest frequently took the form of organised visits. There was, paradoxically, prestige to be gained from the presence of an eminent personage, and records of the Owenite and Chartist communities, especially, are adorned with the names of visiting princes and government ministers. In addition there were organised tours and gala days, with processions from nearby towns, salad teas provided by the colonists, bands and speeches on the green. The ritual of the visit expressed the role of communities as phenomena that were both outside the normal run of working-class existence and aspirations, and which were at the same time harmless to the ruling class – worthy of inspection by the rest of society, in the way that the *voyeur* sees but does not partake.

Instead, it was not from the capitalist, but from rival radical factions that the communities attracted most opposition. Over most of the period the communities were no more of a challenge to alternative political movements than they were to capitalism itself. And yet, perhaps remembering the brief period before 1848 when communities exhibited a real potential as vanguards of the new society, there was always the feeling that they could only serve to distract working-class support from more urgent activities. It was Marx and Engels who, in their critique of utopian socialism, raised the spectre of communities – ironically, at the very time that the 'golden age' of communitarianism had passed.

From 1848 Marx and Engels developed a case against communitarianism, in favour of a new strategy for political change, namely 'scientific socialism'. The contribution of the early socialists in criticising existing society is recognised, but their schemes – which were presented before the true nature of the emerging class conflict between bourgeoisie and proletariat could be seen – are dismissed as 'merely utopian'. They showed no relation to historical forces, and Engels asserted that they might equally have been presented 500 years earlier [3]. All they were based upon was the inventiveness of their designers:

Future history resolves itself, in their eyes, into the propaganda and the practical carrying out of their social plans . . . they reject all political, and especially all revolutionary, action; they wish to attain their ends by peaceful means, and endeavour, by small experiments, necessarily doomed to failure, and by the force of example, to pave the way for the new social Gospel [4].

What was seen to be more inhibiting to change was that the critical impulse that was evident amongst the first utopian socialists had already been overtaken by historical events:

In proportion as the modern class struggle develops and takes definite shape, this fantastic standing apart from the contest, these fantastic attacks on it, lose all practical value and all theoretical justification. Therefore, although the originators of these systems were, in many respects, revolutionary, their disciples have, in every case, formed mere reactionary sects. . . .They still dream of experimental realisation of their social Utopias, of founding isolated 'phalansteries', of establishing 'Home Colonies', of setting up a 'Little Icaria' duodecimo editions of the New Jerusalem – and to realise all these castles in the air, they are compelled to appeal to the feelings and purses of the bourgeois [5].

There had always been doubts as to whether communities were the best way to proceed, but after 1848 new schemes seldom escaped the uncompromising criticism of the scientific socialists. The main theoretical response – arguing for immediate social reconstruction, if necessary in advance of political changes – came with the development of anarchism [6]. But even among the anarchists there were those who were not prepared to support the establishment of communities before a political revolution. Bakunin dismissed the idea of agrarian colonies as:

... beautiful, extremely magnanimous and noble, but scarcely realizable. Even if they do succeed somewhere it will be a drop in the ocean, and a drop is far from sufficient to prepare, rouse, and liberate our people; it will take many resources and a great deal of vital energy, and the results will be negligible.... Let them try it if they see no alternative, but at the same time let them recognize that this is too little, much too little to liberate and save our martyred people.

The other path is the militant one of insurrection. That is the one we believe in, and it is the only one from which we expect salvation [7].

Later in the century the parliamentary socialists joined the attack by portraying the communities as 'withdrawals from the general fray' as opposed to 'the duty of maintaining one's place in the individualist scrummage and pushing for socialism there'[8]. Or, as George Bernard Shaw phrased it – 'one to sit among the dandelions, the other to organise the docks' [9]. As the intellectual voice of parliamentary socialism, the Fabian Society – which had itself been conceived in a dispute as to whether the right way to change society was through communities or through a political pressure group – was an articulate opponent of communities:

Home colonisation and all cognate experiments in sectional communism are distinctly foreign to the Fabian method. This society first arose out of an association for the purpose of communal life, which came near to such an experiment, but which, after a careful examination into the history of the numerous attempts which had already been made in England and America, deliberately abandoned that purpose, and advisedly and expressly excluded it from its methods of action as more likely to retard than to advance the attainment of socialist aims [10].

Among the communitarians, too, there were doubts. Ruskin, for instance, who actively promoted his own schemes, speculated whether it was not, perhaps, all a little too late – 'mere raft-making amidst irrevocable wreck' [11]. And in the case of Chartism the movement was split on the question of communities. While Feargus O'Connor argued that his land schemes would pave the way for lasting change and that they would in no way distract from the achievement of the Charter, his opponents in turn warned working men to reject the schemes which could only be a government plot to stifle in embryo the movement for the full nationalisation of land and property. Even Nellie Shaw, for all her enthusiasm with Whiteway, conceded that it was 'impossible to live in a capitalist world and not become mixed up in it' [12].

Factional struggles were part and parcel of the community

movement. A rare reminder that they were all working towards common ends, opposed to the capitalist system, came in correspondence to the *Labour Annual* in 1900:

The reformers' army can well spare a few sappers and miners for this arduous task. At the worst, the development of character and deepening of experience which always results to those who thus boldly take their welfare in their hands, and go out to seek new forms of life under the sun and stars, is a gain. To us who do not follow their path, their example may be a stimulus to the work we have chosen. . . . The fortresses of injustice, inequality, and all evil, are very many and very strong; they must be assailed from many sides [13].

But apart from the opposition of local villagers, and factional struggles over the best way to overthrow capitalism, there were also important internal reasons why the communities failed to make a greater impact. For a start, the communitarians faced serious practical difficulties – a shortage of suitable land, the lack of training of many of them in farming and self-sufficiency techniques, and inadequate capital to support them through their first harvests. The chances were that they could not survive the difficult initial years, and yet most of their experiments were intended to be long-term. The point was made by the nineteenth-century observer, George Holyoake, that it takes much longer to build a new society than a new technology:

Schemes of social life require the combination of means and intelligence, and have to be attempted many times before they succeed. . . . Establishing a new world is naturally a more elaborate and protracted work than establishing a new manufacture. Electro-plating turbulent and competitive man with pacific and co-operative habits, is a more serious affair than electroplating metals [14].

There are also more fundamental reasons for their lack of durability. The question of leadership and direction is illustrative. While the communities were generally committed to the idea of a cooperative society, there was a marked tendency to subvert this idea to the more immediate attraction of following a leader who claimed to know the way forward. In place of collectively-formed objectives it was not un-common for communitarians to fall in behind a charismatic figure, with the result that the communities persisted for only as long as the leader remained in favour or control of his own faculties. In more than one case the motive force behind the community foundered with the emotional collapse of their leader. As well as the question of leadership, there was also the persistent question as to whether or not there should be a selection process for new entrants. Unlike the political vanguards in other factions, there was a tendency to allow free access, with the result that there was an undoubted mixture of motivations and abilities. For some the communities were a positive force for change, and for others a means of escape from the pressures of the rest of society. At times, they also offered the attraction of temporary refuge from an impoverished winter – 'until the mild spring sun tempts them to a freer life' [15].

Understandably, those communities which did manage to survive over a long period have attracted special attention as possible exemplaries of the process. In particular, attention has frequently been directed to the sectarian communities in the United States which have a very much better record of survival than their secular counterparts (either in that country or in England). Kanter (1972) (A) has provided details of nine communities and societies (with more than one community) in nineteenth-century America, lasting for more than thirty years, and all were of sectarian origins.

The temptation has been to attribute this longevity simply to the cohesive force of absolute standards of religious belief and social practice – the view that this type of community is held together by an unquestioning obedience. Some writers have tempered this view by taking account of other factors – like Charles Nordhoff, who, on the basis of his personal observations, looked to the material source of religious dissent for a fuller explanation: 'I believe that success depends – together with a general agreement in religious faith, and a real and spiritual religion leavening the mass – upon another sentiment – upon a feeling of the unbearableness of the circumstances in which they find themselves ... communism is a mutiny against society' [16]. Writing at the turn of the century, Morris Hillquit dismissed the religious argument, and related the longevity of these communities to the presence of a large number of German peasants – 'experienced farmers and men of modest needs' [17] – who were capable of making a success of an agrarian venture.

There is the alternative view that if communities are committed to change then there are structural reasons why they cannot – and, indeed, should not – survive over a long period. Where they have, in fact, endured, the view is that they have done so either at the expense of individual freedom, on the basis of unbending rules and restrictions on behaviour (as in the case of some of the sectarian communities), or through so many compromises that their original political aspirations no longer hold good. A more helpful measure of their relative success might be less one of longevity, and more one of their role as a seedbed for new ideas. Significantly, the only secular community in England to survive into the twentieth century was Whiteway, and this it could do only by abandoning its original principles of 'pure communism'.

'A commitment to process'

It is right to be sceptical about the achievements of the communities. They did not transform Albion into their New Jerusalem, and at the end of the century capitalism was more firmly rooted than at the start. Yet to leave a critique at that level – on the basis of their limited numbers, the few years they survived, and the empirical evidence of failure – would be to present only part of the story. Instead, it is necessary to look more closely at the 'process' of community formation – at how the communities related to established society and how the participants themselves were involved.

There is, firstly, the point that (regardless of whether they were effective or not in terms of immediate achievement) the communities represented a moral challenge to the existing order. They were sustained, without exception, by a holistic view of an alternative society – a view which shared common assumptions, from one community to another. It rested on an underlying belief that humans are either naturally good or, at least, would recognise it not to be in their interest to be bad – but that they had been corrupted by the persistent hold of the Established Church and by the rise of urban-based capitalism. It was believed that given the restoration of a less constrained setting (of a type that was often assumed to have existed in a more natural age) the inherent goodness of human nature would be released to the benefit of each and all. The establishment of communities would enable this natural development by providing an environment where individuals would be freed from the moral interference of religious doctrine, and from the alienating oppression of the capitalist system of ownership and wage-labour. In the communities, production and consumption would be in their own hands, but governed by principles of cooperation rather than competition. Society would be changed over a period through their example and persuasion, rather than by sudden and violent revolution.

While the communities have been frequently criticised for isolating themselves from the general struggle, the fact remains that most of them went to considerable lengths to spread their particular version of the alternative society. It is no coincidence that a number of the communities accommodated printing presses which were used to spread the message through pamphlets, handbills, newspapers and books. Far from cutting themselves off from the rest of society, they took numerous opportunities to identify with the wider working-class struggle and, on their own account, to persuade others to follow their example. They spoke out against the evils of established society, and looked forward to an alternative where communities would no longer be an exception – like the Owenites who envisaged a 'happy band of communities' from Harmony Hall in Hampshire to the Hodsonian Community on the Cambridgeshire fens; or J. Bruce Wallace's more formalised scheme, fifty years later, for a 'voluntary cooperative commonwealth'.

Alternative communities were, in this sense, society's conscience – constantly exposing where it was going wrong and providing glimpses of how very different things could be. But it was not simply a finger wagging from the pulpit. It is more instructive, perhaps, to understand alternative communities and established society as a dialectical relationship, in the way that Karl Mannheim, for instance, has related utopian thought to the existing order. The value of utopias is not that they are realised *in toto* – if that were the criterion they would, like alternative communities, be regarded as unqualified failures. Instead, Mannheim's argument is that every age gives rise to ideas and values which represent the unrealised and unfulfilled tendencies of that age. These intellectual elements then become the explosive material for bursting the limits of the existing order. In other words, the existing order gives birth to utopias which in turn break the bonds of the existing order, leaving it free to develop in the direction of the next order of existence. To different degrees the alternative communities introduced ideas and forms of organisation that were in contradiction to the established order, and which represented the aspirations of a revolutionary process that took a variety of forms and was to continue long after the communities themselves had disappeared [18].

As well as seeing communities as a challenge to society in a general process of historical change, it is important to recognise them as immediate revolutionary acts in their own right. Their philosophy was one of political change through social revolution, rather than the reverse, and while they may have had little effect beyond their own boundaries, one must acknowledge the likely depth of experience for those who actually participated in the experiments. Their importance might be assessed less in terms of their material impact, and more in terms of what Rosabeth Kanter (referring to contemporary American communes) describes as a 'commitment to process rather than structure' [19].

Without adequate personal case histories it would be purely speculative to suggest individual levels of fulfilment and the personal meaning of involvement. There is sufficient evidence, though, in letters to newspapers at the time, reports in their own journals, and observations by visitors to note the occurrence at times of an almost ecstatic belief that a revolutionary process was being lived through. And as a means of heightening political awareness the process of alternative forms of organisation, where each and every institution of society could be undone and rebuilt in a new form, must have been immense. If only for short periods, time and again the communities appeared capable of arousing powerful concentrations of revolutionary potential, and of engendering unusual levels of commitment and faith.

As a political strategy the communities were founded on the indivisibility of theory and practice – on the value of direct action. No matter how incomplete its fulfilment, the essence of the communitarian belief is to close the gap between the outlines of a new order and the steps that have to be taken to achieve it:

we must create here and now the space *now* possible for the thing for which we are striving, so that it may come to fulfilment *then*; (the communitarian) does not believe in the post-revolutionary leap, but he does believe in revolutionary continuity ... in a continuity in which revolution is only the accomplishment, the setting free and extension of a reality that has already grown to its true possibilities [20].

Finally, one must not neglect the tangible achievements of the communities. While they failed to transform the whole of society, they made undoubted progress in specific fields. Reference has been made in earlier chapters to their achievements in applying and advancing methods of intensive farming. In spite of frequent difficulties encountered by communitarians with an urban background the quality of their farming was widely appreciated. Nordhoff noted the same thing in the American communities, where 'almost without exception the communists are careful and thorough farmers' [21]. There was no lack of originality, too, in their ideas on many of the accepted features of everyday life – with alternative ideas on education, on the place of the family and relative roles of men and women, on the balance and integration of work and leisure, on modes of dress, and on inventions and labour-saving devices (ranging from idiosyncratic contraptions like the model railway to carry dishes at Harmony Hall, to more applicable ideas on ventilation and efficient laundries). On the question of food they were. in the vanguard of concern for a more balanced and wholesome diet, and through their example and in their writings did much to advance the case for vegetarianism. And while the standard of living in the communities was generally frugal, for many it was to mean a material improvement on what they had previously experienced.

6.2 Communities and twentieth-century decentralism

The process of community formation has continued into the twentieth century. It is a process which is consistent with that of the past – namely, one of the communities formed within a framework of utopian thought which, in turn, is derived from the historical circumstances of the period. It is the continuing tripartite relationship between community, utopia and history that was noted in Chapter 1.

The relationship has persisted, but the details of the communities have changed to reflect new historical circumstances. It is no longer the early nineteenth-century question of putting forward the idea of communities as the basic unit of social and economic organisation, at a time when capitalism was itself at an embryonic stage. Instead, by the twentieth century, capitalism was firmly entrenched not only in the first industrialised countries but, increasingly, on an international scale. Nor is it simply a question of contemplating whether society could be rebuilt on cooperative rather than competitive lines, and of romanticising about past forms of community. The scale of economic and political control, and the democratic place of the individual had (especially from the 1930s) become a central and unavoidable political issue. Idealists were now faced with the spectre of growing State control in traditionally-defined democratic countries like Britain and France, with the evidence of totalitarianism in the only country which had achieved a successful communist revolution, and with the emergence of Fascism in Germany, Italy and Spain. In the post-1945 period the economic control of multi-national corporations has been added to the political control of nation states.

It is this pattern of growing national and international control that is seen to be the historical backcloth for the twentieth-century communities. Their response to the situation reflects not only a general desire for a new socio-economic order, but a specific rejection of centralised control. As such they can be located within the vanguard of decentralist movements in this century. They can be seen as part of what Martin Buber described as 'the decentralist counter-tendencies which can be perceived underlying all economic and social evolution, and ... something that is slowly evolving in the human soul: the most intimate of all resistances – resistance to mass or collective loneliness' [22].

Already these tendencies were in evidence in the anarchist communities of the 1890s, but in the early years of the twentieth century it was to mass movements that more people turned. New peaks of community activity did not come again until the 1930s and the 1970s, though then at a scale much greater than at any time in the past. To conclude the historical review of communities we can look in turn, at each of these phases.

'Moscow or Jerusalem'

Martin Buber's polemical challenge that the choice that faced the world of the 1940s was between 'the central authority in a highly centralised State' (which he terms 'Moscow') or the 'social units of urban and rural workers, living and producing on a communal basis, and their representative bodies' (which, referring to the success of the *kibbutzim* in Palestine, as well as to the utopian associations of the city, is 'Jerusalem') [23], illustrates a perception of history that had a strong influence on the communities of that era. From the 1930s onwards 'Evil' is epitomised, variously, in terms of Stalinism; of Fascism in Germany, Italy and Spain; of the dramatic failure of international capitalism in this period; and of the militaristic nature and growing control of the State in avowedly democratic countries. It was seen in apocalyptic terms. 'Again the rains are descending and the floods are out. What will emerge when the waters have subsided none can know' [24].

But, equally, 'the green blade of new life has been breaking for long past' [25], and those who were involved in communities 'while the floods were out' were in little doubt as to where hope lay. Not for the first time the motives for community formation in England were a mixture of religious and political aspirations, and though some are clearly 'socialist' and others avowedly 'Christian', there are many where the various threads are drawn closely together.

In the inter-war period, at the very time that parliamentary socialism was gathering strength, others were turning, instead, to a decentralised version of socialism:

The inertia of the government at home and the spectacle of an almost doomed democracy on the continent ... has led us to look elsewhere than to political action for a real solution, and to ask ourselves, has the stage of action passed from government to the people? This has brought us to the conclusion that governments cannot do everything for us, but that a new approach must be found by the people themselves and that those who really mean their socialism can live it 'here and now' [26].

The 'here and now' was presented in the form of voluntary cooperative communities which rested on a mixture of socialist principles. For some it was a question of reviving the ideals of the 'Rochdale Pioneers', and of reorientating the cooperative movement towards its original aim of 'as soon as practicable, proceeding to arrange the powers of production, distribution, education, and government, or in other words to establish a self-supporting home colony of united interests, or assist other societies in establishing such colonies' [27].

Others subscribed to a model of socialist decentralisation in the form of democratic units of industrial production, which bore resemblance to many aspects of the mediaeval revival championed by Ruskin fifty years earlier. Their arguments for a new economic orthodoxy were rooted in a basic distaste for the increasing scale of industrial organisation and State control – to a point where 'the human mind is unable to get a grip of all the details necessary to its proper ordering' [28]. To reverse this trend, the 'Guild Socialists' had, for some years, been advocating the adaptation of the mediaeval guild system as a more acceptable basis for modern industrial production, and schemes were devised for self-government in industry through the establishment of a system of national guilds working in conjunction with other democratic organisations in the community [29].

By no means a concerted movement in a formal sense but, alongside the Guild Socialists, there were other pressure groups such as the 'Anti-Collectivists' (enjoying the literary support of G. K. Chesterton and Hilaire Belloc) and the 'Anti-Statists' [30]. Their common foe was what Belloc termed the 'Servile State' – where 'a comparatively small class of . . . men shall control under the guardianship of public laws, the lives of all the rest' [31]. Later, in the 1930s, their intellectual forebodings were given a new dimension by the failure of western governments to meet the problems of mass unemployment. Against a background of industrial crisis, new schemes were launched, like that of J. W. Scott, who likened his brand of socialism to Robert Owen's – 'a socialism which begins at home, which builds from the bottom upwards and not from the top down' [32]. He thought the answer lay in the resettlement of the unemployed on the land, in 'brotherhoods' of fifty to 20,000 people, working for one another 'in the family spirit'.

The decentralists of this period aroused interest, but failed to capture a wide following – their schemes seemed far-removed from the scale and urgency of the massive reconstruction that most radicals saw to be necessary. Inevitably, they stimulated some community experiments [33], but these were far from becoming the seeds for a new society of communal organisation.

There was also, in this period, a conscious attempt, through communities, to reconcile socialism with Christianity. In the light of a growing disillusionment with the Bolshevik Revolution it was common to ask whether socialism could be meaningful without a religious basis. John Middleton Murry, an influential figure in the community movement at this time [34], was not alone in his belief that revolution without religion was impossible, and that 'social community and Christian communion must go hand in hand' [35]. In the chaos and barbarism of a society on the brink of war he saw communities as an Ark in the flood, 'the sole indigenous vehicle of the continuity of civilisation [36]. Murry's ideal was that of a society composed of communities with both a spiritual and an economic basis:

The only genuine solution ... lies in the revivification of the national society from below, by the creation of communities with a sense of concrete social responsibility – communities of such a size that men can grasp and understand them as a whole, and be continually conscious as a matter of daily experience of their obligations to one another with them. This requires that the community shall be comprehensive as an economic unit. Mere neighbourhood is insufficient. If the conditions of work of my neighbour are controlled by some huge corporation, managed by people on whom I can have no conceivable influence, my neighbour might as well be living in another continent as far as effective community is concerned. Conditions of work within the community must be controlled within the community if the community is to be real [37].

The advocacy of Christian communities was not mere words, and practical schemes flourished in this period. Some were of a worldly nature, seeking to demonstrate the virtues of community to others through their own example and through involvement in everyday affairs; others attempted egalitarianism through monastic-type retreats from the iniquities of secular life [38]. There was also the interesting example of the Bruderhof communities, the product of a modern revival of the sixteenth-century Swiss sect, the Hutterites. They established themselves in community 'to witness the practical possibility here and now of a way of life based on love and lived in accordance with Christ's teaching about the Kingdom of God' [39]. They came to England from Germany and Lichtenstein to escape Nazi persecution, and eventually most of them moved on to North and South America. But their presence provided an unusual glimpse of the type of rigid but durable sectarian community that, for reasons of intolerance, had for several centuries been more familiar in the United States than in the continent of their origins. The literature of the period suggests that it was not uncommon for communitarians to spend some time with the Bruderhof in the Cotswolds, though the rigidity of their regime was not to everyone's liking [40].

But in terms of numbers at least, a more important contribution to the communities resulted from the pacifist movement, before and during the Second World War – it is estimated that there were several hundred pacifist communities, many of them based on the land [41]. The association of pacifist groups with community experiments had its origins in the First World War, when 'conscientious objectors were seeking alternatives to military service – some also a way out of the competitive system . . . There was a great wave of spiritual endeavour – deep resolves were made, and in that tense atmosphere miracles seemed possible'[42]. Many of the pacifists of the 1930s and 1940s continued to link military aggression with 'the competitive system', and their communities were important seedbeds for a wide range of radical ideas. The very process of groups of people with strong principles of dissent, coming together for a number of years, was sure to provide a rich mixture of alternative theories. Intertwined around the core of pacifism were varying degrees of support for cooperative socialism; for the anarchist traditions of Thoreau and Tolstoy, and the concurrent teachings and practice of Mahatma Gandhi (including his work in reviving the *Ashram* communities in India); and for the brotherhood derived from the principles of primitive Christianity and the monastic ideal. There is also considerable reference to international examples of cooperative land schemes – especially to the *kibbutzim* in Palestine which were idealised as a way of rebuilding society on a communal basis.

As the Second World War approached, many pacifists, who had for long talked about communities, tried to put their ideas into practice. John Middleton Murry was one who did so, later claiming that 'the pacifist has a peculiar duty to the national society . . . to prove that a society of peace is a real possibility and not an idle dream. The primary cell of such a society is a farming community, or a cooperative farm' [43]. And in *Community Journey*, George Ineson provides a fascinating account of the origins of another community – of the network of pacifists in the 1930s and the mixture of ideals which brought them together, and of the added practical difficulties in starting a new community when most people regarded them as traitors rather than as champions of the democratic struggle. Like a number of pacifists, he also looked increasingly towards an inner spiritual will as a basis for community, as opposed merely to external circumstances. He expressed the belief that fundamental change in people is possible, and that 'a community is simply a group of people sharing their intention to submit themselves to change' [44].

From a variety of sources, then, by the end of the 1930s there were probably more communities than at any time previously. Two conferences were held in 1937, on the face of it to take stock of the situation, but with a vision of an emerging federation of communities not far in the background [45]. The conferences revealed a rich diversity of community experiments and though many of the experiments had not gone far towards achieving an alternative order, the belief was that this would come about gradually, through a 'progressive realisation' of communal qualities from simple neighbourliness to economic viability. For most of the experiments, though, the momentum for this 'progressive realisation' subsided with the return of peace in 1945. With the ending of War, and the defeat of Fascism, the sense of urgency diminished. It is not until the end of the 1960s that a new wave of communities begins.

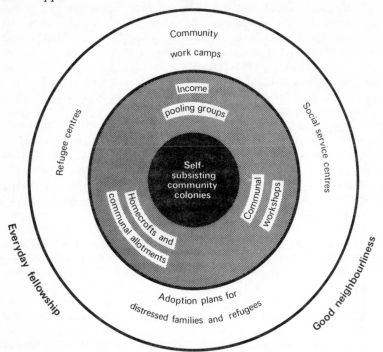

Fig. 6.1 'Community begins where we are and with our nearest neighbour. But it need not end there. This chart indicates the progressive realisation of Community through personal services and group activities to collective units socially integrated and economically self-subsisting' (from Community Service Committee, 1940).

Alternative society

People are wanted to develop a rural village cooperative on the Welsh borders. A group of cottages and some land is available. Anyone interested should be concerned to relate personal growth to a wider political perspective of alternative, feminist and socialist ideas. Long-term aims would be to develop local community ties, build more houses, be relatively self-supporting with a mixed workshop agricultural economy. Capital is not essential, willingness to work hard is [46].

The above advertisement for a community in rural Wales could almost have appeared in one of the early cooperative movement publications, 150 years ago. In the comparable rejection of a competitive system and its replacement by one based on cooperative principles; in a commitment to sexual equality; in the search for more acceptable methods of production than large-scale industrialisation and growing division of labour; and in an attachment to the land – in all these ideas and associated activities, there is much in the modern commune that would be recognisable to the nineteenth-century communitarian.

There is also much that would be different. The modern commune movement is less dominated by charismatic leaders, than was characteristic of its early days; there is a more even distribution between urban and rural locations; and there is a growing tendency in both urban and rural areas to forge close links with the surrounding community, as part of a more gradual and broad-based process of change. In the balance of membership, especially, the nineteenth-century communitarian would be sure to note striking differences. Probably self-taught and from a working-class, factory background, he would find a dominance of middle-class members, most of them young and well-educated, and with a high involvement of women and children. Although not acquisitive himself, he would surely want to explore the motives behind their decision to forego a life of material abundance (that would have been far beyond his own realisation) for one of comparative poverty.

With direct experience of working-class politics, the nineteenth-century communitarian may also wonder at the frequent reluctance of contemporary communes to align to organised movements with a formalised ideology – though if he came from Clousden Hill or Whiteway, rather than Harmony Hall or O'Connorville, he would find this less problematic. For all their differences in what they do and how they are organised, modern communes will generally tend towards an anarchist philosophy, far removed from the more rigid political and religious ideologies that underlay most of the communities before the 1890s. The mainstream modern commune has been likened to an extended family, where the 'idea of friendship envisages an enrichment of self through interaction with others who are in effect second selves' – in contrast to the traditional model of a utopian community, which seeks 'to create an instituted social order existing over and above its individual members and on the basis of the willed subordination of their selves' [47].

At first sight, the size of modern communes may seem to be little different to those of the past century – most of those in the 1970s are small, with a membership of between five and twenty-five [48]. In practice, most of the nineteenth-century communities were of a comparable order. The Chartist colonies were the main exception but it is significant that others – notably the utopian socialists – aspired to far greater totals (sometimes advocating a membership in terms of thousands rather than tens). In contrast, modern communes are consciously concerned to restrict numbers to a level that will enable meaningful social relationships to flourish [49]. Where growth is envisaged at all, it is more likely that it would be directed towards a federation of communes rather than through larger individual settlements.

Far more striking for the nineteenth-century observer would be the extensive variety and number of modern communes. Although there have been changes in the balance between different types of commune since the early 1970s, Andrew Rigby's typology [50] can still provide a helpful introduction to their range. The main groupings that he identifies are, firstly, 'self-actualising communes', where the emphasis is on individual realisation within a community context; secondly, 'communes for mutual support', which provide a supportive environment where members with similar ideas can relate more easily to each other; thirdly, 'activist communes', which take the form of bases for urban (and more recently rural) social and political activity; fourthly, 'practical communes', where economic and material advantages of communal living are stressed (and where one might include the opportunities to develop and practice alternative technologies); fifthly, 'therapeutic communes', where an environment is created which is considered to be helpful to specific groups in need of care and attention; and, finally, 'religious communes', both ascetic (where the commune is separated from the rest of society to lead a way of life according to God's will) and mystical (where the group is concerned to achieve a unity of body and soul, in accordance with a belief that God is immanent).

In respect of numbers, various estimates have been made but, in a constantly changing situation and where many communes consciously eschew publicity, it is difficult to arrive at a precise figure [51]. While numbers undoubtedly increased during the first half of the 1970s it is less certain whether they are continuing to do so, or whether the peak is already past [52]. It is fair to assume, though, that in the late 1970s the total number of communes in existence at any one time exceeds that which was reached during the whole of the past century. While the nineteenth-century communitarian may have dreamt of comparable developments taking root in other parts of the country, his contemporary counterparts have the outlines of their own map of alternative England. The situation is constantly changing, but informal communications are good and the relative fortunes of the various communes and related projects are well-known to those within the network.

Of all the contrasts, though, perhaps the most significant lies in the extent to which modern communes are themselves part of a wider network of alternative, decentralist activity – a 'Fourth World of decentralised, small-scale forms of organisation, structured organically rather than mechanically and directed towards the fulfilment of human values rather than materialist objectives'[53]. In some cases, this activity shares the revolutionary assumptions of many of the communes – in other cases, it extends into the realm of new pluralist institutions and reforms within mainstream society. It is manifested in a variety of forms, by no means mutually exclusive to each other:
– in new ideas on 'self' and 'group relationships', directed towards achieving a greater control over one's own life. This tendency embraces alternative theories of psychology, the emergence of a significant feminist movement, and a wider critique of the nuclear family as a source of many contemporary problems. The search for individual expression, and a rejection of traditional patterns of

Figs. 6.2 and 6.3 Two impressions of modern communitarianism (illustrated by C. Harper): (6.2) the one stressing a 'back to the land' ethic, and the attraction of alternative technology; (6.3) the other exploring the possibilities of the modern commune as a new version of the extended family.

authority have also encompassed a wider use of drugs, new forms of music and drama, and a revived interest in mysticism and mythology;
– in forms of 'alternative technology', (or 'radical technology'), involving not simply new techniques but also a rejection of the capitalist mode of production. It is not necessarily opposed to technology as such, but rather to the way it has been used as a means of exerting social control. Alternative technology schemes include experiments in the use of renewable fuel sources, organic farming methods and a reassessment of diet and food supplies, simpler methods of construction and self-help housing, and a greater

emphasis on crafts and small-scale industrial production;
- in a proliferation of cooperative projects in town and country. These include cooperative shops and workshops, printing works and tool-sharing schemes, cooperative buying and community play projects;
- in organisations which have been formed to promote a return to the land, either through direct action in creating new communities, or through other means of revitalising rural areas. Taken to its extreme is the ideal of a national network of self-sufficient, self-regulating communities;
- and in a wide range of ideas and schemes for the radical restructuring of various institutions along decentralist lines. These include workers control in industry; greater consumer control and a challenge to professional authority, with self-help schemes in, for instance, planning, health and medicine; participation in government and support for devolution at all levels of organisation.

The range of alternative activities is richer and more varied than these few examples can portray [54]. They are enough, though, to indicate what can be expressed as a 'decentralist' tendency which underlies the contemporary critique of established society. It is decentralist in both a socio-psychological and a spatial sense. The former is that of a general resistance to isolation and exploitation in mass society, and of a reassertion of the worth of the individual in his own right. The latter reflects (against a continuing tide of centralisation and consolidation) a preference for small groups, widely diffused and sensitive to changing needs. This tendency has been evident since the 1960s, gathering momentum in the 1970s. For reasons why it should occur at this particular time, and why it should assume such a decentralist form, one can turn (as in previous phases of commune activity) to the specific material circumstances of the period.

In essence, the contemporary commune movement and associated decentralist activities, can be explained in relation to the material structure of advanced capitalist society – to the scale and working conditions of the productive process itself, to the proliferation and control of bureaucracies in both the private and the public sector, and to the exploitative nature of modern technology. It is a response which has been evoked by the growing experience of alienation in relationships between individual and society, and between individual and Nature. An increase in State intervention, the 'rationalisation' of living and working conditions (in the form, for instance, of redevelopment areas and industrial mergers, of standardised housing and automation), the advent of multi-national corporations, the unparalleled rate of destruction of natural resources and environmental quality to serve the unlimited appetite of consumerism and, beyond any single set of events, the disorientating pace of change itself – are material conditions which have produced their own contradictions. At the very time that freedom has become a technical possibility, in that new technologies have greatly increased productive capacity and available wealth, the prospects for its achievement in a competitive, capitalist economy have receded.

Above all, the alternative society (or 'counter culture') has been defined as a search for a free society, emerging in a 'struggle against violence and exploitation where this struggle is waged for essentially new ways and forms of life'[55]. It embraces a notion of 'freedom' which rests not simply on the ability to do what one wants, nor even on the ability of others to do the same – but also on a shared consciousness of the limits of individual action. If there is one thing that can distinguish the communes of the 1970s it is, perhaps, their role as 'the outward form of a movement in consciousness'[56]. How much can one do and have without transgressing the freedom of others, and without destroying natural conditions in the process? A consciousness of these limits is derived, in turn, from an awareness of existing conflicts, and from the results of a shared experience in working towards new structures. In raising consciousness, communes provide both a base from which to understand mainstream society, and an environment within which to work towards something different.

As in the late 1930s, when communities were often envisaged as sanctuaries of hope in the face of encroaching totalitarianism, there is again something of a spiritual mission. Satish Kumar defines a role for communitarians 'as preserving the most fundamental and practical skills, which would otherwise be lost from the lives of many people. They are the Arks for saving human, spiritual and communitarian values, leaving behind the money-motivated cult of material success' [57]. In similar vein Patrick Rivers describes those who pioneer an alternative life-style as 'the survivalists' [58], while George Ineson – continuously involved in community experiments since the 1930s – considers that the role of communities has increased over the period, from one of a 'prophetic gesture' outside the mainstream of society, to that of a 'crucial growing point' [59]. Likewise, Robert Houriet argues that the 'dropout' image is inappropriate, and that it might be more realistic to regard contemporary communitarians as 'pioneers in a movement that will soon have to include most of civilisation' [60].

What is more – and this is a significant departure from earlier phases – as a result of the world-wide spread of those conditions of advanced capitalism which have induced new experiments in this country, communes are now an international 'movement'. In the rest of Western Europe, in Japan and in North America a marked increase in the number of communes has been recorded over the past ten years. In one sense the international character of the commune movement is nothing new. It is the case that past phases of communities have seldom been confined to one country, but often it was such that their spread to other countries was to escape conditions of localised persecution. In the 1970s it is much more the situation that communities are a response in a wide variety of countries to the common problems posed by comparable systems of development.

Significantly, the United States – with its strong tradition of communities (a reminder of which persists in the form of a number of religious sects, such as the Hutterites and the Amish Mennonites, which have survived through to the present day), and with its highly advanced form of capitalist industrialisation – provided the earliest and most extensive evidence of modern communes. Moreover, specific incidents in the mid 1960s – the black ghetto riots, the use of police violence at the Democrat Convention in Chicago in 1968 and the escalation of the Vietnam War – have been variously cited as final points of departure from the mainstream world of pluralist politics and industrialised culture.

At least until the mid 1970s the number of communes in the United States would appear to have increased quite considerably [61], and this was accompanied by a greater variation in their ideological leanings and in their geographical coverage. The favoured locations for the early communes (in California and New England, especially) have been balanced by an apparent dispersal into the town and country of 'middle America' – to Wyoming, Montana, Tennessee, West Virginia. In part, this reflects a move away from the limelight of the early radical 'ghettos' and, in part, a constant search for cheap, available land:

Just as their predecessors did, contemporary groups often settle on poor land which is all they can afford: vacant land – arid and infertile, like Greeley, Colorado, or Llano del Rio, California; abandoned farms; derelict urban space such as abandoned city centre warehouses or decrepit, 'funky' nineteenth century houses in older sections of the cities [62].

Comparable to (but a few years in advance of) the English experience, there has also been a shift in the ideological basis of American communes – away from a total separation from mainstream society and the search for absolute ideals, and towards more practical schemes and a greater tolerance of existing personal and social shortcomings. Many of the early communes took the form of uncompromising rejections of established society, of paths to new forms of consciousness, heavily steeped in drugs and 'hippie' culture; characteristically, they went to great lengths to assert their distance from the rest of society. While no less committed to a long-term rejection of established society, more recent communes have tended to seek a closer understanding of the surrounding community as it now exists and to work from that basis.

There has been a greater involvement in immediate social and political issues (in free schools, drug addiction centres, welfare aid, theatre groups) in an attempt both to effect immediate improvements and to extend a consciousness of contemporary conditions. There has also been a more recent emphasis on practical attempts to create a more acceptable environment, with experiments not only in group relationships but also in alternative farming and technology. It is no longer 'work' that is rejected, so much as the 'work ethic' of capitalist society.

Robert Houriet, in tracing changes in American communes through his own experience, observed that by the early 1970s there was a tendency towards less rigid rules, and more of a balance between freedom and stability, individuality and cooperation, tradition and innovation. There would be room in the new communities for the old as well as for the young, and for those who want to maintain links with the rest of society as well as for those who want to cut themselves off. His view is that the 'new society resembles pluralist, provincial America as it had been under the Articles of Confederation. It is intently decentralised. What organisation exists is based on the anarchist principle of voluntary sharing or mutual assistance . . .' [63].

But also, beyond the advanced industrial countries where communes reflect a growing disaffection with the Western way of life, there are the models of communities in developing countries. There are instances where, instead of rejecting the traditional pattern of village life in favour of a capital-intensive development programme, new and existing small-scale communities are seen as the social growth points for a new society. The best examples are to be found in societies that are moulding their own form of socialism – in the 'communes' of China, and the '*ujamaa*' villages of Tanzania.

Of the latter, President Nyerere has described *ujamaa* villages as settlements based upon the extended family system ('*ujamaa*' itself means 'familyhood'), but involving more people and with modern techniques where these are beneficial. He defined their role as being to reverse the drift towards individualism that was in evidence in the 1960s, and looked forward to the gradual achievement of 'a nation of *ujamaa* villages where the people cooperate directly in small groups and where these small groups cooperate together for joint enterprises' [64].

For Western observers this type of concept is of more than peripheral interest. They can be seen, not as a method of growth that is peculiar to less-developed societies, but as working examples of how small-scale communities can develop as the 'organic' base of a larger structure – providing a human scale for national development. Just as the *kibbutzim* were so attractive to a generation of communitarians in the 1930s and 1940s, so the ongoing examples of communes in China and Tanzania offer, at least, a partial model of the simpler form of society that many would now regard as preferable, if not inevitable.

At the same time, these very examples also serve to highlight the fundamental contradiction that surrounds the issue of communes in the more advanced, capitalist economies. The Chinese communes and Tanzanian *ujamaa* villages are promoted as a means of decentralisation, but this is possible only because in those countries a form of socialism already exists. They leave unanswered the question that dogged the nineteenth-century communities in England, and which now confronts contemporary communes – namely, is it realistic to contemplate an alternative life style within capitalist society, to the extent that it will first challenge and then replace the existing system?

The arguments currently levelled against communes as a means of social change are severe, and their sources – from Marxists who favour mass revolutionary action, and from parliamentary socialists who argue for legislative change – would not be unfamiliar to the nineteenth-century communitarian. An important contemporary critique is that which has been marshalled by Abrams and McCulloch (1976) (F). They argue that the attempts by communes to create pockets of freedom within market societies is contradictory, because the members are unable to free themselves from the hold of 'possessive individualism'. It is not that communes, in themselves, as small units of social organisation are without potential in the right situation, but so long as their members retain an individualistic approach that is shaped by a petty bourgeois culture, this potential is restricted. Thus, the 'material advantages of communes consistently fail to meet the spiritual needs of commune members – for the former are rooted in sharing while the latter presuppose possession' [65].

The revolutionary claims of the communitarians are dismissed as being peripheral to the main foci of class struggle, their aspirations for change being limited to a revolution of private life – of personal salvation rather than of social transformation. The radicalism of the commune is likened to a moral crusade, that eschews both the compromise and the commitments of mundane organised politics in order to proclaim the integrity of a symbolic posture:

Communes are an attempt on the part of those who have belatedly and unexpectedly discovered their true situation in market society to follow the example of the working class and construct a little bit of power through combination. But it is an attempt made on distinctively petty-bourgeois terms, from 'within' the ethos of individualism and denying the profound contradiction between that ethos and the requirements of effective combination [66].

Whitworth (1975) (F), in a comparative statement on nineteenth- and twentieth-century communities, is no less sanguine about the prospects for communities in modern society. In many ways the difficulties faced by contemporary communitarians are greater than for those in the nineteenth century. Among these 'external' difficulties is the fact that, even in America, cheap and fertile land is a thing of the past and many recent communities have foundered in marginal locations; it is also more difficult now than in the days of the American frontier, to avoid the economic and legislative restrictions of mainstream society that are opposed to new growth. Ideologically, modern secular communities lack the unifying force of belief systems of the type that sustained earlier religious groups, such as the Shakers. Moreover, it is Whitworth's view that the success of contemporary communities is seriously inhibited by a tendency among their members to see communitarianism as no more than a phase in their own personal development. He concludes that 'urbanisation, the claims and provisions of the modern bureaucratic state and aspects of the 'social climate' of western industrial societies render the life chances of introversionist communitarian groups, and even the 'birth chances' of utopian groups, extremely small' [67].

The critics of communes are supported by the absence of any serious evidence that capitalism finds itself threatened either by their scattered existence, or even by the more pervasive ideas of the alternative society. The media has been especially active in presenting to the rest of the population an image of communes which is either sensational (concentrating on piecemeal if not peripheral aspects of communal life, that would be enough to deter all but the most avid supporter), or patronising (where communitarians are shown toiling on a Welsh hillside, remote from what matters in the rest of society). The central issue as to why an alternative to capitalism is even contemplated is quite frequently ignored. There are also many instances where the revolutionary potential of alternative ideas and criticisms of capitalist society have been checked through absorption into the existing system. A total vision of an alternative society is fragmented into High Street health food shops, a marketable image of 'crafts' in mass-produced furniture and clothes, and consumerised packages of solar heating.

In response to their critics, the communitarians can argue that the criteria against which they have been judged are unrealistic. It may well have been the case that some of the nineteenth-century groups (notably, the utopian socialists of the 1840s) equated the formation of a community with the simultaneous collapse of the corrupt society around them, but this is not a vision that can fairly be attributed to the communitarians of the 1970s. The fact that they have not resolved, in a few short years, the fundamental tensions between individual and group values (that are themselves a product of generations of competitive existence), and that they have failed to stimulate an immediate and total revolution in the rest of society, is a misleading measure of their impact. Communitarianism is not about sudden change for the whole of society. It is a process with revolutionary potential, but its progress is, inevitably, gradual – proceeding through local initiatives and through a steady diffusion of ideas and experiments. Like the revolutionary society it seeks to create, the revolutionary process is itself local-based and non-violent – a means of achieving change that is consistent with the ends sought. Communitarianism is, therefore, different to other methods of achieving change, but that is not to deny its own revolutionary potential. This potential can be seen at two levels. Firstly, for those who are directly involved in the communes there is the immediate chance to make a start in creating a new life-style. Established patterns of social, economic and technological organisation are not only questioned but, to a varying degree and over a period of time, replaced by alternative forms. In this sense, communes can be seen as important sources for experimentation and innovation. And, among many communitarians, the view is held that this in itself is a revolutionary act – that the first essential step towards wider revolution lies in individuals taking greater control over their own lives. It is this belief which is expressed in various ways as 'living the revolution now' and of 'changing society everyday as you live your own life'.

But, at a second level, the revolutionary potential lies in their role as a model that can encourage others to question the basis of their own lives.

'I don't think you can remould society by taking it *en bloc*. But one can do so, I think, by setting up lots of little examples' [68]. The process is one of non-aggressive demonstration, and there is a clear tendency among communitarians to regard change as rippling outwards to the rest of society. This process can have the effect, either of comparable experiments or, among a wider population, a new questioning of structures which had previously been accepted as normal:

By living our own lives here we can develop a kind of seed that can grow while the old is dying around it. In this way they may begin to think in new ways. . . . By living in communes and by living a different way of life we can make some people sit up and think – 'maybe there is another way of life, maybe we ought to change our way of life' . . . [69].

It is a process of 'quiet revolution', but in its attack on the roots of oppressive structures, a revolution none the less. In this approach one is mindful of the Tolstoyan communities of the 1890s – seeking, through their own example, to extend a consciousness of one's own ability to challenge existing systems of power.

To assess how far the modern communitarians have been successful in this way, in extending their beliefs beyond their own boundaries, is problematic. The relationship is more complex than one of simple cause and effect, where changes in mainstream society could be attributed directly to the example of communes. What can be noted, though, is that many of the ideas that are espoused in communes appear to have gained something of a foothold in a variety of established institutions. The desire for a greater control over one's own life – a basic motivation in the communes – is also a discernible trend in mainstream society. Against the tide of material forces which have continued to reinforce centralisation, an important element of popular feeling has looked, instead, to an alternative emphasis on decentralisation, cooperation and direct action. There are, undoubtedly, characteristics of radical change in the 1970s – manifested in new values, and in a wide variety of innovatory projects and reforms – which share many of the assumptions of the communes. Though these wider changes will generally take a less extreme form than in the communes, their source can be traced to a common core of alienation in modern society. Seen in this light, communes are neither unique nor without foundation, but can be regarded as exemplars of a wider network of social change.

6.4 Concluding note

The main purpose in extending the history of alternative communities into the twentieth century has been in order to locate the nineteenth-century experiments within a sharper comparative perspective, and a number of concluding points can be made.

Firstly, while the nineteenth-century communities exhibit the specific characteristics of their own historical milieu, it is clear that as a social phenomenon they were not unique. Both before and after the nineteenth century, alternative communities have been formed in opposition to the main tenets of established society. What is more they are themselves within a wider tradition of utopian thought and political action which has looked to the community rather than the State as the focus for social reorganisation.

Secondly, it is also clear that neither in the nineteenth century nor in earlier periods have communities represented a sustained challenge to the established order – at no time have they neared the ideal of a new society composed of freely cooperating communities. As a means of achieving widespread social change the question has been raised repeatedly as to whether they are, indeed, structurally capable of doing so. Empirically, it has been shown that they were generally of limited impact, yet the same empirical evidence has also demonstrated their historical persistence – fading sometimes for long periods, but then reappearing to pose new routes for mainstream society. In all cases, the emergence of alternative communities has occurred within a wider matrix of political dissent – amidst the political and religious turbulence of the seventeenth century; as part of the new working-class response to industrial capitalism in the second quarter of the nineteenth century and, again, in the context of a varied pattern of socialist and anarchist activity in the 1890s; as one among a number of extreme political reactions to the domestic and international crises of the 1930s; and from the late 1960s, in a wave of dissaffection with advanced capitalism, articulating new possibilities for post-industrial society. It is at these times that alternative communities have emerged to challenge established society – constantly provocative though incapable of winning major battles. Their strategy predetermines neither total victory nor total defeat but, in the essence of the dialectic, neither side remains entirely unchanged.

Thirdly, for all the differences between communities from one period to another, there are also characteristics and issues which retain a striking relevance for later observers. There is still some value in looking back to the nineteenth-century communities – not so much because there are examples to be emulated (though there are indeed some which retain their own lure), but because they reveal the record of a process from which much can be learnt. One can look both to what was achieved and to reasons why, sooner or later, they all foundered. In some ways it is the latter aspect which is of greater interest, and other writers have made the point that the sociological value of a study of utopian schemes lies less in their details and more in an understanding of why they can never be fully implemented. Did the nineteenth-century communities collapse, simply because of local obstacles that one would not expect to see repeated? Was it because they asked impossible things of people, an outcome that would have occurred in any period because of their unrealistic view of human nature? Or did they collapse because they failed to appreciate their historical situation, erroneously trying to gain a foothold at the very time that capitalist growth was gaining momentum! And what are the implications for contemporary communitarianism in the answers to any of these questions?

All this is not to deny the positive lessons of nineteenth-century communities. Above all, for the twentieth-century observer, the communities remain as a vivid example of direct involvement. They amounted to practical steps to overcome the experience of alienation that was, and still is, endemic in capitalist society – expressing basic desires for identity, for land, for salvation, for involvement. Indeed, perhaps the most positive lesson is that those who participated in the communities were excited and involved. What is revealed is not just the vision of a decentralised society, but a process where the gap between theory and practice breaks down. For contemporary institutions such as town planning, education and health services, where the emphasis is currently on 'product' rather than 'process' – on what should be provided rather than on how it should be done – the communities can offer an alternative model for a higher level of involvement.

Finally, alternative communities of any period are (whether they 'succeed' or not) an expression of popular history and political will. The names of some of the nineteenth-century communitarians – Robert Owen, Feargus O'Connor and John Ruskin are well-known (though primarily for their other activities), but how many have heard of William Hodson, Thomas Smith or Nellie Shaw? This is not to suggest that these latter figures changed the course of history – but they may have come closer to reflecting common ideals and aspirations than many who are better known and who achieved more tangible results.

Christopher Hill has made the point that historians are interested in ideas not only because they influence societies, but because they reveal the societies which give rise to them [70]. It is certainly the case that the ideas underlying the communities can exemplify both what many thought to be wrong with nineteenth-century society, and ways in which common people wanted to see it put right. Whether, in hindsight, they were misguided or not, the fact remains that for the communitarians at the time it was by no means inevitable that England had to continue along the path of capitalist industrialisation. In this sense, as a challenge to orthodoxy, their ideas for an alternative England are of interest in themselves. The communities are of added significance, though, to the extent that they also revealed the existence of what were, undoubtedly, more widely-felt grievances and aspirations.

Appendix

Alternative communities in nineteenth-century England

Name of Community	Date of Inception	Location
The Cooperative and Economical Society	1821	Spa Fields, Clerkenwell, London
Devon and Exeter Cooperative Society	1826	Rockbeare, Devon
Hodsonian Community	1838	Manea Fen, Cambridgeshire
Harmony Hall	1839	East Tytherley, Hampshire
Concordium	1842	Ham Common, Surrey
Moreville Communitorium	1843	Hanwell, Middlesex
O'Connorville	1846	Heronsgate, Hertfordshire
The Agapemone	1846	Spaxton, Somerset
Lowbands	1846	Lowbands, Worcestershire
Charterville	1847	Charterville Allotments, Oxfordshire
Snigs End	1847	Staunton, Gloucestershire
Great Dodford	1848	Great Dodford, Worcestershire
The Cokelers	1850	Loxwood, Sussex
Christian Israelite Institution	1857	Wrenthorpe, Yorkshire
The New Forest Shakers	1872	Hordle, Hampshire
The New and Latter House of Israel	1875	Gillingham, Kent
Totley Colony	1876	Totley, Sheffield
Methwold Fruit Farm Colony	1889	Brookville, Norfolk
Starnthwaite Home Colony	1892	Crosthwaite, Westmorland
Clousden Hill Communist and Cooperative Colony	1895	Forest Hall, Newcastle
Mayland Colony	1896	Mayland, Essex
Norton Colony	1896	Norton, Sheffield
Purleigh Colony	1896	Purleigh, Essex
The Brotherhood Workshop	1897	Victoria Road, Leeds
Ashingdon Colony	1897	Ashingdon, Essex
Wickford Colony	1898	Downham, Wickford, Essex
Whiteway Colony	1898	Whiteway, Gloucestershire
The Blackburn Brotherhood	1899	Victoria Street, Blackburn

The names of the communities are as generally known and reported at the time of their existence. Place names are as used today, a number of which result directly from the presence of a community on the site in the last century.

Notes and References

Chapter 1

Capital letters (in parentheses) indicate the part of the bibliography in which full details may be found.

1. Mannheim, (1960), p. 173 (A).
2. The term 'ideology' has a variety of possible meanings – which are explained in Williams (1976), pp. 126–30 (A) – but it is used in this book in the sense of an 'idea system', usually pertaining to a particular model of social change (such as 'the ideology of religious anarchism').
3. Starting with the late-mediaeval period is not to deny an earlier history of alternative communities, but it is the few centuries which saw the break with theological paradigms and the rise of a merchant class that provide the most immediate context for the nineteenth century experiments.
4. Mannheim, (1960), p. 174 (A).
5. Benjamin Disraeli, *Sybil, or the Two Nations* [1845] Book ii, Ch. 5, p. 146.
6. From Oliver Goldsmith's *The Deserted Village* [1769]. This tradition of rural nostalgia is explained in Hill (1958) (C) and Williams (1973) (A).
7. Central to this tradition is the loss of rights to land and this is explored in Ch. 3.
8. The full titles of the publications in which these utopian lands are featured are Francis Bacon, *New Atlantis*, London, 1627; Samuel Hartlib, *A Description of the Famous Kingdom of Macaria*, London, 1641; Samuel Gott, *Nova Solyma*, London, 1648; John Sadler, *Olbia: The New Island Lately Discovered*, London, 1660.
9. Winstanley (1973), p. 294 (C), *The Law of Freedom in a Platform* [1652] The ideas and importance of Gerrard Winstanley are more fully dealt with in Ch. 3, in the context of agrarian socialism.
10. Winstanley (1965), p. 409 (C), *An Appeal to all Englishmen* [1650].
11. Peter Chamberlen [1647], in Hill (1975), p. 115 (A).
12. Winstanley (1973), pp. 87–8 (C): *The True Levellers Standard Advanced* [1649]. Again, the nature of this experiment receives further consideration in Ch. 3.
13. Hill (1975), p. 124 (A).
14. Armytage (1961), p. 16 (A). A reference to Armytage's *Heavens Below* cannot pass without acknowledging the exceptional value of this book as a source of historical material on the subject of alternative communities.
15. The scheme is described and assessed in Sister Eugenia's 'Coleridge's scheme of Pantisocracy and American travel accounts', *Proceedings of the Modern Languages Association of America*, Vol. XLV, pp. 1069–84, 1930. See also C. Garrett, 'Coleridge's Utopia revisited', (in Teselle, 1972) (A).
16. Southey, in Teselle (1972), p. 122 (A).
17. From Coleridge's poem, *On the Prospect of Establishing a Pantisocracy in America*. Coleridge wrote another poem on the subject, *Pantisocracy*, in the same year, 1794. Both are reprinted in E. H. Coleridge (ed.), *Coleridge: Poetical Works*, Oxford University Press, London, 1969.
18. Coleridge, in Teselle (1972), p. 132 (A).
19. Godwin's ideas are more fully considered in Ch. 5.

20. Coleridge, in Teselle (1972), p. 135 (A).
21. Tönnies (1974), p. 263 (A).
22. From William Cobbett's notes on his visit to Sheffield in January 1830 – see Cobbett (1967), p. 495 (A).
23. Engels (1969), p. 76 (A).
24. D. H. Lawrence, *Phoenix*, Heinemann, London, 1936, p. 135.
25. Further reference is made to Quaker and Salvation Army communities, and to philanthropic land schemes, in Chs. 3 and 4.
26. Arthur E. Bestor (1948) (A) presented a comparable historical interpretation, arguing for the revival of terms that had been derived from 'community' to describe that form of modern socialism which seeks to change society by means of small experimental colonies or communities. The ensuing years have seen Bestor's claims met, and 'communitarianism' is again an accepted term for this type of approach.
27. In the United States there were many schemes where, not only was their design and layout of prime importance, but also where they managed to implement their plans to a greater extent than was common in England. In part, they were helped by the lower cost of land and abundance of natural resources. The importance of design in the history of American communities is explored in Hayden (1976) (G).
28. In spite of a restricted number of examples where communities have been established in other parts of Britain, there is little to suggest that the Celtic countries were consistently used in the way that has occurred in recent years. In part, their contemporary attraction lies in the availability of cheaper land and, in part, in the mystical associations of Celtic culture. In the past century, greater stress was laid on the political importance of remaining in contact with working-class movements in the industrial areas and, even at the end of the century it was still possible to find relatively cheap land not far from a big city (the popularity of the Essex countryside in the 1890s being a case in point).
29. This estimate is derived from the work of Bestor (1970) (G) and of Robert Fogarty of Antioch College – both sources of which are assessed in Hayden (1976) (G). Bestor has catalogued 106 communities in the period 1800 to 1860, which Hayden regards as an underestimate, and Fogarty has compiled a record of 150 communities for the period from 1860 to 1918.
30. Bestor (1970), p. 20 (G).
31. These twenty-eight communities have been located through a variety of journals and newspapers circulating at the time, through secondary source books, and through contact with county archivists and librarians, and letters to local newspapers. But much of the source material is obscure and, with little evidence of their former presence in the landscape, it is freely admitted that a number of communities may well have been omitted from the survey.

Chapter 2

1. Babeuf's original ideas were published as the *Manifesto of Equals* in 1796, and republished by Buonarroti in 1828.
2. Adam Smith's *An Inquiry into the Nature and Causes of the Wealth of Nations* was published in 1776. For an account of this and the subsequent contributions of Thomas Malthus and David Ricardo, see Eric Roll (1973), Ch. IV (B).
3. There is an important (though, amongst the utopian socialists, not widely acknowledged) debt to Rousseau who, especially in *Emile*, 1762, developed the argument that Man's inherent qualities had been corrupted in society, and that it was essential to design an appropriate form of education to allow these natural qualities to flourish.
4. Owen (1967), p. xliii, first published in 1857 (B).
5. William Thompson showed some resistance to this general tendency, believing that cooperative industry could be achieved throughout England through the workers' own efforts. See pp. 29–32.

6. Of special value in relating the history of Robert Owen's ideas and political activities to the various community experiments in this period are Harrison (1969) (B) and Garnett (1972) (B).

7. It is important to note that neither Rousseau nor Godwin were arguing for a return to a state of nature. On the contrary, as Colletti (1972) (B) says of Rousseau, 'for Rousseau man's nature is definitely not realised in the "State of Nature" but can be achieved only "in and through society" ' (p. 151). The point is that it was changes in society that were a precondition for greater equality, not the abandonment of society as such.

8. This is the estimate of Harrison (1969) (B). Apart from the six communities in England (see pp. 42–64), the total of ten would appear to include Orbiston, 1825, in Scotland, Ralahine, 1831, in Ireland, and two communities in Wales, Pant-Glas, 1840, and Garnlwyd, 1847. In both America and England, the majority were initiated by the 'Owenites' (supporters of Owen who tried to put his ideas into practice with or without the direct involvement of Owen himself).

9. Owen (1927), p. 260: *Report to the County of Lanark*, [1820], (B).

10. Owen (1927), p. 299: *An Address to the Inhabitants of New Lanark* [1816], (B).

11. Owen (1967), p. 61 (B).

12. The 'Poor Law' scheme is explained in Robert Owen's *Report to the Committee for the Relief of the Manufacturing Poor*, [1817], while the later scheme of 'villages of cooperation' is set out in the *Report to the County of Lanark* [1820].

13. Owen (1927), p. 246: *Report to the County of Lanark*, [1820], (B).

14. Owen posed this question at various times. This particular extract is from *The Revolution in the Mind and Practice of the Human Race*, [1849], p. 21.

15. Owen (1927), p. 284: *Report to the County of Lanark* [1820], (B).

16. Thompson (1830), p. iii (B).

17. Thompson (1830), pp. 2–3 (B).

18. Thompson (1824), p. 393, (B).

19. Garnett (1972), p. 47 (B).

20. Garnett (1972), p. 59 (B).

21. Barmby, *The Apostle and Chronicle of the Communist Church*, 1 Aug. 1848, p. 1.

22. Frost (1880), p. 61 (B).

23. Barmby, *The Apostle and Chronicle of the Communist Church*, 1 Aug. 1848, p. 1.

24. Barmby, *The Communist Credo*, 1841, p. 23.

25. Barmby, *The Promethean; or, Communitarian Apostle:* A Monthly Magazine, of Societarian Science, Domestics, Ecclesiastics, Politics, and Literature, Mar. 1842.

26. See pp. 63–64.

27. See his brief reference to this in *The Apostle and Chronicle of the Communist Church*, 1 Aug. 1848; and the account in Armytage (1961), pp. 202–3 (A).

28. Frost (1880), p. 64 (B).

29. Garnett (1972) (B), provides an excellent account of the intricate relationships between Owen, the Owenites and the cooperative movement.

30. *The Economist*, Aug. 1821, p. 43.

31. In Garnett (1972), p. 52 (B).

32. Thompson (1830), p. ii (B).

33. Darley (1975), p. 82 (A), includes a summary of the work of one such follower of Owen, John Moggeridge, a Monmouth Magistrate and industrialist who established three model villages – Blackwood, Yuisdd and Trelyn.

34. *The Economist*, 20 Oct. 1821, p. 205.

35. See pp. 43–46.

36. See pp. 46–48.

37. From *The Cooperative Magazine and Monthly Herald*, in Garnett (1972), p. 51 (B).

38. See pp. 49–53.

39. In Garnett (1972) p. 135 (B).

40. *New Moral World*, 8 Nov. 1834, p. 9.

41. Harry Howells Horton, 'Community the only salvation for man. A lecture delivered in the social institutions, Salford on Sunday morning, September 16th, 1838', A. Heywood (etc.), Manchester, 1838.

42. *New Moral World*, 11 July 1839, p. 595.
43. See p. 52.
44. See pp. 53–58
45. See Loubère (1974), Ch. 6 (B). In addition to communities in France there were a number of 'socialist' communities established by French settlers in North Africa.
46. See Loubère (1974), Ch. 6 (B).
47. Sung by Owenite communitarians on board ship, 'en route' for New Harmony, in Lockwood (1971), p. 82 (G).
48. Thomas Hunt, *'Report to a meeting of intending emigrants comprehending a practical plan for founding cooperative colonies of united interests, in the north-western territories of the United States . . .'*, p. 2, W. Ostell (etc.), London, 1843.
49. Hunt (1843), *op. cit.*, p. 3.
50. In Lockwood (1971), p. 70 (G).
51. In Lockwood (1971), p. 70 (G).
52. See Harrison (1969), pp. 165–8 (B).
53. See Harrison (1969), pp. 173–5 (B).
54. From *The Economist*, 11 Aug. 1821. *The Economist* provides the most consistent record of the formation and early history of this community.
55. See Garnett (1972), pp. 44–5 (B).
56. *The Economist*, 27 Jan. 1821.
57. There are various accounts of this phase of the community's formation in *The Economist* between October and December 1821.
58. *The Economist*, 2 Mar. 1822.
59. Mudie's editorial in *The Economist*, 2 Mar. 1822.
60. Bagnigge Wells Road (which at the time contained a spa and bordered open meadows) is now Kings Cross Road, but the course of Guildford Street East has largely disappeared beneath Mount Pleasant Sorting Office on the west side of Kings Cross Road, and new residential development to the east.
61. The pamphlet was advertised in the *Exeter Flying Post*, 20 Apr. 1826; in the same advertisement was Veysey's request for suitable land.
62. From indications given that the site was about 7 miles from Exeter and 10 miles from the coast and, given Veysey's preference for the London Road (in the advertisement he placed in the *Exeter Flying Post*), it is probable that the community was located in the vicinity of Rockbeare, to the east of Exeter. Further local searches would be especially valuable in this case.
63. *The Cooperative Magazine and Monthly Herald*, July 1826.
64. *The Cooperative Magazine and Monthly Herald*, July 1826.
65. *The Cooperative Magazine and Monthly Herald*, Aug. 1826.
66. Letter to W. Hebert from M. Martin, dated 5 Aug. 1827, in *The Cooperative Magazine and Monthly Herald*, Sept. 1827.
67. These two publications provide an important record of both the Hodsonian Community and the concurrent community of Harmony Hall, and of the essence of the socialist debate at that time. They also provide an indication of factional differences amongst Owenites.
68. Letter from William Hodson, *The New Moral World*, 25 Aug. 1838.
69. From a description in *The Working Bee*, 3 Aug. 1839.
70. *The Working Bee*, 28 Nov. 1840.
71. From a *Liverpool Albion* report, in *The Working Bee*, 28 Nov. 1840.
72. *The Working Bee*, 3 Aug. 1839.
73. In a letter to John Finch of Harmony Hall, in *The Working Bee*, 19 Dec. 1840.
74. Garnett (1972), p. 235 (B).
75. George Jacob Holyoake, *A Visit to Harmony Hall!*, p. 10, H. Hetherington, London, 1844.
76. *New Moral World*, 20 June 1840.
77. Alexander Somerville, *Notes from the farming districts. No. XVII. A journey to Harmony Hall in Hampshire, with some particulars of the socialist community, to which the attention of the nobility, gentry, and clergy, is earnestly requested*, p. 7, printed by W. Ostell, London, 1842.

78. Holyoake (1844), *op. cit.*, pp. 8–10.
79. It is interesting to note that Owen had been impressed by the high quality of craftsmanship in Shaker and Rappite communities, and sought to emulate their example in this respect.
80. Somerville (1842), *op. cit.*, p. 8.
81. Holyoake (1844), *op. cit.*, p. 3.
82. Holyoake (1844), *op. cit.*, p. 7.
83. Somerville (1842), *op. cit.*, p. 5.
84. See D. Thompson, 'Queenwood College, Hampshire: A mid 19th century experiment in science teaching', *Annals of Science*, Vol. XI, pp. 246–54, 1955.
85. It was known initially as 'The First Concordium', but reference to its primacy was later dropped. As George Holyoake (1906), p. 152 (A) later remarked with evident satisfaction, it was called the 'first' Concordium but it was also to be the last.
86. One interesting link was that between Alcott House and the American educational reformer, Bronson Alcott, after whom it was named. Alcott visited the English school and brought with him news of experiments and contacts in America. See F. B. Sanborn, *Bronson Alcott at Alcott House, England and Fruitlands, New England, 1842–1844*, Torch Press, Cedar Rapids, 1908.
87. *New Moral World*, 6 Dec. 1844.
88. Holyoake (1906), p. 265 (A).
89. There is much in the mysticism and vegetarianism of Concordium that anticipates the Tolstoyan communities half a century later. It is significant, too, that through Bronson Alcott there was a link with Ralph Emerson and Henry Thoreau, who are later (see pp. 162–5) described in that same tradition. It is mainly through its associations with some of the Owenites and, especially, in its emphasis on educational reform, that it is considered as a utopian socialist rather than as an anarchist community. But the typological distinction is by no means sharp in this case, and should not obscure the areas of overlap.
90. *The New Age*, 1 Sept. 1843.
91. *The New Age*, 6 May 1843.
92. In *The New Age*, 1 Sept. 1843, there was confidence that 'association will be brought into practice in many other localities, and some pleasure in hearing that a small experiment has commenced near Sheffield, and that one is contemplated near Manchester'. Thomas Frost, undeterred by his failure to join Harmony Hall and Concordium, for a while considered establishing his own community in Surrey or Kent. He was again to be disappointed, 'and the dream of planting an Atlantis among the breezy hills of Surrey was not realised' (1880) p. 52 (B).
93. *The New Age*, 1 Oct. 1844.
94. Frost (1880), pp. 46–7 (B).
95. *The Promethean*, Vol. 1, p. 69, (1842).
96. An extensive search has failed to reveal the location of Barmby's house.
97. In an advertisement for future Barmby publications, in *The Communist Miscellany*, Vol. 1, no. 5, 1843.
98. *The New Age*, 20 May 1843.
99. In his utopian *Book of Platonopolis*, which was serialised in *The Communist Chronicle*, Barmby outlined a romantic view of 'communisteries' at the heart of a regenerated world.
100. *The Apostle and Chronicle of the Communist Church*, 1 Aug. 1848.

Chapter 3

1. The origins of 'agrarian' and 'agrarianism' as radical terms, stem from the Roman 'Agrarian Laws', which governed the allocation of surplus public land to private individuals. Between about 500 B.C. and 27 B.C. the administration of these laws was an important source of social reform.
2. This definition is included in a discussion of terms in Bestor (1948) (A).

3. The term 'agrarian socialism' is preferred, in its nineteenth-century context, to 'agrarianism' – indicating that it was a specific tendency within socialism.

4. Collings (1906), p. 103 (C).

5. Reference is made in Ch. 1 to Hill's account (1958) of the 'Norman Yoke' (C).

6. More (1965), p. 47 (A).

7. More (1965), p. 75 (A).

8. In Hill (1975), p. 128 (A).

9. For sources on Winstanley see Winstanley (1965) (C), Winstanley (1973) (C) and Hill (1975) (A).

10. *The Diggers Christmas-Caroll*, verses 21–3, in Winstanley (1965), p. 671 (C).

11. Winstanley (1973), p. 295: *The Law of Freedom in a Platform* [1652] (C).

12. Winstanley (1973), p. 128: *A Watch-Word to the City of London, and the Army* [1649] (C).

13. Winstanley (1973), p. 367: *The Law of Freedom in a Platform* [1652], (C).

14. Winstanley (1973), p. 275: *The Law of Freedom in a Platform* [1652], (C).

15. Apart from separate reference to their original works see, especially, Hill (1958) (C) and Thompson (1968) (A).

16. Spence (1882), pp. 13–16 (C). *The Nationalisation of the Land* was originally published in 1775.

17. See p. 82.

18. Spence (1795), p. 84 (C).

19. Evans, in Hill (1958), p. 107 (C).

20. Paine, in Hill (1958), pp. 100–1 (C).

21. Paine (1797), p. 6 (C).

22. Paine (1797), p. 7 (C).

23. In explaining the context of the agrarian socialist communities there does not seem to be a specific connection with the American communities (as there is in the case of utopian socialism, sectarianism and anarchism). The land issue was radically different in the two countries – in America, land was abundant and freedom lay in the open frontier; in England, land was a continuing point of conflict between those who already owned it, and those who struggled to regain it. Furthermore, the more advanced stage of urbanisation in England produced its own form of reaction and commitment to the land. For those who identified a return to the land with greater freedom, America – a republic of small, independent farms – was an attractive model, but the land movements in the two countries followed their own paths. In the late twentieth century there are more similarities, and this connection is pursued in the last chapter.

24. In O'Connor, F. and Jones, E., *The Labourer*, London, 1847, p. 81.

25. Apart from specific references to O'Connor, helpful sources on the Chartist colonies are *The Northern Star* (from 1842, when O'Connor first outlined his land scheme); *Parliamentary Papers, 1847–48*, vol. XIX (which record the inquiry into the Land Company); Armytage (1958) (C); and Hadfield (1970) (C).

26. John Revans, in his submission to the Select Committee on the National Land Company, *Parliamentary Papers, 1847–48*, vol. XIX, p. 244.

27. O'Connor, in Armytage (1961), p. 227 (A).

28. O'Connor's description of himself, in Hadfield (1970), p. 46 (C).

29. From an appeal by O'Connor in April 1848, in Armytage (1961), p. 231 (A).

30. Ruskin's attempt to put his ideas into practice was developed in *Fors Clavigera: Letters to the Workmen and Labourers of Great Britain*, published between 1871 and 1884. See Ruskin (1871–84) (C) and Spence (1957) (C).

31. Ruskin (1871–84), Letter V, 1871, p. 21 (C).

32. Ruskin (1871–84), Letter XXXVII, 1874, p. 7 (C).

33. Ruskin (1871–84), Letter VIII, 1871, p. 14 (C).

34. Ruskin (1871–84) Letter V, 1871, pp. 21–2 (C).

35. Riley, in Armytage (1961), p. 296 (A).

36. The most comprehensive explanation of this difference between Ruskin and Morris is that in Thompson (1977) (E).

37. Blatchford (1976), Ch. VII (C).

38. Blatchford's articles were published under the pseudonym of 'Nunquam', in *The*

Clarion, 1892–93, and republished as a book in 1893. Cheaper editions followed and over a million copies were sold.

39. George (1953), p. 128 (C). The original publication of *Progress and Poverty* was in 1879.

40. George (1953), pp. 29–30 (C).

41. The Small Holdings Act of 1882 was dependent on County Council support.

42. A tradition of charitable 'home colonies' extends back well before this period. An early nineteenth-century model of a colony to relieve rural distress was that of Lindfield in Sussex, the work of William Allen. His ideas were outlined in a pamphlet, *Colonies at Home*, 1827. Similar schemes were often proposed as alternatives to the workhouse – such as the Hollow Meadows Farm Experiment near Sheffield in 1848 (see John Salt, *Isaac Ironside and the Hollow Meadows Farm Experiment*, Yorkshire Bulletin of Economic and Social Research, Vol. XII, 1960, pp. 45–51). A more ambitious plan for colonies was that of General Booth, outlined in *In Darkest England and the Way Out* (1890) (C); as a result, the Salvation Army was responsible for a number of interesting and influential schemes.

By the end of the century, home colonies were promoted by a wide variety of philanthropic organisations, and a coordinating body, 'The Central Council of Home Colonies and Rural Industries' was established ' . . . to supply a bond of union between the different Societies and Individuals working in various ways to assist the transference of unemployed individuals from the towns to work in the rural districts, and to stimulate the growth and consumption of products derived from English land.' The societies that affiliated serve to illustrate the intensity of interest in home colonisation at that time: 'The Agricultural Banks Association', 'The Allotments and Small Holdings Association', 'The Association for Improving the Conditions of the People', 'The Christian Union for Social Service', 'The English Land Colonisation Society', 'The Home Colonisation Society', 'The Mansion House Unemployment Committee', and 'The Rural Industries Cooperative Society'. See Hobson (1895) (C).

43. Hill (1958), p. 108 (C).

44. The settlement is now known as Heronsgate.

45. Letter from 'A true Englishman' to *The Suffolk Chronicle*, in *The Northern Star*, 22 Jan. 1848.

46. Ironically, the only serious criticism of the Chartist housing came from some of the unallocated members of the Land Company, who considered that the housing was better-equipped and more extravagant than it need have been.

47. The evidence of John Revans, in *Parliamentary Papers, 1847–48*. vol. XIX.

48. Thomas Martin Wheeler, 'Notes of a journey from O'Connorville to the Chartist estates . . .', in *The Northern Star*, 12 Feb. 1848.

49. *The Northern Star*, 8 Jan. 1848.

50. *The Northern Star*, 17 June 1848.

51. Thomas Martin Wheeler, in *The Northern Star*, 12 Feb. 1848.

52. From *A Dodford Ditty, or A Song of Home*, in P. Searby, 'Great Dodford and the later history of the Chartist land scheme', *Agricultural History Review*, Vol. 16, 1968.

53. Searby (1968), *op. cit.*, discusses the occupational backgrounds of the Great Dodford colonists.

54. Ruskin (1871–84), Letter LXXVI, 1877, p. 113 (C).

55. Ruskin (1871–84), Letter LXXIX, 1877, p. 182 (C).

56. Ruskin, in Spence (1957), p. 192 (C).

57. Edward Carpenter's own ideas are considered in Ch. 5, pp. 170–1.

58. Carpenter, in *Commonweal*, 9 Mar. 1889.

59. Herbert Rix, 'A visit to Methwold', in *Seed Time*, October, 1893.

60. W. C. Sambrook, 'A fruit farm colony in Norfolk – how to live and be happy on two acres', in *The Cable*, 25 Feb. 1899.

61. *The Cable*, 25 Feb. 1899.

62. *The Cable*, 25 Feb. 1899.

63. *The Cable*, 4 Mar. 1899.

64. *Seed Time*, October, 1893.

65. Robert Blatchford wrote three articles on 'The Westmorland commune', in *The*

Clarion, 14 May, 4 June and 11 June 1892.

66. Mills, in *The Clarion*, 11 June 1892.
67. Reprinted in *The Clarion*, 14 May 1892.
68. *The Clarion*, 4 June 1892.
69. *The Clarion*, 1 Apr. 1893.
70. See pp. 184–6.
71. T. Bulmer and Co., *History, Topography and Directory of Westmorland, c.* 1905.
72. Sources for the Mayland Colony include *The New Order, Essex County Chronicle*, Fels (1920) (C); also, see Ronald Webber, 'The printer who came back to the land', *Essex Countryside*, June 1975.
73. *The Labour Annual*, 1897, p. 154.
74. R. Hedger Wallace, in the *Essex County Chronicle*, 9 May 1902.
75. Fels (1920), p. 78 (C).
76. *The New Order*, January 1897.

Chapter 4

1. This is the dialectical explanation offered by Ernst Troeltsch, *Social Teachings of the Christian Churches*, Macmillan, New York, 1931 (originally published in 1912).
2. For an extended account of sectarian characteristics and types, see Wilson (1970) (D).
3. An explanation of the radical origins of the Quaker movement is pursued later in this chapter, but there is little doubt that in the nineteenth century the Quaker settlements were more akin to model villages than to alternative communities. The Salvation Army 'colonies' were rather different, being part of a scheme to save bodies as well as souls – to rescue the destitute from slum conditions, and through the colonies to prepare them for a new moral and physical life. The farm colony at Hadleigh in Essex is an interesting example of this type of venture. Undoubtedly, in General Booth's *In Darkest England and the Way Out* (1890) (C) there is an attack on capitalism, but the effect is to chip away at the excesses of the system rather than at the roots. Wilson (1970, p. 62) (D) takes a similar view – 'Booth's scheme was over-ambitious but he was far from being a revolutionary. His plan was not in the usual sense a millennial dream: he did not advocate overturning the social system, nor did he expect the advent of Christ to signal the time when his plan might be implemented. It was rather a reformatory scheme to be run in harness with revivalist and evangelistic effort'. See also Note 28 in Ch. 3.
4. 'Messianism' is closely associated with other terms used in this chapter, and it may be helpful to offer an explanation of their differences. Associated terms are 'eschatology' and 'chiliasm'. Kohn (1967) (D) defines eschatology as the doctrine of the final things concerning man and the world, and the theory of the ages of the world, as the basis of chiliasm, or millenarianism. But he warns that messianism should not be conflated with these other ideas: 'Speculation about final things, such as death, life after death, and the end of the world, which is quite general in religious doctrine, does not necessarily involve a distinct messianic belief; on the other hand, Jews often thought of the coming of the Messiah without implying thereby the end of the world or even the transformation of the whole world. Messianism, moreover, is never mere theoretical speculation about things to come; it is always a living practical force'.
5. For a comparative picture of messianism, see Thrupp (1962) (D) and Wilson (1970) (D).
6. *The Acts of the Apostles*, 2: 44, 45.
7. Cohn (1970), p. 15 (D).
8. A classical explanation of the social basis for sectarian activity is that provided by Niebuhr (1957), originally published in 1929 (D).
9. See Cohn (1970), p. 282 (D).
10. Weber (1965), p. 106 (D).
11. Lawrence (1975), p. 11 (D).
12. Mannheim (1960), pp. 193, 195 (A).

13. See, for instance, Cohn (1970) (D) and Wilson (1970) (D).

14. Armytage (1961) (A) is particularly helpful on this subject for this period.

15. For more information on Quaker involvement in model communities see, for instance, Arthur Raistrick, *Quakers in Science and Industry*, David and Charles, 1968; and Darley (1975) (A). More detailed references are indicated in Anthony Sutcliffe, *A History of Modern Town Planning: A Bibliographical Guide*, Centre for Urban and Regional Studies, 1977.

16. For details on these see Dobb (1951) (D).

17. Charles Kingsley, in Darley (1975), p. 79 (A) in the context of an illustrated account of the Moravian communities.

18. In Davies (1963) p. 64 (D).

19. A good account of this is provided by Sanford (1961), Ch. 5 (G).

20. This estimate is derived from the work of Bestor (1970) (G).

21. See pp. 41–42.

22. In Lockwood (1971), p. 28 (G).

23. William Hebert, *A Visit to the Colony of Harmony in Indiana, in the United States of America, recently purchased by Mr Owen for the establishment of a Society of Mutual Cooperation and Community of Property*, p. 2. Printed for G. Mann, London, 1825.

24. There is an extensive literature on the Shakers. Useful introductory accounts of their communities are included in Nordhoff (1965) (G), Whitworth (1975) (F) and Hayden (1976) (G).

25. Nordhoff (1965), pp. 117–18 (G).

26. For an outline of the movement, see Armytage (1961) (A) and Wilson (1970) (D), and for the design implications of the City of Zion, see Reps (1965) (G).

27. This interpretation is pursued in Thompson (1968), Ch. 11.

28. For references to Brothers and Southcott, see Thompson (1968), pp. 127–9 and 420–6 (A).

29. Mary Girling's community was widely referred to as the 'New Forest Shakers'. See pp. 145–50.

30. An account of J. N. Tom (or 'Sir William Courtenay') is provided in P. G. Rogers, *Battle in Bossenden Wood*, Oxford University Press, London, 1961.

31. Harrison (1969), p. 122 (B).

32. Smith, Rev J. E., *Lecture on a Christian Community*, London, 1965, p. 11.

33. Various works relating to the 'Peculiar People' are held in the Essex Record Office Library. These include works by members of the sect, notably, Isaac Anderson's *The Origin of the Peculiar People* (1882), and *The First Fifty Years of the Peculiar People* (*c.* 1884).

34. I Peter (2:9) – 'But ye are a chosen generation, a royal priesthood, an holy nation, a peculiar people . . .'

35. Sources for this community include the *Illustrated London News*, 29 March 1851; Montgomery (1962) (D); and Donald McCormick's *Temple of Love*, Jarrolds, London, 1962.

36. *Illustrated London News*, 29 March 1851.

37. Of a number of references available in the West Sussex Record Office, two articles have proved to be particularly helpful – that of Earl Winterton, 'The Cokelers: A Sussex sect', *Sussex County Magazine*, vol. 5, pp. 717–22, 1931; and Donald MacAndrew, 'The Sussex Cokelers: A curious sect', *Sussex County Magazine*, vol. 16, pp. 346–50, 1942. There is also an account in Montgomery (1962), Ch. 13 (D).

38. The most commonly-held explanation is that 'Cokelers' is a derivation of 'cocoa-drinkers' – a term applied to the sect on account of their abstinence from alcoholic drinks, and their apparent habit of drinking cocoa between services.

39. From the letter to John Sirgood, in Winterton (1931), *op. cit.*

40. A valuable source of material on this community is a collection of tracts produced by the sect and local newspaper cuttings, held in Wakefield Library.

41. *Free Press*, 28 Feb. 1874.

42. John Wroe had an active following in Australia (as a result of two visits he made) and many of the donations were from these supporters.

43. From a poster entitled 'Christian Israelite Church Sanctuary: Prophet Wroe and the

Wrenthorpe Sanctuary'.

44. *Wakefield Express*, 6 June 1857.
45. *Free Press*, 28 Feb. 1874.
46. Apart from local newspaper cuttings, two informative sources are T. A. Wylie's articles, 'The New Forest "Shakers"', Milford-on-Sea Record Society, June 1927; and 'Arnewood Tower', Milford-on-Sea Record Society, June 1927.
47. Wylie, *op. cit.*, p. 21.
48. Mary Ann Girling, in Wylie, *op. cit.*, p. 29.
49. Wylie, *op. cit.*, pp. 32–3.
50. Sources for Jezreel's community include newscuttings in the Kent County Library at Gillingham; the *Pall Mall Gazette*, 6 Mar. 1885 and 2 July 1888; P. G. Rogers, *The Sixth Trumpeter*, Oxford University Press, London, 1963; and publications currently produced by the 'New and Latter House of Israel', in England and North America.
51. The figure of 144,000 was prescribed in the Bible: 'And I heard the number of them which were sealed: and there were sealed an hundred and forty and four thousand of all the tribes of the children of Israel' (Revelation, 7:4).
52. A copy was included in the *Chatham and Rochester Observer*, 4 July 1885.
53. *Chatham and Rochester Observer*, 4 July 1885.

Chapter 5

1. For an introduction to anarchism, with their own helpful bibliographies, see Woodcock (1975) and (1977) (E).
2. Berkman (1973), p. 42 (E).
3. This is the view of Woodcock (1975), p. 24 (E).
4. Editorial in *The Free Commune*, June 1898.
5. The main source of his ideas is to be found in *Enquiry Concerning Political Justice and its Influence on Modern Morals and Happiness*, first published in 1793, see Godwin, (1976) (E).
6. See Roll (1973), p. 195 (B).
7. Of these poets, Shelley – 'the greatest of anarchist poets' – was the most consistent voice of Godwin's principles. See Woodcock (1975), p. 85 (E).
8. See pp. 170–72.
9. Godwin (1976), p. 254 (E).
10. Godwin (1976), p. 610 (E).
11. Godwin (1976), p. 745 (E).
12. Godwin (1976), pp. 746–7 (E).
13. For suggestions of possible links see Woodcock (1975), Ch. 3 (E), and the introduction by Kraminck in Godwin (1976) (E).
14. For a development of this critique see p. 214.
15. From Proudhon, (1970), 'Economic contradictions', pp. 410–11 (E).
16. From Proudhon, (1970), 'Property', p. 144 (E).
17. For a helpful analysis of the development of American anarchism, see Schuster (1932) (G).
18. The term is used by Schuster (1932) (G), who provides a valuable explanation of the way in which Proudhon's ideas were absorbed alongside an independent development of 'mutualist' ideas. She argues that the French and American strains of mutualism are eventually synthesised in the work of Benjamin Tucker. Another helpful reference to Warren is Bailie (1906) (G).
19. This is the view of Woodcock (1975), p. 432 (E).
20. Warren did, in fact, participate in Robert Owen's New Harmony experiment. The story is that, after hearing Owen lecture during a visit to Cincinnati, he sold his lamp factory and moved with his family to New Harmony. 'If New Harmony were not sufficiently noteworthy as one of the first socialist experiments in the United States and for its large assemblage of famous scientists and educators, it would be worthy of mention because it produced an anarchist', Schuster, (1932), p. 93 (G).

21. Joseph Warren, in Schuster (1932), p. 94 (G).
22. Joseph Warren, in Bailie (1906), pp. 54–5 (G).
23. Thoreau (1960), p. 221 (G).
24. Thoreau (1960), p. 240 (G).
25. Thoreau (1960), p. 66 (G).
26. Thoreau (1960), p. 67 (G).
27. Thoreau (1960), p. 46 (G).
28. Thoreau (1960), p. 143 (G).
29. Thoreau (1960), p. 210 (G).
30. *Freedom* is still produced in London as a weekly publication.
31. The presence of a number of revolutionaries in London at this time is the theme of the book by Hulse (1970) (E).
32. See pp.184–6.
33. See pp.182–3.
34. From Kropotkin, (1970), *Anarchism: its Philosophy and Ideal*, p. 129 (E).
35. Kropotkin (1976), pp. 30–1 (E).
36. Kropotkin, in Buber, (1949), p. 42 (A).
37. Kropotkin (1969), pp. 23–4 (E).
38. Kropotkin (1974), p. 26 (E).
39. In Kropotkin (1974), pp. 105–6 (E).
40. Kropotkin's vision of labour with 'many charms' compares with Morris's 'joyful labour' in *News from Nowhere*. Both held the view that it was not work as such that was objectionable, but 'alienated' work.
41. Kropotkin (1974), p. 106 (E).
42. Carpenter (1911), p. 21 (E).
43. See Morris (1970) (E) and Thompson (1977) (E).
44. Carpenter (1917), p. 58 (E).
45. Carpenter (1917), pp. 61–2 (E).
46. Wilde (1966), p. 916 (E).
47. Wilde (1966), p. 918 (E).
48. Wilde (1966), p. 924 (E).
49. The words of John Kenworthy, in *Seed Time*, Apr. 1895.
50. Extract from *The Cossacks*; where Olenin compares life in the Caucasus with the sophistications of the city.
51. Tolstoy (1894), Preface (E).
52. Tolstoy (1894), pp. 118–20 (E).
53. Tolstoy (1894), p. 285 (E).
54. Tolstoy (1972), pp. 34–5 (E). *The Slavery of Our Times* was written in 1900.
55. Tolstoy (1972), p. 38 (E).
56. Tolstoy, 'Address to the Working Class': an article that first appeared in English in *Reynold News*, August 1903.
57. Shaw (1935), p. 49 (E).
58. A good account of these origins is given in Shaw (1935) (E). The author, Nellie Shaw, was a founder member of the group that gathered at Croydon and, subsequently, of the Whiteway Colony.
59. The point of division was reached at a meeting in December, 1883, after which Frank Podmore called a subsequent meeting to constitute the Fabian Society – as an intellectual pressure group.
60. Extract from editorial in *Seed Time*, Oct. 1894.
61. Herbert Rix, 'The return to Nature', in *Seed Time*, Oct. 1889.
62. Shaw (1935), p. 19 (E).
63. Shaw (1935), p. 21 (E).
64. *The New Order*, Jan. 1897.
65. Kenworthy's letters were published in *The New Age* during 1896.
66. Shaw (1935), pp. 29–31 (E).
67. W. MacQueen, in *The Free Commune*, June 1898.
68. *The Labour Annual*, 1896, p. 23.
69. *The Clarion*, 24 Dec. 1897. Other sources on the community's organisation include a

report in *Le Temps*, cited in Gide (1930), p. 165 (A), and occasional references to the community in *The New Order*.

70. Frank Kapper, *The Clarion*, 22 Feb. 1896.
71. Frank Kapper, *The Clarion*, 22 Feb. 1896.
72. Extract from an account by Ben Glover, in Armytage (1961), pp. 313–14 (A).
73. Extract from editorial in *Freedom*, Sept. 1891.
74. Hugh Mapleton, in *The New Order*, Oct. 1898.
75. Hugh Mapleton, in *The New Order*, Oct. 1898.
76. From an article, 'Four bachelors were Norton's colonists', in the *Sheffield Telegraph*, 30 Sept. 1957.
77. Frank Johnson, *Sheffield Telegraph*, 30 Sept. 1957.
78. Shaw (1935), p. 31 (E).
79. In the 1840s both Thomas Frost and the Concordists of Ham Common had been unsuccessful in their searches for land in Surrey. See pp. 62 and 243 (n.92).
80. Shaw (1935), p. 36 (E).
81. The point was not lost in reports on the community, which was monitored regularly in *The New Order* (in the form of 'Purleigh Notes'), and, locally, in the *Essex County Chronicle*. The latter carried titles such as 'Bread labour at Purleigh' (23 Apr. 1897), 'The new order at Purleigh' (22 Oct. 1897), and 'Religion of labour and self-denial' (12 Nov. 1897).
82. *Essex County Chronicle*, 22 Oct. 1897.
83. *Essex County Chronicle*, 19 Aug. 1898.
84. *The New Order*, Oct. 1897.
85. W. Hone, in *The New Order*, Oct. 1897.
86. This contradicts the views of some colonists who actually left Purleigh because they disagreed with the selection process for new members.
87. *The New Order*, Apr. 1898. ,
88. Aylmer Maude lived at Wickham's Farm, adjoining the colony.
89. *The Labour Annual*, 1898, p. 94.
90. *The New Order*, Apr. 1898.
91. This particular comment is from a report in *The New Order* in December 1898. The publication carried regular reports ('Leeds Notes') on the community between 1897 and 1899.
92. *The Free Commune*, June 1898. No. 6, Victoria Road was within an inner zone of Leeds that has now been extensively redeveloped.
93. *The New Order*, August, 1898.
94. Shaw (1935), p. 120 (E).
95. *The New Order*, Dec. 1898.
96. 'Community Directory', in *The Labour Annual*, 1897, pp. 153–4.
97. *Essex County Chronicle*, 24 June, 1898.
98. From *The Centenary of a 'Crank' Publisher: Charles William Daniel (1871–1955)*, published by the C. W. Daniel Company in 1971.
99. The Wickford Colony in question is not to be confused with another scheme in the district at the same time. In the 1897 edition of the *Labour Annual* (a year before the above) it was announced that a colony had been started at Wickford by John Orme, formerly president of the 'Nationalisation of Labour Society'. But in 1902 a local newspaper report showed little sympathy for its apparent demise: 'What is termed a Socialist experiment at Wickford is, in reality, a private venture. A Mr Orme, after trying for some years to establish a colony on Socialist lines, got tired of waiting, and himself bought 5½ acres of land and, with the help of his two sons, and the kindly offer of a neighbour, this land is being cropped' (*Essex County Chronicle*, 9 May 1902).
100. Jack Goring, in *The New Order*, Oct. 1898.
101. *The New Order* provides a useful source of information on this community, with a limited number of 'Wickford Notes' in 1898.
102. Henry Power in *The New Order*, March 1898.
103. Henry Power in *The New Order*, March 1898.
104. Jack Goring in *The New Order*, Aug. 1898.

105. Henry Power in *The New Order*, March 1898.
106. Joseph Burtt, one of the pioneer colonists at Whiteway, in Shaw (1935), p. 5 (E).
107. Shaw (1935), p. 43 (E).
108. Shaw (1935), p. 52 (E).
109. *The New Order*, June 1898.
110. Shaw (1935), p. 54–5 (E).
111. Shaw (1935), p. 128 (E).
112. Shaw (1935), p. 56 (E).
113. William Sinclair, in Shaw (1935), pp. 81–2 (E).
114. Shaw (1935), pp. 59–60 (E).
115. Shaw (1935), p. 88 (E).
116. Shaw (1935), p. 229 (E).
117. From time to time there are reminders of its local history. For instance, at a recent Rating Valuation Panel, the valuation officer spoke of the problems posed by the burning of the original property deeds.
118. Shaw (1935), p. 225 (E).
119. Joseph Burtt, in Shaw (1935), p. 6 (E).
120. Tom Ferris, in *The New Order*, Aug. 1899.
121. Tom Ferris, in *Blackburn Times*, 15 July 1899.
122. Tom Ferris, in *Blackburn Times*, 15 July 1899.
123. Tom Ferris, in *Blackburn Times*, 15 July 1899.
124. Tom Ferris, in *The New Order*, Nov. 1899.
125. The shop in Victoria Street, where onlookers could once see the works of Tolstoy, is now a second-hand furniture store. There was also a Brotherhood Church in the London Road in 1900, but this, too, seems to have gone by 1903.

Chapter 6

1. These were the Chartist settlements of Snigs End and Lowbands.
2. Jasper Veysey, in *The Cooperative Magazine and Monthly Herald*, July 1826. For details of Veysey's community, see pp. 46–48.
3. Engels (1962), p. 119 (A).
4. Marx and Engels (1972), p. 71 (A).
5. Marx and Engels (1972), p. 72–3 (A).
6. Buber (1949) (A) provides a good account of the communitarian response to the Marxist critique in the century from 1848. The debate continues, and more recent responses are included in contemporary literature on communes and the alternative society, as referenced later in this chapter.
7. Bakunin, M., 'Statism and Anarchy' in M. S. Sharz (ed.), *The Essential Works of Anarchism*, Bantam, New York, 1971, pp. 178–9.
8. From the editorial in *The Clarion*, 22 Feb. 1896.
9. George Bernard Shaw, in Armytage (1961), p. 332 (A).
10. Edward R. Pease (Secretary of the Fabian Society), in *The Clarion*, 29 Apr. 1893.
11. Ruskin (1871–84), Letter I, 1875, p. 42 (C).
12. Shaw (1935), p. 228 (E).
13. *The Labour Annual*, 1900.
14. Holyoake (1906) pp. 166 and 199 (A).
15. Nordhoff (1965), p. 395 (G).
16. Nordhoff (1965), p. 408 (G).
17. Hillquit (1965), p. 126 (G).
18. Mannheim (1960) (A).
19. Kanter (1972), p. 224 (A).
20. Buber (1949), p. 13 (A).
21. Nordhoff (1965), p. 391 (G).
22. Buber (1949), p. 14 (A).
23. Buber (1949), pp. 148–9 (A).

24. Community Service Committee (1938), p. 9 (F).
25. Community Service Committee (1938), p. 9 (F).
26. Sisley Tanner, *Cooperation and Community* in Community Service Committee (1938), p. 132 (F).
27. For details of this revival of cooperation, see Dent (1931) (F).
28. A. J. Penty, one of the main advocates of Guild Socialism, in Williams (1958), p. 188 (A).
29. This case is developed in G. D. H. Cole (1920) (F).
30. An account of these groups is included in Carpenter (1922) (F).
31. Hilaire Belloc, in Carpenter (1922), p. 62 (F).
32. Scott (1935), p. 11 (F).
33. See Armytage (1961), pp. 408–9 (A).
34. In addition to Murry's own schemes he was a prolific writer on what he saw to be the basis of a new society, and was at one time secretary of the Community Service Committee.
35. Murry, J. M., *The New Community* in Community Service Committee (1938), p. 126 (F).
36. Murry, *op. cit.*, p. 125.
37. Murry (1942), pp. 118–9 (F).
38. For details of some of these schemes, see the Community Service Committee's *Community in Britain*, 1938 (F).
39. Community Service Committee (1938), p. 202 (F).
40. See Rigby (1974a), pp. 26–8 (F).
41. See Armytage (1961), pp. 398–9 (A).
42. Dent (1928) (F).
43. Murry (1952), p. 34 (F).
44. Ineson (1956), p. 96 (F).
45. The findings are recorded in the publication of the Community Service Committee (1938) (F).
46. Advertisement in *In the Making*, a directory of cooperative projects, No. 4, 1977, p. 53.
47. Abrams and McCulloch (1976), p. 33 (F).
48. There seems little disagreement that communes are of this order. Abrams and McCulloch (1976, p. 39) (F) cite this range as a well-confirmed observation both in this country and in the United States. Whitworth (1975), p. 131 (F) speculates that probably more than 90 per cent of contemporary communes have less than twenty persons.
49. Again, Abrams and McCulloch (1976, p. 39) (F) assert that so long as communes wish to promote friendship they will find that a total membership of twenty-five represents a limit beyond which intense relationships among all members of a group becomes impossible.
50. Rigby (1974a) (F).
51. Rigby (1974b, p. 4) (F) estimated a total of around 100 communes in 1972, and there is every sign in the reports and advertisements in alternative publications to believe that this figure has increased.
52. Writing primarily about North American communities, Whitworth (1975, p. 117) (F) takes the view that the peak is indeed past. He locates its heyday in the six or seven years after 1965. The English movement has generally followed a comparable course to that in America, but has been two or three years behind in its developments. On that basis, one might expect the peak to have been reached in the mid 1970s. An alternative speculation is that there has been not so much a falling-off in numbers as a qualitative change in communes, from their original form as uncompromising critics of society and towards more practical, less isolated schemes. This transition is explained later in this section.
53. This notion of a 'Fourth World' is defined and developed in the publication *Resurgence* (*Journal of the Fourth World*).
54. Various references to these and other examples are included in the bibliography, but for a helpful introduction to a wide range of experiments and source material see Leech (1973) (F), Saunders (1975) (F), and Boyle and Harper (1976) (F).

55. Marcuse (1969), p. 25 (F).
56. Houriet (1973), p. 12 (G).
57. From the editorial in *Resurgence*, Vol. 7, no. 5, Nov.–Dec. 1976.
58. Rivers (1975), Ch. 1 (F).
59. Ineson, G., 'Reflections on Community' in *Resurgence*, Vol. 7, no. 5, Nov.–Dec. 1976. For the beginnings of his involvement in communities, see Ineson (1956) (F).
60. Houriet (1973), p. 10 (G).
61. No less than for the number of communes in England, estimates are notoriously difficult. Houriet (1973, p. 10) (G) cites alternative sources which suggest that the number may have been between 2,000 and 3,000 in 1970; and Jerome (1975, Ch. 1) (G) makes the claim that there could be as many as 30,000 communes in rural areas alone. Set against this latter type of claim is the note of caution offered by Whitworth (1975) (F) that the peak of commune activity may now have passed.
62. Hayden (1976), p, 323 (G).
63. Houriet (1973), p. 364 (G).
64. Nyerere (1968), p. 143 (F).
65. Abrams and McCulloch (1976), p. 205 (F).
66. Abrams and McCulloch (1976), p. 200 (F).
67. Whitworth (1975), p. 135 (F).
68. A communitarian response, in Rigby (1974a), p. 252 (F).
69. A communitarian response, in Rigby (1974b), p. 42 (F).
70. Hill (1975), p. 17 (A).

Bibliography

Detailed references to specific communities are included in the preceding 'Notes' and are not repeated here. Special mention can be made of those references to periodicals produced in the communities themselves – providing, as they do, a rich source of material for further work on this subject.

A. General

Armytage, W. H. G., *Heavens Below: Utopian Experiments in England, 1560–1960.* Routledge and Kegan Paul, London, 1961.

Armytage, W. H. G., *Yesterday's Tomorrows: A Historical Survey of Future Societies.* Routledge and Kegan Paul, London, 1968.

Bauman, Z., *Socialism: The Active Utopia.* Allen and Unwin, London, 1976:

Bell, C. and R., *City Fathers: The Early History of Town Planning in Britain.* Penguin, Harmondsworth, 1972.

Berneri, M. L., *A Journey through Utopia.* Routledge and Kegan Paul, London, 1949.

Bestor, A. E., 'The evolution of the socialist vocabulary', *Journal of the History of Ideas*, Vol. 9, pp. 259–302, 1948.

Buber, M., *Paths in Utopia.* Routledge and Kegan Paul, London, 1949.

Chandler, A., *A Dream of Order: The Mediaeval Ideal in Nineteenth Century Literature.* Routledge and Kegan Paul, London, 1971.

Cobbett, W., *Rural Rides.* Edited by G. Woodcock, Penguin, Harmondsworth, 1967.

Darley, G., *Villages of Vision.* The Architectural Press, London, 1975.

Engels, F., 'Socialism: utopian and scientific', in *Selected Works*, Vol. II, Foreign Languages Publishing House, Moscow, 1962.

Engels, F., *The Condition of the Working Class in England.* Introduction by E. Hobsbawm. Panther Books, St Albans, 1969.

Fromm, E. (ed.), *Socialist Humanism.* Allen Lane, London, 1967.

Gide, C., *Communist and Cooperative Colonies.* Harrap, London, 1930.

Hill, C., *The World Turned Upside Down: Radical Ideas During the English Revolution.* Penguin, Harmondsworth, 1975.

Holyoake, G. J., *The History of Cooperation.* T. Fisher Unwin, London, 1906.

Kanter, R. M., *Commitment and Community: Communes and Utopias in Sociological Perspective.* Harvard University Press, Cambridge (Mass.), 1972.

Mannheim, K., *Ideology and Utopia: An Introduction to the Sociology of Knowledge.* Routledge and Kegan Paul, London, 1960.

Marx, K. and Engels, F., *Manifesto of the Communist Party.* Foreign Languages Press, Peking, 1972.

More, T., *Utopia.* Introduction by P. Turner. Penguin, Harmondsworth, 1965.

Morton, A. L., *The English Utopia.* Lawrence and Wishart, London, 1969.

Mumford, L., *The City in History.* Penguin, Harmondsworth, 1966.

Rexroth, K., *Communalism: From its Origins to the Twentieth Century.* Peter Owen, London, 1975.

Teselle, S. (ed.), *The Family, Communes and Utopian Societies.* Harper, New York, 1972.
Thompson, E. P., *The Making of the English Working Class.* Penguin, Harmondsworth, 1968.
Tönnies, F., *Community and Association.* Routledge and Kegan Paul, London, 1974.
Williams, R., *Culture and Society, 1780–1950.* Chatto and Windus, London, 1958.
Williams, R., *The Country and the City.* Chatto and Windus, London, 1973.
Williams, R., *Keywords: A Vocabulary of Culture and Society.* Fontana/Croom Helm, Glasgow, 1976.

B. Utopian socialist communities

Benevolo, L., *The Origins of Modern Town Planning.* Routledge and Kegan Paul, London, 1967.
Carpenter, K. E. (ed.), *The Rational System (Seven Pamphlets, 1837–41).* Arno Press, New York, 1972a.
Carpenter, K. E. (ed.), *Cooperative Communities: Plans and Descriptions (Eleven Pamphlets, 1825–1847).* Arno Press, New York, 1972b.
Carpenter, K. E. *(ed.), Owenism and the Working Class (Six Pamphlets and Four Broadsides, 1821–1834).* Arno Press, New York, 1972c.
Colletti, L., 'Rousseau as critic of "civil society"', in *From Rousseau to Lenin: Studies in Ideology and Society.* N. L. B., London, 1972.
Fourier, C., *Design for Utopia: Selected Writings of Charles Fourier.* Introduction by F. E. Manuel. Schocken Books, New York, 1971.
Frost, T., *Forty Years Recollections – Literary and Political.* Sampson Law and Co., London, 1880.
Garnett, R. G., *Co-operation and the Owenite Socialist Communities in Britain, 1825–1845.* Manchester University Press, 1972.
Harrison, J. F. C., *Robert Owen and the Owenites in Britain and America: The Quest for the New Moral World.* Routledge and Kegan Paul, London, 1969.
Haworth, A., *Planning and Philosophy: The Case of Owenism and the Owenite Communities.* Urban Studies, Vol. 13, pp. 147–53, 1976.
Johnson, C. H., *Utopian Communism in France: Cabet and the Icarians, 1839–51.* Cornell University Press, Ithaca, 1974.
Loubère, L., *Utopian Socialism: Its History since 1800.* Schenkman Publishing Co., Cambridge (Mass.), 1974.
Owen, R., *A New View of Society, and other writings.* Introduction by G. D. H. Cole. Dent, London, 1927.
Owen, R., *The Life of Robert Owen, written by himself,* Vol. 1. Frank Cass, London, 1967.
Plamenatz, J., 'The early socialists, French and English', in *Man and Society,* Vol. 2. Longman, London, 1963.
Podmore, F., *Robert Owen: A Biography.* Hutchinson, London, 1906.
Roll, E., *A History of Economic Thought.* Faber and Faber, London, 1973.
Thompson, W., *An Inquiry into the Principles of the Distribution of Wealth most conducive to Human Happiness applied to the newly proposed System of Voluntary Equality of Wealth.* Longman, London, 1824.
Thompson, W., *Practical Directions for the Speedy and Economical Establishment of Communities, on the principles of Mutual Cooperation, United Possessions and Equality of Exertions and of the Means of Enjoyment.* Cork, 1830.

C. Agrarian socialist communities

Armytage, W. H. G., 'The Chartist land colonies, 1846–48', *Agricultural History.* Vol. 32, No. 4, 1958.
Blatchford, R., *Merrie England.* Reprinted by Journeyman Press, London, 1976.
Booth, William, *In Darkest England and the Way Out.* Salvation Army, London, 1890.

Collings, J., *Land Reform: Occupying Ownership, Peasant Proprietary and Rural Education.* Longman, London, 1906.

Collings, J., *The Colonization of Rural Britain.* Rural World Publishing Co., London, 1914.

Fels, M., *Joseph Fels: His Life-Work.* Allen and Unwin, London, 1920.

George, H., *Progress and Poverty.* Hogarth Press, London, 1953.

Hadfield, A. M., *The Chartist Land Company.* David and Charles, Newton Abbott, 1970.

Hill, C., 'The Norman Yoke', in *Puritanism and Revolution: Studies in Interpretation of the English Revolution of the Seventeenth Century,* Secker and Warburg, London, 1958.

Hilton, R. H., *The English Peasantry in the Later Middle Ages.* Clarendon Press, Oxford, 1975.

Hobson, J. A. (ed.), *Cooperative Labour upon the Land.* Swan, Sonnenschein and Co., London, 1895.

Hyndman, H. M., *England for All: The Text Book for Democracy.* Harvester Press, Brighton, 1973.

Jebb, L., *The Small Holdings of England.* John Murray, London, 1907.

Merrington, J., 'Town and country in the transition to capitalism', New Left Review, Vol. 93, pp. 71–92, 1975.

O'Connor, F., *A Practical Work on the Management of Small Farms.* A. Heywood, Manchester, 1843.

Paine, T., *Agrarian Justice as opposed to Agrarian Law and to Agrarian Monopoly.* T. Williams, London, 1797.

Ruskin, J., *Fors Clavigera: Letters to the Workmen and Labourers of Great Britain.* George Allen, Orpington, 1871–84.

Spence, M. E., 'The Guild of St George: Ruskin's attempt to translate his ideas into practice', *Bulletin of the John Rylands Library,* Vol. XL, pp 147–201, 1957.

Spence, T., *Description of Spensonia.* London, 1795.

Spence, T., *The Constitution of Spensonia: A Country in Fairyland situated between Utopia and Oceana.* London, 1801.

Spence, T., *The Nationalisation of the Land in 1775 and 1782.* Edited by H. M. Hyndman, E. W. Allen, London, 1882.

Thompson, E. P., *Whigs and Hunters: The Origins of the Black Act.* Allen Lane, London, 1975.

Winstanley, G., *The Works of Gerrard Winstanley.* Edited by G. H. Sabine. Russell and Russell, New York, 1965.

Winstanley, G., *The Law of Freedom, and Other Writings.* Edited by C. Hill, Penguin, Harmondsworth, 1973.

D. Sectarian communities

Cohn, N., *The Pursuit of the Millennium: Revolutionary Millenarians and Mystical Anarchists of the Middle Ages.* Temple Smith, London, 1970.

Davies, H., *The English Free Churches.* Oxford University Press, London, 1963.

Dobb, A. J., *History of Moravian Architecture in England.* Thesis in typescript. R. I. B. A. Library, London, 1951.

Hobsbawm, E. J., *Primitive Rebels: Studies in Archaic Forms of Social Movement in the 19th and 20th Centuries.* Manchester University Press, 1959.

Kohn, H., 'Messianism'. In *Encyclopaedia of the Social Sciences,* pp. 356–64. Macmillan, New York, 1967.

Lawrence, D. H., *Apocalypse.* Penguin, Harmondsworth, 1975.

Matthews, R., *English Messiahs.* Methuen, London, 1936.

Montgomery, J., *Abodes of Love.* Putnam, London, 1962.

Niebuhr, R. H., *The Social Sources of Denominationalism.* Meridian Books, Cleveland, 1957.

Thrupp, L. (ed.), *Millennial Dreams in Action.* Mouton and Co., The Hague, 1962.

Wallis, R., (ed.), *Sectarianism: Analyses of Religious and Non-Religious Sects.* Peter Owen, London, 1975.

Weber, M., 'Religion of non-privileged classes'. In *The Sociology of Religion*, Ch. VII. Methuen, London, 1965.

Whitley, W. T., 'Sects (Christian)'. In *Encyclopaedia of Religion and Ethics*, pp. 315–29. T. and T. Clark, Edinburgh, 1920.

Whitworth, J. McKelvie, *God's Blueprints: A Sociological Study of Three Utopian Sects.* Routledge and Kegan Paul, London, 1975.

Wilson, B., *Religious Sects.* Weidenfeld and Nicolson, London, 1970.

E. Anarchist communities

Berkman, A., *A. B. C. of Anarchism.* Freedom Press, London, 1973.

Berneri, C., *Peter Kropotkin: His Federalist Ideas.* Simian, London, 1976.

Carpenter, E., *Non-Governmental Society.* A. C. Fifield, London, 1911.

Carpenter, E., *My Days and Dreams.* Allen and Unwin, London, 1916.

Carpenter, E., *Towards Democracy.* Allen and Unwin, London, 1917.

Godwin, W., *Enquiry Concerning Political Justice.* Edited by Isaac Kraminck. Penguin, Harmondsworth, 1976.

Hulse, J. W., *Revolutionists in London: A study of Five Unorthodox Socialists.* Oxford University Press, London, 1970.

Kenworthy, J., *A Pilgrimage to Tolstoy.* The Brotherhood Publishing Co., Croydon, 1896.

Kropotkin, P., *Ethics: Origin and Development.* Prism Press, Dorchester, 1976.

Kropotkin, P., *The State: Its Historic Role.* Freedom Press, London, 1969.

Kropotkin, P., *Kropotkin's Revolutionary Pamphlets: A Collection of Writings by Peter Kropotkin.* Edited by R. N. Baldwin. Dover Publications, New York, 1970.

Kropotkin, P., *The Conquest of Bread.* Edited by Paul Avrich. Allen Lane, London, 1972a.

Kropotkin, P., *Mutual Aid: A Factor of Evolution.* Edited by Paul Avrich. Allen Lane, London, 1972b.

Kropotkin, P., *Fields, Factories and Workshops Tomorrow.* Edited by Colin Ward. Allen and Unwin, London, 1974.

Morris, W., *News from Nowhere.* Routledge and Kegan Paul, London, 1970.

Proudhon, P. J., *Selected Writings of Pierre-Joseph Proudhon.* Ed. Stewart Edwards, Macmillan, London, 1970.

Shaw, N., *Whiteway: A Colony in the Cotswolds.* C. W. Daniel Co., London, 1935.

Shaw, N., *A. Czech Philosopher in the Cotswolds: being an account of the life and work of Francis Sedlak.* C. W. Daniel Co., London, 1940.

Thompson, E. P., *William Morris: From Romantic to Revolutionary.* Merlin Press, London, 1977.

Tolstoy, L., *The Kingdom of God is Within You.* W. Scott, London, 1894.

Tolstoy, L., *To the Working People.* London, 1900.

Tolstoy, L., *The Slavery of Our Times.* Briant Colour Printing Joint Chapel, London, 1972.

Wilde, O., *The Soul of Man under Socialism.* Collins, London, 1966.

Woodcock, G., *Anarchism: A History of Libertarian Ideas and Movements.* Penguin, Harmondsworth, 1975.

Woodcock, G., *The Anarchist Reader.* Fontana/Collins, Glasgow, 1977.

F. Twentieth-century communitarianism

Abrams, P. and McCulloch, A., *Communes, Sociology and Society.* Cambridge University Press, 1976.

Bishop, C. H., *All Things Common.* Harper, New York, 1950.

Bookchin, M., *Post-Scarcity Anarchism.* Wildwood House, London, 1974.

Boyle, G. and Harper, P., *Radical Technology.* Wildwood House, London, 1976.

Carpenter, N., *Guild Socialism.* D. Appleton, New York, 1922.

Clark, D., *Basic Communities: Towards an Alternative Society.* S.P.C.K., London, 1977.

Cole, G. D. H., *Guild Socialism Restated.* Leonard Parsons, London, 1920.

Community Service Committee, *Community in Britain: A survey of contemporary thought and work at home, with some indications of parallel activities from other parts of the world.* London, 1938.

Demant, V. A., *This Unemployment: Disaster or Opportunity?* Student Christian Press Movement, London, 1931.

Dent, T., *War and the Social Order.* Society of Friends, London, 1928.

Dent, T., *Voluntary Socialism.* Society of Friends, London, 1931.

Dickson, D., *Alternative Technology and the Politics of Technical Change.* Fontana/Collins, Glasgow, 1974.

Dunn, N., *Living Like I Do: An Exploration of Alternative Life-Styles.* Futura, London, 1977.

Ecologist, The, A Blueprint for Survival. Penguin, Harmondsworth, 1972.

Girardet, H., *Land for the People.* Crescent Books, London, 1976.

Ineson, G., *Community Journey.* Sheed and Ward, London, 1956.

Kanter, R. M. (ed.), *Communes: Creating and Managing the Collective Life.* Harper and Row, New York, 1973.

Leech, K., *Youthquake: The Growth of a Counter-culture through Two Decades.* Sheldon Press, London, 1973.

Marcuse, H., *An Essay on Liberation.* Allen Lane, London, 1969.

Mills, R., *Young Outsiders: A Study of Alternative Communities.* Routledge and Kegan Paul, London, 1973.

Murry, J. M., *Christocracy.* Andrew Dakers, London, 1942.

Murry, J. M., *Community Farm.* Peter Nevill, London, 1952.

Musgrove, F., *Ecstasy and Holiness: Counter Culture and the Open Society.* Methuen, London, 1974.

Nyerere, J. K., *Ujamaa: Essays on Socialism.* Dar es Salaam, 1968.

Rigby, A., *Alternative Realities: A Study of Communes and their Members.* Routledge and Kegan Paul, London, 1974a.

Rigby, A., *Communes in Britain.* Routledge and Kegan Paul, London, 1974b.

Rivers, P., *The Survivalists.* Eyre Methuen, London, 1975.

Roberts, A., *Consumerism and the Economic Crisis.* Spokesman Press, Nottingham, 1975.

Roszak, T., *The Making of a Counter Culture: Reflections on the Technocratic Society and its Youthful Opposition.* Faber and Faber, London, 1971.

Saunders, N., *Alternative England and Wales.* Nicholas Saunders, London, 1975.

Scott, J. W., *Self-Subsistence for the Unemployed: Studies in a New Technique.* Faber and Faber, London, 1935.

Schumacher, E. F., *Small is Beautiful: A Study of Economics as if People Mattered.* Blond and Briggs, London, 1973.

Speck, R. V., *The New Families: Youth, Communes and the Politics of Drugs.* Tavistock Publications, London, 1974.

Ward, C., *Anarchy in Action.* Allen and Unwin, London, 1973.

Whitworth, J. McKelvie, 'Communitarian groups and the world'. In R. Wallis (ed.), *Sectarianism.* Peter Owen, London, 1975.

Windass, S., *Where do we go from here?* Alternative Society Working Papers, Oxford, 1976–77.

G. American communitarianism

Bailie, W., *Joseph Warren: The First American Anarchist.* Small, Maynard and Co., Boston, 1906.

Bestor, A. E., *Backwoods Utopias: the Sectarian and Owenite Phases of Communitarian Socialism in America, 1633–1829.* University of Pennsylvania Press, Philadelphia, 1970.

Hayden, D., *Seven American Utopias: The Architecture of Communitarian Socialism, 1790–1975.* M. I. T. Press, Cambridge (Mass.), 1976.

Hillquit, M., *History of Socialism in the United States.* Russell and Russell, New York, 1965.

Hinds, W. A., *American Communities.* Corinth Books, New York, 1961.

Holloway, M., *Heavens on Earth: Utopian Communities in America, 1680–1880.* Dover Publications, New York, 1966.

Houriet, R., *Getting Back Together.* Sphere Books, London, 1973.

Jerome, J., *Families of Eden.* Thames and Hudson, London, 1975.

Lockwood, G. B., *The New Harmony Movement.* Dover Publications, New York, 1971.

Nordhoff, C., *The Communistic Societies of the United States.* Schocken Books, New York, 1965.

Noyes, J. H., *History of American Socialisms.* Dover, New York, 1966.

Reps, J. W., *The Making of Urban America.* Princeton University Press, 1965.

Sanford, C. L., *The Quest for Paradise.* University of Illinois Press, Urbana, 1961.

Schuster, E. M., *Native American Anarchism: A Study of Left-Wing American Individualism.* Smith College Studies in History, Vol. 17, pp. 6–187, 1932.

Thoreau, H. D., *On the Duty of Civil Disobedience.* New American Library, New York, 1960.

Thoreau, H. D., *Walden or, Life in the Woods.* New American Library, New York, 1960.

Index